SOVIET
SST

SOVIET
SST

THE
TECHNOPOLITICS
OF THE
TUPOLEV-144

HOWARD MOON

Orion Books • New York

for my parents

Copyright © 1989 by Howard Moon

Published by Orion Books, a division of Crown Publishers, Inc., 201 East 50th Street, New York, New York 10022.

ORION and colophon are trademarks of Crown Publishers, Inc.

Manufactured in the United States of America

Library of Congress Cataloging-in-Publication Data

Moon, Howard.
    Soviet SST: the technopolitics of the Tupolev-144 / by Howard Moon.
        p.   cm.
    Bibliography: p.
    Includes index.
    1. Tupolev 144 (Jet transport)—History.   I. Title.
TL686.T77M66 1989
387.7'0947—dc19   88-39736
                                                                            CIP

ISBN 0-517-56601-X
Book design by Linda Kocur
10 9 8 7 6 5 4 3 2 1

First Edition

CONTENTS

CONTENTS

FOREWORD

Walter J. Boyne

If Secretary General Gorbachev needs further evidence of the ills and errors of the Brezhnev regime, he will find in this book a perfect—and tragic—exposition of the problem. As much a spy novel as a technical history, it is a compelling look at the fascinating, ill-fated Soviet SST program. Howard Moon, drawing on his broad knowledge of both aviation engineering and political in-fighting has presented the first full-fledged exposé—no other word really fits—of the misguided national leadership that destroyed a dramatic Russian aviation first.

Glasnost has not yet revealed much about Soviet aviation history, and there are pitifully few books on the subject. Most are derived from stock Soviet sources, presenting only what the Soviets want people to know. Others are mere encyclopedias of types, cataloguing year by year the very impressive variety of civil and military aircraft. In contrast, Howard Moon's research ability, combined with his integrative faculties, produce an insightful look at the people and the politics that characterize not only the SST program, but beyond, the very fabric of the Soviet techno-political network.

The Soviet SST was sneeringly and incorrectly dubbed "Konkordski" by the uninformed because of its almost inevitable resemblance to the slightly later and far more successful Anglo-French Concorde. Although, as we will see, the Soviets worked very hard to take advantage of every scrap of information, their SST was in fact an astounding achievement. If the father of the Soviet SST was that designer of genius, Andrei Tupolev, then its mother was the broad base of Russian experience in building gigantic aircraft. Unfortunately, there was also an unskilled midwife, the creaking Soviet top leadership, that interfered with the birth and development of the airplane, letting concerns about being the first take precedence over the solid engineering of which Tupolev's teams were capable.

Tupolev's bravery and composure during the long, agonizing, and eventually disastrous development of the SST are all the more remarkable because of his previous experience at the hands of the regime. He was arrested on fabricated charges of high treason during the purges of 1937, and actually continued his career in a prison "Design Bureau". There, despite the personal design intervention of the notorious L. P. Beria, Tupolev succeeded in producing the Tupolev TU-2, a twin engine bomber that won not only the Stalin Prize, but also restoration of his rights as a citizen.

After the war, Tupolev designed both jet bombers and jet transports, including the sensational TU-104, which revolutionized Soviet civil aviation. He would be joined by his son, Alexei, in an even greater project as the pace of Western progress accelerated. By the 1960s, Premier Nikita Krushchev was demanding that the Anglo-French effort to create a supersonic transport be matched—and beaten—by a Russian effort. The SST fever had begun!

No little part of the fever's heat was the necessity for the Soviets to catch up by any means, including espionage, which ranged from the analysis of runway scrapings (to determine the composition of tires used on Western supersonic aircraft) to intensive analysis of Western academic papers to full fledged spy networks.

The latter were enormously successful. In one case, a high level French technocrat, the son of a White Russian émigré, provided the entire technical documentation of the Concorde prototype! In the time-honored fashion, microfilm was transferred on trans-European trains by being hidden routinely behind the heating grill in the first-class lavatory of the Ostend-Warsaw Express.

Ultimately the pace of SST development was matched by the pace of espionage, so that it became of concern which "Koncordski" was a copy of which "Concorde."

Yet the espionage—and the heroic Soviet design efforts—

resulted in the Russian SST being the first of its type to fly. On December 31, 1968, Andrei Tupelov, the "old man" recently turned eighty years old, arrived by limousine at Zhukovsky airfield in the Moscow suburbs. He was met by his son, Alexei, the Chief Designer of the Tupolev TU-144, the 120th aircraft to bear the Tupolev name. Not mentioned in *Pravda* was the grumbling and discontent among other senior engineers that the "Czarevitch" was going to succeed his father by right of primogeniture, not skill.

The first flight, only twenty-eight minutes long but totally successful, was an amazing achievement; the Concorde would not fly until more than two months later.

The effect on the West was spectacular. The United States, still reeling from the disastrous blows to morale of Sputnik and Gagarin, was shocked once again, particularly since it was still in the midst of an agonizing debate over whether an American SST was to be built. It was particularly galling that initial analysis indicated that the Soviet SST would be a far more formidable commercial competitor than the Anglo-French Concorde. One American businessman even announced that he had signed a contract for the SST sales rights in the Western hemisphere.

Salt was poured into SST proponent wounds two days before the 1971 Paris air show, when a Senate vote finally killed all hope for building the Boeing SST. Observers compared the Soviet SST and the Concorde both statically and in flight, finding to their surprise that the Soviet aircraft was smaller, carried more passengers, and was quieter and cleaner, at least in subsonic flight.

This was probably the high point in the Soviet SST's career, for the Soviet engineers were becoming overwhelmed with the enormous problems of developing the design from a prototype to a successful commercial vehicle. Worse, there was tragedy to come; tragedy caused by political hubris.

Matched against the sparkling flying routine of the Concorde at the 1973 Paris air show, and burdened by lax discipline upon the part of the air show managers, the Soviet TU-144 was flown beyond its design envelope, broke up in the air, and crashed into a Paris suburb. Moon's trenchant analysis of this crash, unique and convincing, is one of the high points of the book.

The path of the Soviet SST led downward after Paris, in spite of the best efforts of the Tupolev team to correct its faults, until a final, off-handed announcement by Aeroflot in August 1984 that the program was terminated. In contrast, the Anglo-French Concorde went into regular, prestigious, passenger service, establishing an enviable safety record that survives to this day.

It is especially rewarding that Howard Moon teaches us even more about Russian scientific and political psychology than he does about the SST, and given our own space and aircraft mishaps, what he teaches is comforting. His conclusions tell us what the SST experience means for Russian efforts in the future, as America begins to warm to the idea of its own Mach Five "Orient Express." Most important, it is a vivid and perhaps frightening example of the way in which the Soviets let a terminally flawed program continue for a decade, like a headless Leviathan, to serve now as the most striking example of the sheer inertia of the stagnant Brezhnev regime.

INTRODUCTION: PIECING TOGETHER THE STORY

There is a dramatic imbalance between what we know of the Concorde and what we have found out about its Soviet counterpart. The Concorde is the subject of at least fifty monographs; its technical data are in the public domain. The controversies attending its birth, development, and deployment are a matter of record. In contrast, the Soviet plane represents a black hole in our knowledge. Information covering the twenty-five years of TU-144 development and the seventeen Soviet supersonic airliners that were built has remained until now scattered, contradictory, and sparse.

The TU-144 story is a hostage of the Soviet tension between publicity and secrecy. Soviet national prestige required *glasnost,* or selective publicity regarding its innovative high-speed airliner, yet many aspects of the Soviet SST story remain veiled and mysterious. Soviet documentation is sparse and cryptic regarding the more interesting aspects of its evolution, and in any case is not available to researchers. The Soviet SST was commissioned during a beach conversation between Khrushchev and the senior Tupolev; many other crucial nuances and decisions were probably not committed to paper.

Behind the fog of secrecy and the lack of sources, the SST's complex technology poses further perplexities. For example, Concorde development history covers the technical problems of sustained supersonic flight, yet the Soviets met these challenges in unique, telling ways. But Soviet secretiveness has occasionally undercut Soviet national interests. The Soviets insisted on suppressing the findings of the Franco-Soviet inquest into the crash of a TU-144 at the 1973 Paris air show. Yet the inquiry found that Soviet technology played no role in the disaster.

Interpreting these elusive clues, doubly shrouded in Soviet secretiveness and innate technical complexity, has required unorthodox sources and research methods. Soviet photos and films yielded insights unavailable from propagandistic press releases. Specialists requesting anonymity in various countries shed light on behind-the-scenes segments of the story. The TU-144 story represents a puzzle with many of its key pieces missing, but by reassembling the scraps of evidence, it was possible to reconstruct the key chain of events.

When the titanium curtain of secrecy surrounding the Soviet SST is lifted, the controversies and factions that swirled about its gestation are revealed. These controversies teach us a great deal about Soviet technopolitics—the issues and interactions involving Soviet technical and political elites and issues. In the Soviet aerospace sector, rivalries between designers and design bureaus, and struggles for official patronage, parallel those among aerospace contractors in the West. The complex struggles associated with a twenty-five-year quest to build and operate a 1,500 mph showcase airliner shed new light not only on Soviet controversies but on the symbiotic nature of pressure groups. In their enthusiasm for a particular technology, sponsors of futuristic projects in different countries band together against their common natural enemies: the skeptics, critics, and budget-cutters.

The leading Soviet protagonists of our story were prisoners of Soviet history and politics. Under Stalin, the "creative technical intelligentsia" was persecuted, and occasionally executed. But in the end, Stalin was dependent upon them to provide the mechanisms to extend his power. Stalin's "barracks communism," characterized by interference and short-term deadlines, gave way to a benevolent despotic technocracy in which engineers and designers could aspire to the leader's innermost circle.

Andrei, the elder Tupolev (1888–1972), was cursed to live in interesting times. The bizarre dynamics of Stalin's paranoid rule saw him exalted as Chief Constructor for the industry, then plunged to the depths as a condemned traitor. He was arrested in October 1937, for allegedly selling plans for a fighter-bomber to Nazi agents. He confessed to avoid torture and was condemned to death. Andrei Tupolev then was reprieved to design aircraft in a unique Soviet institution, the *sharashka* or prison design bureau. He worked his way back from the obscurity of the war years, when his designs were subject to interference from the infamous Beria, to become a confidant of Khrushchev.

Tupolev's second great period of creativity in the fifties and sixties saw him produce with great skill and speed a series of turboprop and jet bombers and airliners, which came to symbolize Soviet technical parity with the West. Khrushchev, mesmerized by technical marvels such as nuclear-powered aircraft, committed the USSR to proceed with SST development. Tupolev, lionized as patriarch of the Soviet aircraft industry, regarded this as his culminating achievement. Unlike most of his peers, who had known Lenin and Stalin, he died in his bed in 1972.

Tupolev's son and heir, Alexei, came to maturity in more settled times. Lacking his father's occasional spark of intuitive design genius, Alexei was more attuned to contextual considerations such as production and operating costs. He is a complex, engaging figure—a Chief Designer with mixed feelings regarding his primary responsibility. Alexei was charged to realize the final legacy of his celebrated father, even while he was among the first Soviets to question its ultimate worth and practicality.

The Tupolev Design Bureau nurtured two generations of leaders in Soviet aircraft design and production. Myasishchev, who married Tupolev's daughter, went on to propose innovative high-speed, long-range jet bombers whose performance fell far short of target. Reassigned to the directorship of TsAGI, he pioneered the earliest Soviet SST proposals. Sergei Ilyushin founded his own design bureau, which in the eighties has usurped Tupolev's traditional role as the USSR's premier producer of airliners. Pyotr Dementiev, a Tupolev ally as Minister of Aviation Production, was an important SST supporter. Boris Bugayev, Chief of Aeroflot, moved from his early enthusiasm for the SST concept to opposing it on grounds of expense, safety, and reliability.

The Soviet SST impacted on other world leaders as well. Reports of a Soviet SST prompted John F. Kennedy to launch a U.S. counterproject in 1963; its priority continued under his successor, Lyndon Johnson. France's de Gaulle personally expelled the Aeroflot spymaster Sergei Pavlov in 1965 for organizing the theft of Concorde blueprints.

Though the broad concepts of the SST are rooted in Soviet history, its technical lineage is Western. The TU-144 broke conceptually with previous Soviet designs and followed German, U.S., and Anglo-French precedents, such as its delta wing. The "Konkordski" myth is misleading. Soviets never actually "copy" foreign aircraft, even when licensed to do so; Soviet technical limitations and operational requirements—such as a specified ability to land on dirt airfields—prevent this. The earliest Soviet SST designs reflect efforts to make it distinctly different from Western archetypes, with original—if crude and impractical— approaches to such matters as wing profile and engine placement. The 144's growing convergence with the Concorde in design matters was forced by technical requirements and a tight development timetable. In short, there is little leeway for originality when preparing an unprecedented 1,500 mph airliner for its first flight within forty months.

The extensive Soviet industrial espionage apparatus made a major contribution to this accelerated development timetable. In the early 1960s, aerospace was the first priority of Soviet technological espionage, and SST data were among the most eagerly sought. Hundreds of agents and thousands of analysts collected and sifted through information on British, French, and American SST designs. One effort, representing a pioneer use of Aeroflot as an espionage front, saw communist sympathizers in Aerospatiale's Toulouse factory steal Concorde blueprints and technical data, later forwarded to Moscow by couriers. Unstinting Soviet efforts to learn the secrets of Concorde engines in Britain were less successful.

Former Soviet engineers provide rare evidence as to the fate of stolen technical information on arrival in the USSR. Concorde data were often indecipherable or not easily understood. Sometimes Soviet technology or metallurgy was not up to the job of interpreting or reconstructing Western technology. Soviets have never constructed "Konkordskis," but instead use analogues that follow Soviet technical traditions and capabilities. Reports that the French fed Moscow doctored technical data through turned agents may have reinforced Soviet reluctance to become dependent on Western ideas. For reasons of national pride or technical advantage, the Soviets opted for technical solutions different from the Concorde, as with the canard "winglets" to ease landing and takeoff speeds. The U.S. Boeing SST design was also carefully analyzed for aerodynamics and construction details.

The Soviet SST project was commissioned and directed from the very top of the Soviet power structure. The number of high-level Soviet leaders associated with it attests to its appeal to the official Soviet mind-set; it represented the values and dreams of a generation of the Soviet elite. Its speed, power, prestige, and glamor were to be a showcase for rapidly advancing Soviet technology. And its slow, sputtering end signaled Soviet inability to match the West's achievement.

If dogged perseverance and marshaling of unlimited resources guaranteed success, a fleet of TU-144s would be serving Aeroflot today. Seven years of design and study work were followed by fifteen years of flight testing. Two major designs were developed that involved at least four major wing designs and two different engines, fixed in four locations. Yet for all their efforts, in the end the Soviets were left with a rugged, powerful airframe, noisy and gluttonous of fuel, unrefined beyond the level of a high-performance military interceptor.

This showcase project represented the pinnacle of Soviet ability. The SST's aerodynamics were progressively improved, its fuselage immensely strong, its engines prodigiously powerful; the last few examples manufactured reflected a high level of craftsmanship and impressive finish. The best that the USSR could produce, however, could not match the West's skill in refinement, creature comforts, or applied electronics. The intricate programs that controlled airflow to the Concorde's engines never had a Soviet equivalent, nor did the Soviets make the vital breakthroughs in sophisticated cooling and metallurgy that made possible efficient, durable, high-thrust engines. Hence the TU-144 was crippled in its range and reliability.

Whereas the Concorde used its fuel mass to cool its kinetically heated skin, the Soviets deployed huge air-conditioners, adding to the deafening cacophony in its passenger cabin. On exhibit, the TU-144 was marred by badly worn tires, testimony that Soviet rubber could not cope with high speed and weight. Production-version TU-144s had canards, or winglets, which lowered its takeoff and landing speeds at the expense of aerodynamic drag, in partial compensation for the absence of the Concorde's thrust reversers, which provided "engine braking."

The twenty-five-year history of Soviet SST development attests to the power of bureaucratic momentum within the Soviet system. Even when the plane's commercial prospects had dwindled alarmingly, and its many technical drawbacks remained unresolved, state funds continued to push the project forward. An inability to call a halt reveals a central weakness of a centralized economy: orders from the top cannot easily be countermanded or reversed.

For all the vaunted scientism of Soviet socialism, the TU-144 survived and flourished because it incarnated cultural myths— largely irrational and unexamined—of prestige, power, and supreme speed. For all the Marxists' acquaintance with immutable laws of history and their superior prescience regarding the future, the 144 proved a dangerous illusion. The future changed and, with it, SST commercial prospects. The TU-144 saga shows the powerful appeal of the myths of power, speed, and futurism. As Goya commented, "the sleep of reason produces monsters."

The TU-144 was always anachronistic, born out of due time, more a realized wish-fulfillment fantasy than a reflection of reality. At its inception it was an intruder from the future, its rakish profile apparently projected from the next century or another planet. The future did not arrive in time to save it; in the end it represented a collection of obsolete, undesirable traits. Noisy, inefficient, elitist—it was an embodiment of yesterday's tomorrows, a frozen dream that never achieved a context. Its pterodactyl profile, now relegated to museums, seems unrelated to the increasingly pragmatic world of civil aviation. Rather, it was an irrelevant tribute to an age of Grand Scale, dedicated to the pursuit of superlatives without regard for cost.

Yet it is possible that the enormous effort devoted to the Soviet SST may find a purpose. HST projects now underway in both East and West promise to revive the SST themes of the 1960s. Now a strategic application—as a low-cost space shuttle—makes defense funding possible. The Soviets exhibited their first HST scale model at Paris in 1981, a probable development of the Mach 3 SST developed in parallel with the TU-144 in the mid-1960s. In the spring of 1988, the Soviet press contained reports of a projected 300-passenger airliner that would fly from Moscow to Tokyo in two hours. If such a project receives backing in the more pragmatic context of the Gorbachev era, it will mean that the Soviet SST anticipated a new type of hybrid aircraft, capable of taking off from normal airports but then achieving a space orbit. Should this plan take concrete shape, the time and treasure spent on the TU-144 may be redeemed, and the quarter-century of feverish work have found a purpose.

The Soviet SST is not a subject that invites arrogance or complacency. Many mysteries have been unraveled, but the full story remains secret and obscure. For example,

• Did the Soviets paint the same prototype number—68001—on two aircrafts to cover themselves in case of an accident?

• Why were no photos ever distributed of the long-range 144D or its engines?

• Is the Soviet SST still serving secretly as a military test bed aircraft today?

This book is the first to examine this intriguing and important topic in detail. It contains much new material never before analyzed and evaluated and also many rare, insightful, and previously unpublished photographs. My hope is that readers will share my fascination with the history of the Soviet SST, that my findings may increase our understanding of the other superpower, and that other seekers of the elusive truth will come forward to shed light on the remaining mysteries of this project.

I welcome your comments, clues, and solutions.

I
ANDREI TUPOLEV
AND THE SOVIET
STATE

In his dotage, Andrei Tupolev (November 10, 1888–December 23, 1972) was lionized by the Soviet regime as the "Patriarch of the Soviet Aircraft Industry." The claim was a valid one: Tupolev witnessed 120 first flights of aircraft bearing his name and was responsible for more aircraft designs than any other single individual. Yet Tupolev's relations with the regime were far more interesting than the official record would indicate. While still in his thirties, Tupolev was made Chief Engineer of the Industry, controlling design and production of everything but fighters. Then, abruptly, he was arrested, charged with treason, and imprisoned, designing aircraft under prison conditions. He was eventually "rehabilitated" and received a succession of Soviet prizes and awards. This cycle of eminence-disgrace-rehabilitation absorbed only five years of a fascinating career.

Tupolev had impressive credentials, both ideological and technical. He was the son of a lawyer exiled for revolutionary activity and had himself been arrested for the same activity as a student in 1911. Two years earlier, he had flown a biplane glider near Moscow under the patronage of Professor Nikolai Zhukovsky. No other Soviet could claim to have been an aircraft designer since the revolution. He helped design the USSR's first wind tunnels. According to the Tupolev legend, at the age of thirty he conceived of an ambitious plan for a national aviation research center, marched resolutely into the Kremlin, demanded to see

9

Lenin, and sold him the idea.[1] Moscow's TsAGI, the Central Institute of Aerohydrodynamics, was created in 1918.

Tupolev's design apprenticeship consisted in adapting the German Junkers all-metal aircraft design ideas to a series of progressively more complex Soviet designs. He later represented this phase of his career as a series of firsts in civil design displaced by military requirements. The ANT-9, designed in 1923, was the "first three-engine metal passenger plane." The ANT-14 of 1932, "the world's first four-engine metal passenger craft," was supplanted in mass production by the TB-3 bomber.[2]

Stalin's call for crash industrialization in 1928 launched the First Five-Year Plan and provided a stage for Tupolev to demonstrate his gifts not only as a designer but also as an organizer of production. By 1932, an impressive 216 of his ANT-4 twin engine bombers, a landmark monoplane, had been produced. They also served as ambassadors for the Soviet state: one example was flown across Siberia and the Pacific to New York in 1929.

Tupolev's ability to deliver impressive numbers of multi-engine aircraft during the First Five-Year Plan, when many other sectors were woefully deficient in meeting plans, led to his promotion in 1931 as Chief Engineer of GUAP, the Chief Directorate of the Aircraft industry. As early as 1929, Tupolev had had 450 engineers working under him.[3] Now he had a huge design bureau under his authority, responsible for everything but fighters. Seaplanes, bombers, transports, and airliners in vast profusion rolled from Tupolev's Experimental Design Bureau (OKB). From 1932 to late 1936, thirty-seven different designs were produced under the ANT house designation: a proliferation of blueprints unlikely to have been equaled before or since.

This productivity was rooted in Tupolev's innovation of "mass development." Tupolev discovered that even a twenty-hour workday did not suffice to develop all the design concepts that crowded his mind. So he developed "Design Brigades" to work out several different ideas simultaneously. Many destined to become heads of the Design Bureaus in their own right—

Ilyushin, Sukhoi, Myasishchev, Gurevitch—began their careers in Tupolev's mass-development scheme, which established his reputation as a supermanager as well as a designer. In 1936, Tupolev's mass-development concept—using parallel design teams to crack open technical puzzles—was adopted throughout the Soviet system. A decade later, it was reportedly used to exploit the secrets of captured German rockets to speed the day of Sputnik. It accelerated the advent of Soviet missiles.[4]

Soviet success in mass production of complex multi-engine types such as the TB-3, and the "aeromania" of the 1930s inspired Stalin to adopt aviation as a prop of the regime. In 1933, Stalin for the first time identified himself with the successes of the aircraft industry and designated April 28 as Aviation Day. This holiday was one in a yearly Soviet liturgy designed to supplant that of Orthodox Czarist Russia. On these occasions, the leaders of the regime would show themselves to the people, clustered on reviewing stands as a technocratic hierarchy. Aeroflot Day and Red Air Fleet Day would follow. Aviation spectacles were exploited to provide legitimacy for the regime.[5]

To compensate for the technical link with Germany severed after the Nazi seizure of power, Stalin in 1933 created an aviator cult. "Stalin's Falcons" were exhorted to master aviation technology by "flying farther than anyone, faster than anyone, and higher than anyone." "Farther, faster, higher" became the bywords of Soviet aviation in the 1930s, and their spirit of record breaking, innovation, and competition has informed Soviet aviation ever since.

The industry assumed many elements of its character as a result of the way Stalin envisioned aviation's role:

• Use of record-breaking flights for purposes of state and ideological prestige.

• Construction of very fast, very long range, or very large aircraft as ends in themselves, exploring the limits of technology at the expense of more rational, economically justifiable designs.

• Comparative neglect of civil aviation and economy as a design goal. While the promise of profit in the West forced the development of airliners that for the first time could pay their way without subsidy, Soviet designers remained relatively un-contaminated by economic discipline. Fuel-consumption rates, high-efficiency engines, and seat-cost per mile factors were not emphasized as design goals. There was no cost-accounting in the Soviet system to push designs in this direction. Rather, system incentives rewarded high-performance aircraft produced in mini-mum time. Resource-allocation patterns were established that are reflected to this day in the inferior fuel consumption and range performance of most Soviet aircraft.

• Development of purely propaganda aircraft whose mission was to glorify the Soviet state.

ANT aircraft of the 1931–36 era embraced several types:

1. Multi-engined bomber/transports (ANT-6, ANT-9)

2. Single-purpose, experimental record-breakers (ANT-25)

3. Propaganda aircraft (ANT-20, ANT-25)

4. Modern airliner (ANT-35)

That dramatic, colorful, and amusing aircraft were developed in the USSR in the 1930s is not remarkable. All industrial states were then engaged in heavily subsidizing a great many experimental designs produced in small numbers. What seems unique in the Soviet case is the perpetuation of these operating patterns into the 1970s. The politicization of aircraft design and deployment, and the absence of the profit incentive as a forcing function, has given Soviet aviation a unique cast.

For reasons predominantly ideological and partly geopolitical, the USSR was untouched by the revolution occurring in Western civil aviation in the later 1930s: the appearance of aircraft capable of returning a profit and repaying their development and operating costs. This development has been obscured by the rise of military air power, technically so close and economically so distant, that followed it. Operational aircraft existed for thirty-two years before the DC-3 appeared as the first profit-producer. Profitability is arguably the most demanding aviation design criterion of all, attained by only a small minority of aircraft designs. The Soviets admired the DC-3 in terms of its superior design; Tupolev was dispatched to the United States in 1936 to negotiate a license for its manufacture in the USSR. Over 2,000 ultimately were built. But the superior economics of the DC-3 escaped the Soviets, for their system has few mechanisms capable of monitoring operating costs.

Tupolev's Design Philosophy

Tupolev's own approach to his craft was more pragmatic than some of his products of the 1930s would suggest. He believed that the USSR needed "planes like it needs black bread." Exotic confections could indeed be proposed, but no ingredients were available to make them. Consequently, aviation thought, he believed, should be restricted to realizable designs. Mass-produced models should be based on existing technology and production capabilities. If these lagged behind the West in performance, "Devil take them, we'll take quantity."[6]

Tupolev proposed that the gap between quantity and quality be minimized by giving the OKBs assignments for mass-production aircraft as well as experimental machines representing a "strong leap forward." He believed in strong, centralized Design Bureaus, arguing that his bureau produced ten types of use to the military in 1927–37, while Poliakarpov's fighter KB produced five, and Ilyushin's "microbureau" two.[7] He did not abolish the "dwarf bureaus" as he could have, preferring open discussion.

In technology, Tupolev was tolerant. He listened to opposing opinions and was capable of having his mind changed. He defended coworkers, was a Puritan in his personal life, "held staunch moral convictions" and demanded almost ascetic dedication from his closest subordinates. "One had to be full of initiative, steadfast, and truthful, not subservient to authority or the administration. Boldly seek new ways and, having found them, do not retreat before any kind of consideration." Those capable of living up to this standard over the years won his trust and were, essentially, unsupervised.[8]

Tupolev's own particular value to the nascent Soviet aircraft industry was his ability to translate ideas into metal on the shop floor—a point where the Soviet system is notoriously weak. When, in 1947, subordinates questioned his intuitive aerodynamic correction of the grafting of a jet engine nacelle to the wing of the TU-14 bomber prototype, he turned on them with biblical vehemence: "Urchins, snivellers, beggars! Why are you confusing the issue?" In time, Tupolev's modification, which looked strange, proved right. Yet design "intuition" in his time was ideologically suspect: considered un-Marxist, "idealist," and akin to black magic.[9]

Tupolev's early talent for designing multi-engined aircraft commended him to the State apparatus. The prototype ANT-9, christened *Wings of the Soviets*, made a 9,000-kilometer tour of European capitals in the fall of 1929 to serve notice that the USSR did not lag in aviation. The four-engine ANT-4 made the first Soviet flight to the United States in the same year, probably for the same purpose. A special air squadron was formed in the Red Air Fleet to undertake propaganda flights. The CPSU (Communist Party of the Soviet Union) resolved in June 1929 to "build up Red aviation to the level of the most advanced bourgeois countries."[10]

Monsters of the Mid-1930s

The *"Maxim Gorky"* was officially commissioned by the Soviet Union of Writers and Editors in 1932 to celebrate the fortieth birthday of the famous writer. Six million rubles, or eight million dollars, was raised by public subscription. In spite of a massive "Technical Soviet" with representatives from 100 institutions,

Tupolev succeeded in bringing the project to rapid fruition. Construction by 800 technicians began in mid-1933 and took nine months, the parts leaving by road for assembly in April 1934. It was planned to be the first of seven, each named for a prominent Bolshevik leader.

It was the largest aircraft in the world, powered by eight engines, with an on-board movie theater and post office. On the underside of its huge and red main wing, lights spelled out edifying revolutionary slogans—while loudspeakers carried the strains of proletarian hymns—to bemused workers and peasants below.

The majestic ANT-20 made a series of propaganda flights in its fourteen-month career, and an accompanying squadron of fighters flew next to it to emphasize its unprecedented size. Its claimed 1,200-mile range, however, was never employed to inspire non-Soviet workers.

The end of the *Maxim Gorky* closed an era in airborne agit-prop. The Khandinka fields in northwest Moscow, scene of czarist coronations and religious pageants, had been converted to the Central Airfield, where air shows and exhibitions provided the sacraments of Soviet futurism and technocracy. Above the Khandinka, on the warm and festive Sunday afternoon of May 18, 1935, the *Maxim Gorky* was carrying families of "shock workers" on an excursion flight, the strains of the "Internationale" drifting down from its loudspeakers to the muscovites below. Abruptly the music ceased. Large pieces of metal crashed into the streets of Moscow. The *Gorky's* fighter escort had recklessly attempted to loop the *Maxim Gorky* while cameras were rolling for a propaganda film. The fighter debris lodged in the wing, but then came loose and destroyed the ANT-20's fin, destroying lateral control. The *Maxim Gorky* broke apart in the air. Both aircraft were completely destroyed and fifty-six lives were lost—the world's greatest airplane disaster recorded up to that time.[11]

Stalin was infuriated. Tupolev escaped punishment: the tragedy had not resulted from any ANT-20 design fault, though rumors to this effect spread through Moscow. Stalin instead vented his wrath on Moscow city officials. A huge state funeral was rapidly organized. Khrushchev and Bulganin carried the victims' ashes in urns before crowds who stretched from the crematorium to the Hall of Columns. The final resting place for the victims was the Novadevichy, oldest and most prestigious cemetery in Moscow. A large tablet commemorated all the victims of the tragedy; below their names, a single line identified the pilot responsible: N. P. Blagin.[12]

Ironically, the *Maxim Gorky* was the *smallest* of a family of projected aircraft characterized by huge wings and relatively short fuselages. The destruction of the world's largest airplane interrupted Tupolev's plans for a series of even larger and more ambitious designs. In 1929, following the successful quadrupling in size on the ANT-9 formula into the ANT-14, Tupolev initiated design studies expanding the dimensions of his basic metal monoplane beyond the "square cube" law of physics: design size is constrained by the molecular strength of the metal used. Tupolev envisaged scaling up to an ultimate aircraft, the TB-6, of 150 tons gross weight with a wingspan of 200 meters, or 656 feet. This monster would surely have collapsed under its own weight.[13]

This Leviathan was to be accomplished by creating two intermediate steps. The first of these was the ANT-26 or TB-6 bomber, developed as a design exercise in 1932–36, following the abandonment of a military version of the ANT-20. It would have weighed 70 tons gross with a 312-foot wingspan, compared with the 42 tons and 206 feet of the *Maxim Gorky*. It would have carried twelve engines and a crew of twelve, but was canceled in 1936 before a prototype was completed. The poor performance of the TB-4 suggested that ultra-large combat craft were lumbering giants vulnerable to attack. The future seemed to lie with small, nimble bombers like Tupolev's SB-2, swarms of which could be produced for the cost of one aerial monster. Tupolev backed away from large four-engine aircraft for nearly a decade.[14]

But public sentiment demanded the building of one final ANT-20. Thirty-five million rubles were collected via public subscription to build a fleet of sixteen additional ANT-20s. This amount was apparently diverted to other purposes, with only one further ANT-20 being completed in 1938. Advances in power plants meant that only six engines were now required, and this aircraft served as a transport with a good reliability record until it was damaged in a heavy landing in December 1942.

Long-Range and Commercial Aircraft

Another of Tupolev's design milestones was the ANT-25, which also featured an extremely wide wingspan and was designed for maximum range to learn lessons useful for bombers. It was built around the supremely reliable AM-34 V-12 engine built for extreme endurance. With its crew of four, it could stay aloft for at least sixty-five hours. On September 10–12, 1934, an ANT-25 broke world long-distance records, attaining 7,712 miles in just over seventy-five hours. Twice during 1937, unprecedented nonstop flights were made from Moscow to the United States: to Portland, Oregon, on June 18–20, and to San Jacinto, California, on July 15. The latter flight still held the FAI record for distance flown in a straight line as late as 1982.[15]

The ANT-25 design had originated in 1931, and twenty had been built by 1936.[16] Following the first transpolar flight to the United States, Tupolev on June 21, 1937, noted that the ANT-25 was now five years old, slow and obsolete, and called for new and better machines.[17]

While the USSR was garnering records, the rest of the world was developing more modern combat aircraft, as shown by the air war in Spain, in which Soviet types were overwhelmed by more modern German designs. And economically viable commercial aviation was beginning in the United States. The Boeing B-9 bomber had evolved into the Boeing 247 airliner, used exclusively by United Airlines. Competitors pressured Douglas to build an aircraft that could cruise at 150 mph and carry twelve passengers 1,000 miles. This became the DC-1 of 1933, superseded by the DC-2 of 1934, and the DC-3 of 1935. The latter carried double the number of passengers through the use of a widened fuselage, and carried 90 percent of world air traffic by 1939.

These dramatic developments were followed closely in the USSR and in 1935, Tupolev introduced the ANT-35. It was smaller and marginally faster than the DC-3, a "courier" plane carrying ten passengers. The DC-3 weighed 64 percent more, but carried over twice as many passengers. The ANT-35 was still an impressive achievement and was flown to the Paris Salon Aeronautique in 1936, in part to publicize the recent Franco-Soviet Pact. In September 1936, it flew a Leningrad–Moscow–Leningrad route at a then-impressive speed of over 220 mph. Based on the SB bomber, eleven ANT-35s were produced in 1937–39.

But a more pragmatic approach was adopted regarding the DC-3. Tupolev was dispatched on at least two trips to Germany and the United States in 1936–37, and in 1938, a license was purchased to produce the DC-3 in the Soviet Union. Myasishchev oversaw its conversion to metric production and the heavier parts required by Soviet operating standards and simpler production techniques. Almost 3,000 "LI-2"s were built over a fifteen-year period. [18]

Tupolev had been strongly influenced by German Junkers construction techniques at the beginning of his aircraft-designing career. German influence remained strong in the Soviet technical sector; German remained the second language of the USSR well into the war. Although the Soviets purchased the license for the DC-3 and a number of less well known military and seaplane types in 1936–38, the Nazi-Soviet alliance of 1939–41 reawakened interest in German technical innovations. Beria's wartime insistence upon the impractical four-engine dive-bomber probably had its origins in a Luftwaffe specification that resulted in the HE-177 of 1939. Tupolev's German connections were certainly suspect during the terrifying purges of the late 1930s. At this time of mass arrests, "confessions" under torture, the executions and deportations of millions, the wonder is not that Tupolev was arrested, but that he survived.

Ruin and Rehabilitation

By the mid-1930s, Tupolev's career had reached a peak that in some sense it was not to reach again. He was not simply a General Designer, the supermanager of the bulk of the Soviet aircraft industry. A contemporary noted: "Among Soviet airmen Tupolev was almost a legendary figure before he went to jail. Each time I saw him he acted supremely self-confident, even barking orders to his Red bosses. He lived like a King: two *dachas* (summer homes), three cars with chauffeurs, an unlimited bank account, an ample supply of the best French wines and cognac, and immunity from the NKVD by order of Stalin. Only the scientist Ivan Pavlov and the writer Maxim Gorky were accorded such priviledges. Tupolev made use of his immunity to say exactly what he thought about the communist rules. He sneered and jeered at them. He was an old-fashioned intellectual, a distinguished scientist and engineer since Czarist days, and he was proud of it. He once defended a group of students arrested by the NKVD. To do so took great courage, even for a man of his unique standing."[19]

The reasons for Tupolev's fall from such empyrean heights were rooted in Soviet politics. Tupolev was associated with Marshal Tukhachevsky, executed in June 1937, and the leadership of the Soviet armed forces, particularly those of the Red Air Fleet that deployed his bombers in such unprecedented quantities. The Soviet High Command by the mid-1930s was reportedly planning a coup against Stalin, having apparently found evidence that he had been a double agent for the Okhrana, the czarist secret police.

Stalin apparently got wind of the plot and outmaneuvered them by arranging through a double agent for the Gestapo to forge documents implicating this group in treason. This was an overture for the Nazi-Soviet Pact of three years later: Stalin had a plausible reason for getting rid of some dangerous rivals, the last threat to his authority in the USSR; the Nazis could help eliminate the most able Soviet military leadership and decapitate a dangerous rival.

Tupolev also was an object for suspicion because he had traveled abroad: he visited designers and aircraft factories in Germany and the United States twice around 1936, in part to negotiate licensed manufacture of the DC-3 in the USSR. Tupolev's arrest on October 21, 1937, illustrates the casual brutalism of Stalin's power. Three secret police entered his inner office and ransacked it while questioning him. Leaving the room littered with technical papers, they led off the Chief Designer who, for the first time, had "a lost look on his face."[19A] One report says the precipitating factor was Tupolev's reported demand to Stalin that arrested Tupolev designers and associates be freed and vindicated. Stalin, according to this account, had Tupolev arrested—like so many others—on fabricated charges of "high treason." The Soviet court accepted as evidence fabricated evidence regarding blueprints Tupolev was allegedly trying to peddle to the Nazis, who in the late 1930s had little to learn from anyone in this category. However, for the Moscow court this "evidence" was "overwhelming," and Tupolev was sentenced to death, with the generous Stalin commuting this to life imprisonment. The Chief Designer might still prove useful.[20] Tupolev disappeared, a "nonperson"; ANT aircraft became anonymous or were renamed.

In the Soviet context, of course, the "Prison Design Bureau" which was to be Tupolev's home was not a bizarre aberration, for the USSR had become a prison society. Under the "Barracks Regulations" that came into effect in 1938, senior Soviet officials were virtually confined to their offices or homes until the end of the emergency in 1946. "Freedom" was relative; even commissars lived in gilded cages.

The bulk of Soviet aircraft designers were arrested during 1937–38 and about a hundred of them perished in the camps. Tupolev himself spent several months in Lubianka prison. Here he confessed to "treason" to avoid torture, on the advice of a friend. Later, in Butyirki prison, his cell contained a drawing table and his wife was present. Months were wasted before surviving designers were brought back from the gulag and concentrated, in early 1938, in "Prison Design Bureaus," or *sharashkas*.

The purge worked havoc in Soviet society in general. Its effect on Tupolev KB was that at least seven designs in progress at the time of Tupolev's arrest were "unbuilt."[21] Tupolev became a number: "011" appeared on all his work. His cot stood in one corner of an oak hall, which every evening became a "technical Soviet." Ozerov and Kerber, fellow prisoners, have provided us an earthy portrait of Tupolev at work as a prisoner-designer.

> A sheet of paper was pulled out from underneath the bed— paper was forbidden in the sleeping areas to guard against information leaks—and some design sketched on it. Tupolev adjusts the design with a soft pencil and explains his thought. . . . "No, the solution still hasn't been found here. You can't stick the engine nacelle to the wing with shit. . . . That's stupid. This isn't a strut but snot." Biting his hangnails (the sharp knife always in his pocket has been taken away . . .) and from time to time laughing in- fectiously—then his fat stomach would heave like a bag of jelly—the Chief Designer instructs his flock.[22]

From the time of his arrest—possibly before—Tupolev's style of work refocused. His work in the thirties had been remarkably prolific and embraced almost all types of aircraft. From this point forward, Tupolev worked in a careful, evolutionary manner, for the most part in two-engine aircraft, whether for civil or military application. Four-engine bomber commissions were imposed upon him by the State, and the four-engine turboprop airliner TU-114 appeared during the 1960s. In the jet era, the only four-engined Tupolev, with the exception of the SST, was the TU-110 (only one of which was produced).

Andrei Tupolev's design career from this point can be sub- divided into the development of a relatively small number of types, extrapolated into different variants. The first of his prison designs was the ANT-58, the same number as the prison cell in which it was conceived. This was a twin-engine fighter-bomber conceived in response to a "vague command" to build something that could outperform the German Junkers 88. The development of this aircraft was long and complex even by Soviet standards, partially explained by the fact that its entire design team was in jail.

This aircraft, ultimately to be known as the TU-2, was begun in 1938. Its first flight occurred in January 1941. A major effort was made to simplify the design in terms of parts and man-hours. Tupolev designed it for ease of mass production, with emphasis on accurate tooling, bench-made wiring looms and pipe runs, with a wide range of subcontracted subassemblies.[23] Production of the TU-2 was threatened by the dilettantish interventions of Beria, who tried to recast its design concept several times. About fifteen months was lost by stopping production at one factory and through prolonged modifications long after the TU-2 was ready for service.

Finally, Tupolev and his team were released, and they organized the production of the TU-2 in their own factory in 1943. That summer, Tupolev was awarded his first Stalin Prize and the equivalent of $25,000 for this feat. According to one account, Stalin apologized to him. Tupolev's decorations were restored and his initials—now "TU"—were restored to the aircraft he designed. Tupolev was promoted to Lieutenant General of Technical Services of the Red Air Fleet.[24]

However torturous its gestation, the TU-2 was an excellent medium bomber, serving into the fifties. Yakovlev, no uncritical admirer of Tupolev, noted that its tactical and flying characteristics outdid the JU-88, and it had a range of 2,100 kilometers (3,360 miles).[25]

About this time, in his mid-fifties, Tupolev began to be called "*Starets*," the "Old Man," or "Boss," partially in wonderment that he, a prominent victim of the purge, had survived. The "Starets" had not lost his earthy touch: he still joked with the mechanics who helped assemble his prototypes and did not forget his friends. But if his professional judgment was questioned, the patriarch could turn tough. Part of the Tupolev legend concerned a shop foreman who argued that a proposed aircraft fitting was not strong enough. The "Starets" ordered him to pound on it with a sledgehammer, and this continued for two days. The fitting survived the ordeal in better condition than the foreman. This test "taught everybody not to doubt."[26]

Tupolev, however, never did regain the position of absolute preeminence he had enjoyed in the early 1930s. The Soviet aircraft industry had matured in the years of his disgrace, when the new Design Bureaus of MIG and Yakovlev produced fighters for the emergency. Stalin summoned Tupolev to build a copy of the American B-29, then incomparably the finest strategic bomber in the world and one of the most advanced designs then in service. It inspired a generation of Soviet analogues, some in service to this day forty-five years later.

The Soviet Superfortress and its Derivatives

Even though the *sharashka* was dissolved in August 1941, the maddening caprices and interventions of Stalin and Beria remained a factor in aircraft design and manufacture until their deaths in 1953. In 1941, Stalin dispatched Khrushchev to the Kharkov Locomotive Works to see if its diesel engines could be mounted in airplanes. Diesels in aircrafts had earlier been tried by the Germans, but had been rejected as too heavy. Beria, regarded by Tupolev as a dangerous dilettante, interrupted the development of the TU-2 by insisting on technically nonsensical projects such as a high-altitude, four-engine dive-bomber "to annihilate the beast in his own den," probably inspired by an equally nonsensical Luftwaffe project. Stalin spurred designers to produce bombers capable of reaching and returning from U.S. targets, a technical task then—and perhaps even today—beyond the range of Soviet engines. Turboprops and projected nuclear-powered bombers with the range were too slow to avoid interception.[27]

By 1944, it was obvious that the USSR was winning the war. The post-1938 "defense emergency" emphasis on fighter and tactical aircraft that aped German thinking and tactics, which had led to the ascendancy of the MIG and Yak Design Bureaus, was ending. Stalin, anticipating a postwar confrontation with Great Britain and the United States, was impressed by the effects of Allied bombing attacks on German cities and, possibly, intelligence reports of Luftwaffe projects to develop long-range bombers that could reach New York City. Beginning around 1943, Stalin began to pester his Allies for Lend-Lease B-17 and B-24 strategic bombers, while designers were secretly ordered to start studying and copying their technology. Mindful that Stalin might be trying to rebuild the Soviet strategic bomber capability he had destroyed in the prewar purges, the Allies were deaf to his entreaties.

Stalin later made at least three requests to the Allies for the B-29. About the same time, in early 1944, the authorities commissioned Tupolev's Project 64, an attempt to reconstruct the B-29 from clandestinely obtained Western data. Stalin reportedly gave Tupolev a deadline of only thirty-six months for the B-29 copy. The prototype was begun in early 1945, but the thirst and low power of its Soviet engines limited its range to a fraction of its archetype. The Shavrov Design Bureau had begun as early as late-1943 to attempt a copy of the B-29's Wright-3350 engine and G.E. turbocharger.[28]

In late 1944, a windfall occurred. Three B-29s crash-landed on Soviet Pacific territory, having been damaged or run short of fuel while on bombing missions over Japan, with which the USSR was not then at war. The Politburo pondered retaining the aircraft for a week or so while the B-29 structure could be studied, but Stalin suggested simple confiscation. The gamble worked: the United States restricted itself to protests and continued to deliver Lend-Lease.[29]

The Soviet Superfortress Project proved to be another mass-development endeavor. In one of those huge concentrations of resources alleged to be an inherent strength of a controlled economy, sixty-four design bureaus and over 1,000 draftsmen were set to work copying the B-29's engines, fuel, metallurgy, navigation, sighting, and internal and external communication systems. This was the most massive reverse-engineering project undertaken by the Soviets—or, possibly, by anyone else—up to that time. Tupolev stated that over 105,000 items were checked for material specifications, function, manufacturing processes, and fit. Few parts of the copy, the TU-4, were identical to their originals when this process was completed.

Switching from U.S. measurements to metric equivalents was slow and costly. Soviet trade representatives in Britain, Canada, and the United States bought up measuring equipment in small quantities. In great secrecy, thousands of technicians were retrained to work in inches, feet, pounds, and foot-pounds. Even though Stalin reportedly ordained that the Soviet copy follow its American archetype "like two peas in a pod," different Soviet operating specifications and shortfalls in such areas as metallurgy militated against literal copying. Plumbing and cable systems were extensively redesigned; even the basic structure used different materials. Technical realities mocked the pretensions of absolute imitation.[30]

A full-scale program was launched in the first week of 1945. Following Tupolev's preference for airliners, a civilian B-29, the TU-70, was first produced as a Tupolev in-house project. This was a more direct copy of the B-29, since Tupolev could make his own design decisions unencumbered by the requirements of an external consumer. The TU-70 flew in November 1946, seven and a half months before the first TU-4 bomber. The B-29's circular fuselage was enlarged 20 percent, from 2.9 to 3.5 meters (10.5 feet). Only one TU-70 appears to have been built, apparently with American engines, landing gear, and tail.[31] As with earlier Tupolev airliners, an ambitious design had been produced that was simply beyond the primitive Aeroflot infrastructure of the time: the TU-70 required concrete runways, and Aeroflot was still stuck in the mire of dirt runways and twin-engine airliners of late-1930s' standard.

The TU-4 bomber prototype, first flown in July 1947, was bedeviled by a host of problems, particularly propellers, turbochargers, and armament. Engines overheated. The Soviets experienced difficulties manufacturing distortion-free Plexiglas required for its flight decks and turrets. The first three TU-4s appeared at the 1947 Air Day celebration and "buzzed" the crowd at an altitude of 600 feet, owing to control-tower error, and were roundly applauded for providing this thrill.[32] The West had already been alerted to the possibility of a Soviet Superfortress; in 1946, Soviet agents in the United States were discovered trying to buy up quantities of B-29 tires and landing gear.

Two more years of development followed. A more impressive group of TU-4s flew over Red Square on May 1948, and Tupolev was given an Order of Lenin for remastering the technically tricky B-29. Production at the war-ravaged site in Voronezh (to serve as the assembly area for the TU-144 forty years later) saw 300 TU-4s in service by 1950 and about 400 produced overall. Its factory workers labeled the TU-4 the "Brick Bomber," since its components arrived from factories all over the USSR. Tupolev coordinated a construction effort that, in fact, engaged the energies of a large part of the Soviet aircraft industry. But by 1950, the TU-4 had been rendered obsolete by the introduction of the B-36, whose range it could not hope to match.

A turboprop version—the TU-85—was flying by 1950 in response to a 1948 requirement for a bomber that could reach the United States and return—a rapid development that Tupolev regarded as one of his greatest achievements. In an effort to increase range, the TU-85 had a higher fuel capacity than any other piston aircraft except the B-36. It was shown at Tushino in 1951, and was said to have a range of 12,000 to 13,000 kilometers from its four twenty-eight-cylinder engines. But only two were produced, a victim of the rapidly approaching jet age.[33]

The ultimate Soviet development of the B-29 theme, the 20/95 Bear, is still in service; its TU-142 variant is still in production. The 20/95 was conceived in 1950 as an improved TU-85, with its design details settled early in 1952. Key to the aircraft's marvelous range was Kuznetsov's NK-12 turboprops, reportedly developed by 800 interned Austrian and German engineers in a postwar *sharashka* in Kubyshev in 1948–54.[34] The Bear variants remain the largest propellor aircraft ever to see regular service. The 20/95, whose fuselage was a stretched version of the TU-85, was first seen on Aviation Day 1955, commencing over thirty years of service in Soviet military aviation.

The civil version of the Bear, the TU-114, first flew in prototype form to celebrate the fortieth anniversary of the October Revolution in 1957. It was eclipsed later only by the Boeing 747 as the largest, heaviest airliner in the world. This turboprop family in essence represented a Soviet design detour around the inefficiencies of Soviet jet engines. Its ultimate 6,200-mile range outperforms any current Soviet jet airliner, and possibly all contemporary Soviet aircraft. It could fly direct to Havana after refueling at Murmansk; the IL-62 in current use requires two refueling stops. In June 1959, a TU-114D, with Deputy Premier Kozlov and Tupolev and his daughter aboard, flew directly to New York from Moscow, to support negotiations for direct air service between the two cities at a time when the United States had no aircraft capable of this feat.[35] The double-decker TU-114 was an awesome artifact in 1959; it stood twelve feet off the ground and could carry 220 passengers on short hauls.

The TU-114 was a study in evolutionary refinement: each of its four turboprops produced 12,000 horsepower and drove two counter-rotating propellors eighteen feet in diameter. Its landing gear, crude and heavy to cope with landing on dirt airfields, recalled the TB-3 of the 1930s. Seen on the ground, its lithe fuselage seemed disconnected from its earthy undercarriage. The greatest problem in putting it into service was upgrading Soviet airports to handle its great weight and size; it forced the pace of Aeroflot's modernization program of the late 1950s. About thirty examples of the TU-114 were built, some with a 220-passenger capacity, with Aeroflot service initiated in 1961. Tupolev told Westerners that it was the most economical airplane then in service: "An 'extremely cost-conscious' Soviet government had insisted on low operating costs." Paradoxically, he added that overhaul time for the huge turboprops was 250 hours, which tended to support suspicions by Western experts that these engines were tricky, indeed. In addition, in long service, TU-114s tended to induce fatigue cracks in the wings.[36]

Three examples of an ultra long range variant, the TU-114D, were also constructed, with a shorter, slimmer fuselage carrying fewer passengers, mail, and urgent freight. These changes extended the 5,560-mile range of the standard version to an unprecedented 6,200 miles. The TU-114D proved invaluable in establishing Aeroflot's longest international routes to Accra, Montreal, and Tokyo—not to mention the politically important service to Havana—until its replacement by the IL-62 jet starting in the fall of 1967.

Tupolev Enters the Jet Age

Paralleling the development of B-29 derivatives, Tupolev began a second family of aircraft, similar in concept to the wartime TU-2, but based on studies of German and British jet engines.

In 1947, Tupolev began developing twin jets, destined to become the focus of its production and eventually to return the Design Bureau to a position approaching its prewar eminence. From 1938 to 1943, Tupolev had been almost exclusively preoccupied with the TU-2 twin-engine bomber and its variants. In 1947, as soon as the TU-4 bomber design entered production, he began development and design studies of twin-engine jet designs. From this point on, Tupolev's only deviations from two-engine designs were the turboprop 95/114, the abortive 110 airliner, which appeared in only a single example, and the TU-144 supersonic airliner.

The postwar Tupolev jet designs at first were based on modified TU-2s, but they soon developed into an independent design family. The first Tupolev twin jet—the TU-12—featured the first Soviet use of Rolls-Royce Nene jet engines bought from Britain. The Nenes were fitted to a modified TU-2 fuselage. This experimental aircraft was completed in May 1947, and took part in the Aviation Day flypast.

The TU-12/177—still based on the TU-2—was a properly developed jet project started in 1946 and shown at Tushino in 1947. A few were quickly built in a short production run, as an interim design.

The third design featured a new fuselage and was designed to meet a 1946 Soviet Air Force requirement. Types 72, 73, and 78 were all variations of the same theme. Because the Soviet Klimov engines were underpowered, the basic design appeared in both twin and trijet applications. The TU-14/81, an up-engined version of the earlier design, was the first Tupolev jet to reach mass production.

In the 1950s, the Tupolev Design Bureau began to focus more directly on its specialty: bombers, transports, and airliners. Mikulin's development of the large AM-3 turbojet made possible the first long-range Soviet jets, and for the first time provided Tupolev with a proper powerplant.

The TU-16, ordered in 1950, was the first Soviet design to exploit this new engine and flew in early 1952. Mass production followed quickly, and the 16/88 was first seen in 1954. The excellence of the TU-16 marked the first time that Tupolev OKB won out over its rival Ilyushin in an official Soviet jet-bomber procurement program. Two thousand TU-16 Badgers were produced up until 1959, not counting bootleg copies still made by the Chinese. Roughly half the Soviet production is still in service. The TU-16 also provided the platform upon which the TU-104—the first Soviet jet airliner—is based.

The Transformation of Aeroflot, 1953–60

His airliner designs of the thirties—the ANT-14, 20, and 35, the TU-70 airliner version of the B-29 of 1947—and his speech to the Supreme Soviet attest to Tupolev's fascination with the technical challenge of airliner design. For twenty-five years before the advent of the TU-104 in 1956, technically advanced Tupolev airliner designs were aborted: those that reflected or exceeded the Western state of the art would have forced the Soviet state to devote scarce funds to modernize Aeroflot's pastoral infrastructure, dominated until the late 1950s by dirt or grass runways complete with grazing herds of unsupervised cows, goats, and pigs.

The low priority accorded civil aviation in the decade of postwar reconstruction kept Aeroflot technology frozen at about a 1935 level for twenty years, dominated by twin-engine designs cruising at 160 to 180 mph and updated solely by portable radar installations. This arrested development ended when Soviet leaders, emerging from the cocoon of Stalin's isolationism, entered the world stage. Arriving at international conclaves, they found themselves upstaged and visually outranked in prestige by capitalist counterparts in shiny four-engine airliners.

This lag in part was rooted in Stalin's ambivalent, paranoid attitude toward aviation. Even while he sponsored the aviation cult as a substitute State religion, the "Boss" feared that aircraft accidents might decimate his entourage. Stalin would have been among the first to contemplate the arrangement of aircraft accidents as an effective mechanism for eliminating awkward rivals. So far as is known, Stalin's control of the State apparatus never forced him to employ such complex and expensive subtleties: aircraft were expensive, bullets and lives were cheap. But Stalin suspected others. Alarmed by reports that Mikoyan had indulged in a risky, acrobatic joyride, Stalin around 1939–40 decreed airplanes off limits for all Politburo members and first secretaries of republics. This ban grossly inconvenienced his satraps, who resented revocation of the coveted privilege of air travel. Many, like Khrushchev, loved to fly and found the prescribed journey by car or train from Moscow to their provincial posts time-consuming and tiresome.[37]

This restriction did not long survive wartime pressures, but Stalin's sensitivity to aviation dangers was reflected in Aeroflot's benchmark airliners of 1945–55: the IL-12 and IL-14. The IL-12 was originally designed for twenty-seven passengers, but passenger capacity was cut back to eighteen to increase safety and compensate for inadequate engine power. The IL-12 weighed as much as a contemporary Western design, the Convair 240, that could carry forty-eight passengers. Soviet civil aviation during these years focused on conveying small numbers of Soviet executives and managers to and from Moscow. The inefficiency of these relatively few airliners was regarded as an acceptable burden.

The IL-14 developed in Stalin's last years, coming into service the year of his death, 1953. It was capable of taking off on one engine even from high-altitude dirt airfields, and represented the nadir of obsession with safety. The "principal aim" of its designers was "absolute reliability under unfavourable conditions." This preoccupation resulted in technical-economic degeneracy: the wartime LI-2—the Soviet version of the DC-3—required 314 kilograms of plane to carry each passenger; the 1947 IL-12, 412 kilograms; and the 1953 IL-14P, 660 kilograms. After Stalin's death, Aeroflot pushed for increased capacity, and an IL-14 variant appeared in 1955 that could carry twenty-four.[38]

1953 was a benchmark year for Soviet civil aviation, highlighted by the end of production for the Soviet DC-3 variant, the LI-2,[39] the death of Stalin, and Mikulin's development of Junkers and BMW jets into the AM-3, then the world's most powerful jet engine. This conjunction of events may explain Tupolev's 1960 observation: "In 1953 our country became sufficiently strong to design and build passenger and military aircraft in serial production."[40]

Tupolev records that the TU-104 jetliner design that revolutionized Soviet civil aviation was approved by Stalin just before his death in March 1953.[41] It represented one of Tupolev's greatest technical triumphs. Entry of the TU-104 into Aeroflot service in September 1956 followed the first flight of the prototype by only fifteen months.[42]

The TU-104 underwent a profound identity crisis almost as soon as it was completed. Stalin apparently approved a state-of-the-art, high-speed executive transport for the minions of his empire. The 104's original passenger salon reflected the tastelessness of the most rapacious of Gilded Age capitalists, with mahogany seats and tables, antimacassars, lace curtains, mohair upholstery, heavy brass luggage racks, cut-glass chandeliers, and cast-iron toilets.[43] This Stalinist Gothic was displaced in subsequent 104 variants by aseptic plastic and aluminum artifacts of efficient mass air travel.

The original TU-104 concept of a high-speed jet transport—later inherited by the TU-144—was superseded by a top-priority political mandate to Aeroflot to expand at all cost. The leisurely elegance and discomfort of pre-1955 Aeroflot was quickly displaced by a modern jet airline. The TU-104, originally a TU-16 bomber variant with a wide body and dropped wings, was quickly redeveloped into a semblance of an economical airliner. A stretched 1957 version carried seventy passengers and improved engines. The four-foot-longer hundred-passenger version TU-104B, which appeared in 1959, was so successful that the four-engine TU-110 design, also carrying a hundred passengers, was canceled in its favor.[44] This recalled the dramatic development of the DC-1 into the DC-3 thirty years before, but with the emphasis on speed instead of profitability. Moscow-to-Peking travel time shrank from thirty-two to ten hours.

The 104's payload doubled in three years, but its lackluster export performance, a bitter disappointment to the Soviets, suggested that Soviet technical milestones were not overly influenced by considerations of efficiency. Only three TU-104s were exported—to CSA Czechoslovak Airlines; one of these was soon mothballed for economic reasons. While the pioneering TU-104 was somewhat resistant to after-the-fact efforts to introduce weight saving and economics into its operating profile, it planted Soviet civil aviation not only in the jet age but also at the top of it. For more than two years, 104s provided the only scheduled jetliner service in the world. Tupolev had enabled Aeroflot to leap directly from the twin-engine airliners of the mid-1930s to the jets of the later 1950s, skipping the generation of four-engine piston airliners that characterized the West during this era.

Soviet leaders, chagrined to arrive at the 1955 Geneva Conference in a prewar style IL-14 twin-engine airliner, exploited the twin-jet 104 to the hilt in a Soviet State visit to London the next year. KGB Chief Serov made advance security arrangements in a preproduction prototype; the Soviet delegation used one for a highly publicized arrival at Heathrow; and three more were deployed as courier aircraft while the Soviet leaders remained in London. Khrushchev commented with characteristic modesty, "We wanted our hosts to know about it." Even Queen Elizabeth II was curious about the craft, having seen it come in for a landing. Khrushchev assured her, "It was an excellent plane—very modern, undoubtedly the best in the world."[45] This may not have been music to the ears of British ruling circles, chastened by the three crashes of their earlier Comet jetliner, which had led to its withdrawal from service.

The TU-104 achieved relative reliability. Aeroflot at first tore down its engines after 300 hours of service, but by early 1960 had extended this interval to 1,000 hours. Its swept wings required long runways, and contemporary observers recorded burned-out brakes routinely cooled by Aeroflot bucket brigades.[46] But it provided service until 1980, with a reliability and safety record better than any other Soviet aircraft,[47] without reports of the metal fatigue that had proved fatal for the Comet. This feat reestablished Tupolev's reputation as the preeminent Soviet aircraft designer for the next twenty-five years.

The precipitate arrival of the jet age revolutionized Aeroflot almost overnight. Robert Hotz, editor of *Aviation Week*, sampled Aeroflot in depth in 1956, and he described it in terms akin to an open-air museum. Unsupercharged, unpressurized IL-12s and IL-14s had to wait days for good weather to charge up the passes to provide service to Kabul. Soviet self-consciousness regarding the primitive nature of Aeroflot's fleet is reflected in their 1955 agreement with SAS. SAS was not allowed to fly four-engine airliners into Moscow, though the distance favored larger aircraft. Instead, SAS was restricted to the twin-engine Scania—the peer in prestige of the IL-14—until the Soviets had the TU-104 in service.[48]

Hotz's second visit only three years later gave the impression that the USSR had compressed twenty-five years of progress into three. Aeroflot travel in 1956 was not for the faint-hearted:

33

"coffee-grinder" IL-12s, their propellors defying synchroniza-
tion, had carried him in from Copenhagen, then Aeroflot's only
bridgehead in Europe, on a "long rattling vibrating grind" to Riga
and then Moscow. Three years later the picture had been transformed: 200-pound female attendants whose only uniform had
been a red sweater were replaced by trim, attractive "nattily
dressed" stewardesses. Instead of fifteen to twenty passengers
bouncing along at 160 mph, ninety-six passengers enjoyed hot
meals at 500 mph in smoothness and silence.[49]

In 1959, of course, Aeroflot technological transformation was
manifest only on its main routes. Here, the strong mandate from
the 20th Party Congress to make air travel "the primary method of
passenger travel" during the 1955–62 Seven-Year Plan was
evident. The USSR was following the West into low-cost, high-
density air operations with ever-larger airliners. Off Aeroflot's
main routes, the passing age could still be glimpsed: grass
runways, haystacks, and cattle pens serving as improvised comfort stations. Even Kiev, the USSR's third city in 1959, was still
served by an unpaved field, alternatively rutted mud or dust.[50]
But the age of democratic air travel was inexorably on the way in,
heavily pushed by Khrushchev and his regime as one of the
foundation stones of the better life prophesied in the 1961 Party
program.

The SST project, starting to be discussed by Soviet leaders and
designers in the late 1950s, straddled these two ages. In concept
it was an executive high-speed transport of the older type, as the
TU-104 had been—at odds with the mass-service airline that
Aeroflot was to become during the 1960s. At the same time, it
countered the USSR's reputation for technical backwardness.
Adding to the laurels of the Soviet space program and Soviet
military aviation now going supersonic, it appealed enormously to
leaders mesmerized by the very real achievements of their leading-edge industries. This tension between Soviet technical and
economic reality and the heightened expectations of the Soviet
elite that commissioned it explains much of its subsequent complex history.

Forerunners of the Soviet SST: TU-104 and TU-114

The dramatic new Tupolev airliners were trailblazers of *détente*, the new Soviet diplomacy of "peaceful coexistence," wider trade, and expanded Aeroflot links. Airborne Soviet delegations sometimes resembled a Tupolev family outing featuring the "Old Man," his daughter Julia, a specialist in internal medicine, or "Aloysha," Alexei, the future Chief Designer of the TU-144. In the late 1950s, two new benchmark Tupolev airliners conveyed Soviet delegations in dramatic circumstances to Western cities months before they entered Aeroflot service. Airliners were crucial to the Soviet economy, but they were also a showcase of technical skill, a invaluable adjunct to Soviet diplomacy.

The unexpected appearance of the TU-104 in London in March of 1956, on the eve of a Soviet State visit, created a sensation. The Soviets showed considerable skill in stage-managing the debut of this advanced Soviet civil technology. A generation after the event, it is difficult to imagine the TU-104's impact on the West, revealed to the world with such studied casualness. Sputnik lay eighteen months in the future; the myth of universal Soviet backwardness still had not been punctured. Evidence that the USSR might lead the West in such a critical category, with strategic implications, was a novel and uncomfortable phenomenon.

The auspicious occasion was the advance visit by KGB Chief General Ivan Serov to coordinate security arrangements for an impending, unprecedented visit to Great Britain by the Soviet leadership. Serov, associated with mass deportations of Baltic and other populations, did not enjoy good press. The *Manchester Guardian* described him as the "latest Russian version of Himmler" with an "odious" record; the *Daily Mail* labeled him a "Russian jackal." Serov, smiling, indicated to photographers that they should take pictures of the plane rather than of him.

Serov's instincts were sound. One London paper reported that British experts watched the TU-104 land with "shaken silence."

The *Daily Express* termed it a "bolt from the Red."[51] It had flown the 1,564 miles from Moscow in three and a half hours, averaging 446 mph, a feat with strategic implications not lost on the British. The TU-104 had no peers. Britain's pioneering Comets had been withdrawn; entry of Boeing and Douglas jetliners lay over three years in the future. Its Plexiglas nose, suitable for a bombardier or navigator, and the transparent blister in the tail for a rear gunner, was noted.[52] Guards surrounded the aircraft at Heathrow, and no one was allowed a close inspection.[53] Six more Soviets guarded the TU-104's interior. The 104 used, in fact, was the first prototype, so new that the pressurization was not yet working: passengers had been issued individual oxygen masks.

The Soviets scored a coup. The London *Times* quoted experts who pronounced it "potentially a formidable aeroplane." The *New York Times* reported that local experts agreed that such an advanced airliner represented a notable Soviet achievement,[54] while *Aviation Week* characterized the event as "harsh proof of rapid Soviet progress."[55] The TU-104, if uneconomic in its fifty-seat version, incorporated imposing technology. Its Mikulin M-109 engines were "particularly impressive," "two of the largest turbojet engines operating in the world today," producing power comparable to that of the Comet's four jet engines. Rolls-Royce designers estimated their thrust at 13,000 to 17,000 lbs. Tupolev revealed in *Pravda* that the TU-104 could cruise on one engine at 16,000 feet. This had its cost: the 104 took on 9,600 U.S. gallons of jet fuel for its return flight to Moscow. Experts agreed that if the Soviets pursued development of a four-engine airliner of this type, they might produce "before the Americans" an aircraft competitive with the 707 or DC-8.

The Soviet press lovingly replayed the awed reactions of Western experts. An *Izvestia* headline chortled "the West has never seen anything like it." The chief of Aeroflot announced that the TU-104 was in mass production and would soon inaugurate high-speed service to New Delhi, Peking, and Tokyo. All Moscow papers published TU-104 pictures and articles, as well as numerous interviews with Tupolev. The designer stressed that the plane was made entirely of Soviet materials, "down to the last little screw" and was the first of a new family of high-speed airliners. To dramatize its speed, *Komsomolskaya Pravda* said a passenger could board a TU-104 at Vladivostok in the morning and attend the Bolshoi Ballet in Moscow that evening. He would travel so fast he would see the sun rising during the entire trip westward across the USSR.[56]

When TU-104s conveyed Khrushchev's delegation to London in April 1956, British experts compared it to the Comet. Its two-engine layout made it less acceptable for flights over long stretches of water or undeveloped countries. Its general standard of finish was regarded as "quite outstanding." It had flown from Moscow at an estimated 518 mph.[57] Khrushchev referred to Tupolev's achievements in the course of his visit, and boastfully compared the TU-104 to British aircraft. "Russians, when compelled to do so, could make any kind of machine." Mr. Tupolev, said Khrushchev, "was building an aircraft to carry 170 passengers" and the TU-104 could carry 50 at 850 kph. Khrushchev himself corrected the translator who had mistakenly said its top speed was only 800 kph (496 mph).[58]

In September 1957, two TU-104s were the first Soviet aircraft to land in the United States since Molotov's 1943 visit to Washington. Landing at McGuire Air Force Base, they carried the Soviet delegation to the annual opening of the U.N. General Assembly. Tupolev reportedly was summoned to the Kremlin's inner sanctum, where he basked in praise from a highly pleased Khrushchev for this propaganda coup.[59] The Soviets shamelessly exploited the TU-104 as a propaganda weapon. The prototype was flown and put on exhibit at the Zurich air show in May 1956. TU-104s were a leading attraction at the 1957 Paris air show. They conveyed the Bolshoi Ballet to London, and they ferried the Soviet Olympic team to Rangoon. Three were assigned to fly from Prague to Damascus, Cairo, and Beirut to carry Soviet experts into the Middle East.[60]

The New York visit reflected Soviet interest in beginning air service to the United States. Alexei Semenov, Aeroflot's Chief of

Flight Operations, intoned on arrival, "Let this flight be the positive forecast of the beginning of regular flights of our civil aircraft between the Soviet Union and the United States of America." The TU-104's range was only 2,000 miles, requiring the crossing of the Atlantic in easy stages, but the Soviets claimed a number of speed and lifting records during the return journey. At the controls sat Boris Bugayev, eventually to become chief of Aeroflot.[61] The next Tupolev craft to come to New York would have no range problems.

The TU-114's debut in New York on June 28, 1959, was even more sensational. It had made a historic nonstop 5,092-mile flight from Moscow to New York in eleven hours, at an average speed of 460 mph. Heading a delegation of seventy, to open a Soviet scientific and technical exhibition in New York, was Frol Kozlov, Khrushchev's second in command. Tupolev and his daughter, also aboard, later toured the California aircraft plants of Lockheed, Convair, and Douglas. The huge Tupolev turboprop dominated the front page of the *New York Times* for two days running. Coverage of its flight was followed by President Eisenhower's study of its scale model at the Soviet science fair the next day. The TU-114 was open to the public at New York's Idlewild Airport for two weeks. It made a powerful impression, even on jaded New Yorkers: the *Times* reporter noted that its height, drooped wings, and "huge black propellors tipped in yellow" gave it an "eerie spider-like" aspect.[62]

That same month, a TU-114 carrying 170 Soviet officials, technicians, and Aeroflot employees made a proving flight to Khabarovsk in eastern Siberia, covering the 4,500 miles in eight hours, forty-five minutes, at 515 mph. This run was shaping up as the fastest-growing segment and future main line of Aeroflot, with traffic growing 30 percent per year. In New York, Tupolev announced that the TU-114, already in mass production, was the most economic aircraft in current service. The Soviet government had been "extremely cost-conscious" in its development.

Tupolev, interviewed in New York before leaving for a tour of aircraft factories in California, predicted that the future of air travel belonged to the large airplane: the TU-114 could handle the load of fourteen to sixteen express trains. The awesome size of the TU-114 in 1959 introduced new dimensions to air travel. It would enter service in three months. It featured a forty-eight-seat restaurant, its engines were torn down every 250 hours of use, and it took on sixty-five tons of fuel for the return trip to Moscow.[63] The Soviets calculated that since the Boeing 707 jet or DC-6 would have to stop to take on fuel, the TU-114 could beat them home from New York to Moscow.

The Khrushchev-Tupolev showmanship used to introduce advanced airliner served notice that the Soviet Union was rejoining the world in a spirit of peaceful competition in civil technology. The crushing of the Hungarian uprising was a reminder that Soviet brutality still prevailed, but circumscribed openness to the West had superseded sterile confrontation. These two Soviet achievements galvanized Western specialists into a rapid reassessment of Soviet civil aviation.

The Soviets were intoxicated by their two remarkable and inexpensive successes. Both the TU-104 and the TU-114 had been developed from military designs in only eighteen months. The speed and ease of these conversions encouraged Soviet leaders, at the end of the 1950s, to consider the mesmerizing concept of an SST. It was heady to imagine a Soviet supersonic airliner landing in London after only an hour's flight, or in New York in three hours, the time it had taken the TU-104 to reach London. Superfast flights to these bastions of capitalism would again augment Soviet prestige. The TU-104 and TU-114 achievements ushered in an era of rash and unconsidered optimism.

2

PREMONITIONS: THE SOVIET PATH TO THE SST, 1951–1965

The debut of the TU-144 in scale-model form at the 1965 Paris Salon Aeronautique was hailed at the time as a great surprise, although reports that the Soviets were seriously pursuing a supersonic transport had repeatedly surfaced in the Western press since 1959. Confirmation of the project's existence by Khrushchev in 1963 was a matter of public record.

Trends that coalesced in the Soviet SST project of the mid-1960s may be discerned in the 1950s: Myasishchev's experiments with large supersonic aircraft, Tupolev's growing confidence following the success of two state-of-the-art airliner designs, Soviet optimism buoyed by ebullient economic growth and a series of high-tech breakthroughs, Soviet sensitivity to Western SST speculation was amplified by a highly articulated intelligence apparatus. All were goaded by the galvanizing eccentricities of Nikita Khrushchev.

The "Adventurism" of Myasishchev

In contrast to all other aircraft bearing the Tupolev name, the TU-144 does not resemble its predecessors. In fact, its most salient characteristic—the signature full-delta wing—was not only without precedent in Soviet production but transgressed an edict of the TsAGI that all Soviet aircraft feature a separate tail plane.[1] The 144's unique appearance in part was dictated by the unprecedented speeds it was designed to reach and influenced by the blueprints of the Concorde prototype stolen in France. Tupolev's traditionally evolutionary approach was overwhelmed by rapidly developing international technology.

In response to U.S. launching of B-57 jet-bomber production in 1951, the Myasishchev Design Bureau was founded specifically to produce a jet for Stalin that could reach the United States with nuclear weapons. Jet engines with this range were not then available in the USSR, so Tupolev turned down the project. Vladimir M. Myasishchev, son-in-law and former deputy to Tupolev, was ready to explore beyond the capabilities of extant technology. In the late 1930s, he supervised the conversion of the licensed DC-3 design to metric measurements and Soviet standards of construction. Myasishchev was "granted considerable financial and technical resources. His own KB was set up at the newly established GAZ no. 23."[2] Development of the USSR's first operational four-engine jet bomber was carried out with Stalinist dispatch. Fifteen hundred designers were collected from all other experimental Design Bureaus, and management of the project was assigned to former prisoner-designers.

Begun in 1951, the M-4 "Hammer's" last blueprint was sent to the factory in May 1952. The prototype flew over Moscow on May 1, 1954. This aircraft, denominated the "Bison" by NATO, was roughly comparable to early versions of the B-52, and was capable of carrying free-falling weapons only.[3] Soviet introduction of the M-4 "Molot" (Hammer) kicked off a mid-1950s bomber scare. Greater numbers of the M-4 flown a year later in 1955 alarmed U.S. defense analysts, who were convinced that Soviet capability to attack the United States directly had finally arrived. The U.S. Air Force estimated that by 1959 the USSR would have a thousand such bombers available. The reality was quite different. In 1955, the Soviets flew eight M-4s repeatedly past Red Square in different formations to create the impression that they had several M-4 squadrons. CIA analysts, mapping Soviet industrial and technical capabilities, argued that the Soviets could not build such a large air fleet; there were not enough machine

41

tools or aluminum forges to do the job. The first U-2 flights in 1956 confirmed that there were no large Soviet strategic-bomber fleets.[4]

The Hammer may have misled Western analysts mesmerized by its potential; to the Soviets it was a bitter disappointment. To Myasishchev's argument that the Hammer could bomb the United States and then land in Mexico, Khrushchev responded, "Do you think Mexico is our mother-in-law? The Mexicans would never let us have the plane back." Khrushchev was bitterly disappointed with the M-4: there was doubt it would survive dense antiaircraft fire, and it killed a number of test pilots. Ultimately, it was scrapped; it contributed nothing to Soviet security at great cost.[5] The M-4's range and ceiling never met the ambitious specifications set for it, and the misnamed Hammer ended its long career primarily as a tanker aircraft. It was withdrawn from front-line Soviet bomber units in the mid-50s: 160 to 180 were built before production ceased in 1962.[6]

Tupolev, more cautious, developed the turboprop TU-20 at the same time as a slower, long-range aircraft. By spring 1958, the TU-114D, its ultra-long-range variant, was flying from Moscow to Irkutsk averaging over 500 mph. While the TU-20 was never deployed as a combat aircraft, its very existence inspired the United States to build advanced warning radar bases.[7]

Tupolev's skepticism regarding Soviet technical ability to mass produce high-speed intercontinental jet-bombers was well founded. But he did pursue more realistic development of twin-engine bombers for mid-range European operations. The TU-88 and IL-46 entered flight testing in the summer of 1952. The TU-16, which was the result of this design competition, made its debut at Tushino on July 3, 1955.

Fomenting bomber scares was profitable. Ignoring the fact that their tactics inspired 1950s "bomber scares," Soviet propagandists charged that the number of Soviet bombers was routinely exaggerated by three or four times.[8] Entrepreneurs occasionally exacerbated tensions between the superpowers. In February 1954, a U.S. aviation journal published photos of new

Tupolev and Ilyushin "intercontinental bombers," with four and six turboprops, 400 of which were reported to be in service. These proved to be concoctions manufactured by an ingenious photographer in Berlin.[9] Soviet realities were less impressive. M-4 production was reportedly ten a month in 1958. The TU-20/TU-95 turboprop was developed in parallel by Tupolev as a real-world, less technologically risky backup.

Undaunted, Myasishchev accepted a second commission for a four-engine intercontinental bomber, this time with the proviso it be supersonic. This became the M-50 or M-52, named the Bounder by NATO—the high point of Soviet supersonic thought in the 1950s. Only one example of this bomber ever appeared in public, on the single occasion of Soviet Aviation Day over Moscow in 1961. It was typical of Soviet transitional supersonic designs, featuring a truncated delta shape for its main wing with a separate tail plane. It is a somewhat mysterious aircraft, with its first flight date ascribed to 1957, 1958, 1960, and 1961 in four separate accounts. It precipitated yet another bomber scare in

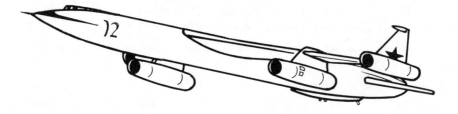

The TU-144's most immediate Soviet ancestor, Myasishchev's M-52 bomber, sparked a bomber scare in the United States when it appeared at the climax of the Aviation Day fly-past in Moscow in July 1961.

the 1960s. Ironically, it appears to be based on a Convair design for an interim SST based on the B-58 Hustler. This fearsome Soviet strategic bomber was rooted in an unknown U.S. civil airliner design.[10]

Its earliest version, for which we have only a "provisional drawing,"[11] featured four engines slung in pods under the main delta wing, like the B-58. The Chief of Staff of the United States

Air Force at the time determined it was "probably configured for supersonic flight." Its limited glass area and sharply raked wing and tail surfaces testified that it represented Soviet state of the art on this subject. It was the basis for two record-breaking Soviet aircraft that set a number of speed-with-payload and payload-to-height records in 1959. Later analysis estimated that it was good for only short supersonic spurts up to Mach 1.4.[12]

The M-50 aircraft that appeared at Tushino in 1961 featured a radical reconfiguration of the engines, with the outboard engines replaced by smaller units installed on the wing tips, with retractable balancing wheels installed in the lower nacelles. Western analysts noted that its fuselage "was much cleaner than that of earlier Soviet strategic bombers" and it carried no apparent defensive armament, the reason being that thoughts of deploying it had been abandoned by the time it appeared in 1961.

Myasishchev's bomber inspired a number of U.S. aircraft industry observers: "Bounder has a wing-fuselage-powerplant combination that some experts believe adequate for prolonged cruise at speeds between Mach 2 and 3." Photographs of the Myasishchev touched off speculation within the U.S. aviation industry that the Soviets would introduce a supersonic civil transport based on this aircraft by 1965.[13] This indicates that Western experts themselves understood very little about supersonic aerodynamics in 1961. Again, the aviation press overrated Soviet technical prowess and ascribed to new designs capabilities they could not necessarily deliver.

Contemporary observers had no way of knowing that the Bounder's first appearance was also its last, and that the design bureau responsible for it had been abolished the year before. *Aviation Week* described it as a "large high delta wing bomber of intercontinental range" approaching the B-36 in size, "with a supersonic dash capability." Over the last three years it had reportedly been flown and tested with a variety of powerplants (in at least two different configurations). With the wisdom of hindsight, it can be said that the M-50 fell short of the full-delta, tail-less configuration that became characteristic of successful supersonic aircraft. Contemporary observers saw in it the rumored nuclear-powered bomber or a potential Soviet SST.

In retrospect, the M-50 supersonic bomber is recognized as an abject failure. Myasishchev was not disgraced, but nominated as Deputy to the Supreme Soviet in 1958, perhaps for effort.[14] His striking delta-wing M-50 powered by four Solovy'ev turbofans developed in the late fifties, in common with the M-4, lacked the range to return from bombing raids on the United States. Western observers were far more impressed by the M-50 than Khrushchev, who closed down the design bureau, terminated future work on strategic bombers, turned the Fili factory over to helicopter production, and provided Myasishchev with a presumably harmless post as head of TsAGI in 1960. When Myasishchev's mighty swept-wing bomber was first revealed at the 1961 Aviation Day Show, it had already been relegated to research and development projects.[15] Unremarked was its resemblance to Convair's proposal for an interim SST.

Soviet Technocracy and Futurism, 1957–61

The advent of Sputnik in October 1957 inspired street celebrations; Soviet media rhapsodized for a month. Soviet lunar probes in 1959 and Yuri Gagarin's historic orbital flight on April 17, 1960 embodied the hopes of successful Soviet technocracy, for which much had been sacrificed. These technological feats were paralleled by dramatic Soviet economic growth, beginning in the early 1960s and continuing for over a decade. Such developments contributed to a political atmosphere in which nothing seemed impossible.

Soviet achievements were paralleled by Western advances that Soviet technocrats wished to emulate. By 1959, the Royal Aircraft Establishment had concluded that the SST had great promise and recommended two design studies: a long-range Mach 2 and a medium-range just above the speed of sound.

In the United States, Lockheed was developing a design study of a Mach 3 SST. Its catalytic proposal, presented in June 1959, in a paper at the Institute of Aeronautical Sciences in Los Angeles, "created considerable international impact." Lockheed declared that an SST was "economically feasible . . . all technical and operational factors could be successfully treated with full utilization of the current state of the art . . . a certification date of 1965 was possible." The International Civil Air Organization (ICAO) met in the United States for the first time the following month. The British, who were until this time convinced that they were ahead of all other nations, were "greatly disturbed" by Lockheed's apparent progress. Britain accordingly lobbied other delegations in an effort to slow down SST development until "its social effects were better understood."[16] This evocation of "environmental impacts" would return to haunt British and other SST advocates.

In 1959, the ICAO, based in Montreal, sent a State Letter to its member states asking questions regarding the impact of an SST in their countries. Though the Soviets were not a member of the ICAO, Czechoslovakia was, and could substitute for the Soviets in this setting. The official ICAO inquiry probably deepened the interest of the Soviet elite in an SST project. In addition to the floods of articles in specialized and general literature discussing the merits and drawbacks of the project, there was now an official international inquiry. The Czech response to the ICAO came in February 1960, after coordination with Moscow.

It was later revealed that SST ideas had been discussed and developed among Soviet aircraft designers as early as 1954–55. In 1958, Minister of Aviation Production Pyotr Dementiev stated that SST designs had been investigated since that time, though no one design seemed to be outstanding—indicating that there were a number of design proposals besides those of Myasishchev. In 1958, design work was in a tentative state: "much remained to be done." But the project approach was already settled; when taking such a large step forward, "it is necessary to do what is technically sound . . . economics will follow later."[17]

M-50 variants considered included a passenger version with a lowered wing, as well as a tanker and military transport. By 1957, SST design issues were being raised in the Soviet aviation press, particularly regarding aerodynamic and powerplant challenges. Highly placed, well-known chief designers were already addressing these issues.[18]

Further confirmation that an SST project was being worked on in Soviet higher circles came in June of 1959. Artem Mikoyan, Chief Designer of MIG and brother of the Soviet Deputy Prime Minister, told officials from British European Airways in Moscow that the USSR "was interested" in the development of supersonic airliners. He noted that the first nation to have supersonic air travel would be the first to operate it economically. He commented that it would have to be capable of twice the speed of sound to operate "at very long range" to reap its maximum benefits. His beliefs were typical of thinking in Moscow, and explain some of the Soviet haste in developing the project.[19]

In January 1960, Andrei Tupolev was the second to rise in the Supreme Soviet to support Khrushchev's reduction in the Soviet armed forces. In this remarkable speech, Tupolev noted that, "There can be no fear that even a total changeover to peaceful production will reduce the pace of the national economy and the scope of the creative search of engineers and technicians." Tupolev was trying to assure his listeners that a normal peacetime economy would not disrupt the Soviet system. He asserted that Soviet technocrats eagerly looked forward to developing the arts of peace and artfully inserted a de-Stalinizing twist: it was only in 1953, the year of Stalin's death, that "our country became sufficiently strong to design and build passenger and military aircraft in serial production."

Tupolev noted that his pioneering efforts in airliners in the 1930s had been supplanted three times in mass production by bombers. Tupolev suggested that Stalin had kept the industry frozen in development of exclusively military types until his death. Now, in 1960, under the patronage of the reformer Khrushchev, Soviet technocrats could move into more productive vistas: "Designers will have even more work, they will be engaged on an even more intensive scale in the solution of most interesting problems." The straitjacket of the *Vozhd* ("Boss") could be cast off. Under these new conditions, Tupolev forecast a "radiant future. . . . We would build all kinds of aircraft—sonic, supersonic, short-distance, and long-distance passenger aircraft; all would be for the benefit of the people . . . as regards passenger aircraft, technical progress is likewise unlimited. In this sphere a mass of very interesting problems are to be solved."

Tupolev expressed no such sentiments extolling the joys and challenges of bomber design. Rather, "I am convinced that I shall be expressing the view held by all scientists and designers if I say that we shall with great pleasure change over to the solving of peaceful tasks for our peaceful economy."[20] Tupolev's comments were cited in the Western press and in U.S. Senate documents.

The new Party Program, announced by Khrushchev in October 1961, resonated with technocratic futurism. It was promised that the USSR would shortly surpass its capitalist rivals: by 1970, the Soviet Union would outstrip the United States in many categories of well-being. Soviet labor productivity would exceed that of the United States by "roughly 100 percent." Accelerated output of consumer goods would see the Soviet people more prosperous than workers in "developed capitalist countries." The eternal Soviet housing shortage would end within the decade. Free midday meals and municipal transport would inspire Soviet workers to leave their U.S. counterparts "far behind" in per capita production by 1970.

In this heady atmosphere, Tupolev's Experimental Design Bureau began SST design studies in 1961. They were begun in the wake of the successful Soviet air display at Tushino and in response to President Kennedy's June 1963 pledge that the United States would launch an SST project in addition to putting a man on the moon by the end of the decade. Peaceful coexistence knew no finer hour.

Yuri Gagarin's epoch-making space flight on April 17, 1961, catalyzed an era of futuristic hopes, inspiring the unprecedented spectacle of Soviet citizens embracing and kissing on the streets. Three months later, the first important Soviet air pageant in five years—at Tushino, a Moscow suburb—reflected great expectations and technical futurism. Knowledgeable Soviets had anticipated that supersonic aircraft might make their debut at the Tushino exhibition, but even they were unprepared for the full range of Soviet supersonics that were displayed. Tushino 1961 was a lavish and expansive pageant even by the standard of previous Soviet air exhibitions. Special efforts were evident. Both chocolates and cherries were freely on sale, something Muscovites had not seen for years.[21]

At Tushino, the Soviets—among other marvels—unveiled two new Mach 2 interceptors and two Tupolev supersonic medium bombers. Last of all, was the debut of the M-50 supersonic bomber, overestimated by informed Western observers at the time as "an exceptionally large, high delta-wing bomber of intercontinental range approaching the B-36 in size and with a supersonic dash capability. . . ."[22] The USSR had entered the supersonic era with a vengeance, on the crest of an unprecedented and historic space success. A supersonic transport could not be far behind; the air was filled with a sense of achievement and expectation.

Yakovlev characterized Tushino as "a creative accounting by the aviators to the Party and to the Soviet people." For the first time, supersonic Soviet jet combat aircraft were shown, all "super fast, super long range, with super high ceilings" that had established world records. The Soviet Air Force was now jet powered, and some of the fighters could approach Mach 3.

Technological prowess had by now assumed the status of a Soviet State religion. Technical progress had become the opiate of the Politburo. Futurism as an antidote for societal ills captured the imagination of the elite, and not only the Soviet. Most major powers were intoxicated by the recent dramatic advances in aviation and space.

* * *

49

SST Fever: East and West, 1959–64

Rumors that the Soviets would convert the M-50 supersonic bomber into an SST circulated within the upper levels of the U.S. government during 1961. This, in fact, had been the path followed for the first Soviet jet airliner, the TU-104, based on the TU-16 twin bomber, and the TU-114 turboprop airliner, which was based on the TU-95 bomber. Najeeb Halaby, President Kennedy's head of the new and then powerful Federal Aviation Agency, was convinced that the Soviets could create a prestigious SST any time they chose by installing a "passenger pod in one of their supersonic bombers and fly their leaders to a politically important spot." Khrushchev "might make such a spectacular flight from Moscow to New Delhi or Peking, or even London or Paris, to demonstrate their technological progress. We could have done the same thing."

This yarn was rooted in mirror-imaging. Halaby had arrived in office early in 1961 to find a proposal from Convair to modify a B-58 bomber as a "Special Air Mission plane"—an SST executive transport for President Kennedy. There were proposals to convert the B-58 into an airliner by carrying forty passengers in a detachable pod, but these fortunately were not followed up.[23] Convair's more realistic proposal to use the B-58's delta wing for an interim SST was not developed in the U.S., but this design served as the base for the Soviet M-50.

The Soviets inadvertently revealed how much they had learned from the design mistakes of the M-50. Colonel-General Yevgeny Loginov, Chief of Aeroflot, was in Washington the week following the Tushino air display to negotiate reciprocal air service between New York and Moscow. Loginov stated that, "The problems of sustained supersonic flight demand an original design concept." It "was not correct" to modify a bomber design "in designing a supersonic transport strictly for carrying passengers."[24] Rather, it was "more economic and useful" to design a civil SST as such from the start.

Soviet candor on this point may have been helped by Khrushchev's decision to cease development of strategic bombers and concentrate Soviet resources on Nedelin's rocket forces. This had the effect of depriving the SST of much of its strategic significance in Soviet eyes, and opened the way to eventual sharing of some of its technical secrets with the West.

Technological evolution meant that supersonic airliners no longer could rely on military aircraft R & D. The development strategy outlined by Loginov, in fact, was that being followed by the U.S. government. Halaby had already testified before Congress that the halting of the B-70 program "would have little or no effect on when a U.S. supersonic transport first earns its type certificate." This did not stop Halaby from repeating the original story—that the Soviets were converting a supersonic bomber to civil use—as late as April 1962.[25]

When *Aviation Week* asked Loginov if the Soviets had an SST "flight target date" under the current Seven-Year Plan begun in January 1959, he answered, "Not specifically . . . we will not be behind." When reminded of "his government's claim that it would be the first to inaugurate SST service," Loginov hedged "that may well be the case."[26] This portion of the *Aviation Week* interview was picked up and widely replayed in the general press. By 1959, the U.S. Air Force was already committed to the development of North American's Valkyrie B-70 bomber, weighing 250 tons—twice the weight of the Concorde—and designed for intercontinental flights at three times the speed of sound. In the United States, it was generally assumed at this time that development of this long-range supersonic bomber would lead to a commercial SST, following past patterns. However, only two B-70s were built as experimental craft after the project was phased out in 1960–61. One of these was subsequently destroyed in a midair collision.

In April 1962, Halaby claimed that one of his counterparts in the Soviet civil air administration had told him Soviet designers were developing a supersonic transport for Aeroflot. This was a public replay of Kennedy administration conjecture of the previous year. Halaby went public with the pronouncement that the

USSR was "trying to rig a 1,300 mph bomber to look like a transport, so it can claim the first supersonic transport." This would "harvest propaganda" like that produced by the TU-104.[27]

Halaby pressed the theme. In a report to the Cabinet in May 1963, he again noted that the USSR was "believed to be actively engaged in building a supersonic craft." Gordon Bain, who headed up the FAA's SST project, noted in a radio interview, that "latest information" indicated the Soviets were "well into the design stage." Information now was that this would be a "brand-new plane," a unique design "not merely a modified military aircraft," as had been the case with previous Soviet airliners.[28] According to Halaby, Kennedy's decision to launch a U.S. SST project in mid-1963 was spurred by reports of Franco-British and Soviet design studies "that might be ahead of anything on our own design boards. . . . We had a pretty good idea that they were at least blue-printing an SST. . . . All we knew for sure, however, was that the Soviet Union wanted badly to get into the SST picture, and eventually we were to learn that there were at least two design teams working on two different models, one of which would become the TU-144."[29]

Kennedy's announcement of a U.S. SST project on June 5, 1963, must have precipitated a final Soviet go-ahead for their own project, if it had not already been given:

> Neither the economics or the politics of international air competition permit us to stand still. . . . Today the challenging new frontier in commercial aviation [is] supersonic flight . . . it is my judgment that this government should immediately commence a new program in partnership with private industry to develop at the earliest practical date the prototype of a commercially successful supersonic transport superior to that being built in any other country in the world. An open preliminary design competition will be initiated immediately. . . .[30]

No Soviet technocrat would have found much to disagree with in these sentiments, but he—and his Anglo-French counter-

The Russian-Prussian connection: at the airport of Königsberg—now Kaliningrad—about 1931, an ANT-9 trimotor rests between two Junkers-52 cousins. Its corrugated aluminum skin attests to kinship with Junkers design practices. *(Lufthansa)*

The TB-3 was the first effective platform for dropping massed paratroops. Tukhachevsky, the innovative Soviet Chief of Staff, introduced paratroops in the 1931 Red Army maneuvers. TB-3s delivered mass paratroop formations for deployment in the 1935 and 1936 maneuvers. Following Tukhachevsky's execution in June 1937, TB-3s were used to airlift officers to Moscow for execution. *(Schoenmaker)*

Closeup of the TB-3, apparently at 1935 Paris air show, showing corrugated skin. *(Ruffle)*

ANT-20 on agitprop mission, revealing all eight engines and a wingspan greater than the total length. *(Ruffle)*

ANT-20, with R-5 escort. Each landing wheel reportedly weighed more than Tupolev's first ANT-1. Electric lights under the wing flashed out slogans, while loudspeakers carried speeches and revolutionary hymns to toiling masses below. *(Schoenmaker)*

ANT-25 in United States, summer of 1937, at the conclusion of a Transpolar flight captained by Chkalov. This sleek 1933 design had slim, wide wings that made possible its impressive range but held its top speed to 125 mph. It was originally developed to serve as a test bed for long-distance bomber research. *(NASM)*

ANT-35 airliner, about 1937, in Aeroflot livery. Clearly inspired by the Douglas DC series, the ANT-35 was a "courier" aircraft with insufficient passenger capacity to pay its own way. Its compound-curve surface development represented a new level of design and manufacturing sophistication. Following a trip by Tupolev to the United States in 1936, the USSR purchased the rights to manufacture the DC-3, reworked by Myasishchev as the LI-2. *(Ruffle)*

The TU-2, which occupied Tupolev in the prison design bureau from 1938 until its entry into service in 1943. Its similarity to the Messerschmitt BF-110 is obvious, though a more likely reason for Tupolev's 1937 arrest was his connection with Tugachevsky and the great resources devoted to slow, oversized bomber projects. *(DOD)*

Tupolev's "copy" of the B-29, circa 1949–1950. *(DOD)*

Myasishchev's M-4 strategic bomber helped spark a bomber scare in the United States in the early 1950s, but it did not have the speed or range to threaten the United States. *(DOD)*

The TU-114, with its massive German-engineered turboprops at Andrews Air Force Base. *(DOD)*

The TU-104 prototype makes its appearance on the stage, at London's airport, March 1956. The impact of this technical achievement was countered somewhat by its notorious cargo: Soviet security chief General Serov was known as the supervisor of mass deportations in the Baltic Republics. *(Schoenmaker)*

Convair's tricky
B-58 Hustler
represented
supersonic
state-of-the-art in
1960, the largest
delta-wing design
up to that time.
Fast and
dangerous, it
helped catalyze the
Soviet decision to
proceed with an
SST.

Staged Tupolev
design conference
from the 1969
Soviet film *Take-
Off*. At left is a
scale model of a
twin-tail prototype,
a rare—and possi-
bly inadvertent—
revelation of one
of the 100-odd
different configu-
rations considered.

In the months following the unveiling of the TU-144 in model form at the Paris air show, it was featured in a number of doctored photos representing future supersonic air travel, this one from *Civil Aviation*, June 1966. The angle dramatizes the single-centerline engine nacelle of the earliest version.

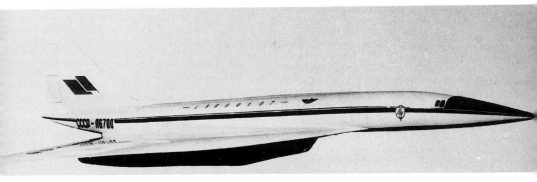

Another variant: a 1967 windowless 144. Chief Designer Alexei Tupolev later indicated that a windowless version had been studied as a means of saving weight, but that this made the cabin too claustrophobic. *(Schoenmaker)*

1967 wind-tunnel test at TsAGI of one-fifth scale model. *(TASS)*

parts—would have done well to have heeded closely what followed:

> If these initial phases do not produce an aircraft capable of transporting people and goods, safely, swiftly, and at prices the traveler can afford and the airlines find profitable, we shall not go further.[31]

This cost-effectiveness in the U.S. SST program, reflecting the hard-nosed analysis of Robert McNamara, explains why the nation most able to afford an SST was the first to back out of it. McNamara's evocations of the dismal science were not an isolated event: Charles Lindberg later pinpointed the Achilles' heel of the SST: it consumed too much energy for its payload. A later RAND study done for the SST based on "abnormal contingencies" predicted that "an unexpected and massive rise in the cost of fuel . . . would be catastrophic to the SST." Even Halaby, an SST fan, eventually recognized that, in the long run, the U.S. SST's "paralysis by analysis" was the best thing, and concluded that by the early 1970s, speed was no longer the sole goal of commercial aviation.[32]

There was no economic analysis comparable to this in the USSR. Tupolev and his colleagues based the economic rationale of the TU-144 on the time saved by transferring travelers from rail to air, without apparent consideration of material and fuel costs. The Soviet SST's prestige factor shielded it from the paralyzing analysis that eventually enveloped its American cousin. Despite this state of affairs, Soviet aircraft designers, and eventually the younger Tupolev himself, would bewail the fact that it had absorbed resources better devoted to other projects. But this would be in 1971, when it was too late. British, French, and U.S. discussions of SSTs were monitored by Soviet intelligence organs and disseminated to important members of the Soviet elite through restricted-circulation periodicals such as TASS's *Bulletin of Foreign Aviation News*. This ensured the steady infiltration of design ideas from West to East. Later, issues of *Aviation Week* would be put aboard Aeroflot flights and be translated into Russian in their entirety before the aircraft landed in Moscow. SST gossip became an important staple in East-West meetings of civil-aviation notables.[33]

In November 1963, Khrushchev himself confirmed reports that the USSR was preparing its own SST: "I can say that we are designing and building a supersonic plane. I can't give you the details because I don't remember technical details. . . ."[34] Halaby, visiting the Soviet Union in December 1963, did not find many Soviets willing to expand on Khrushchev's revelations. He was not allowed "even to see a sketch of it," but found the Soviets radiating "pride and confidence" regarding their SST project, enough to convince him they'd be flying it "before the early 1970s."[35]

In 1963, Julian Amery, Britain's Minister of Aviation, led a high-powered delegation of British scientists and aircraft industry leaders to Moscow. Their concern was the IL-62, which they concluded was a copy of their VC-10. Toward the end of the visit, British-Soviet discussion of SSTs led to the British delegation's being shown a model of an SST design the Soviets were considering. Although it was "no more than a little model on the table . . . they were absolutely staggered by its resemblance to Concorde." On return, Amery initiated a ministerial inquiry into whether design data had been leaked to the Soviets, alerting the Concorde builders to the possibility of industrial espionage.[36] The startling appearance of the SST model at the 1965 Paris air show crowned six years of rumors and reports filtered out of the USSR. In mid-1964, Loginov had provided anticipatory details at a news conference. He confirmed that Soviet designers were at work on an SST they hoped to have flying before an American version appeared. Its top speed would be superior to the Mach 2.2 projected for the Concorde.[37]

For the next ten years, the Soviets almost invariably defined their aircraft in terms of its superiority to Western counterparts: it was bigger, faster, and cheaper or would appear sooner than its capitalist competitors. These claims were welcomed by SST proponents in the West, who pointed to the progress of the

TU-144 as evidence of the soundness of the SST concept. Later they claimed that the Soviet Union would steal the SST market if the West were lax in developing its own versions.

This symbiotic publicity supported SST projects East and West. Soviet bombers had been useful in arguing for expansion of Western air defenses. In the new age of "peaceful coexistence," references to Soviet SST progress were used to counter doubters and economists in the West. Western SST experts had sparked the SST project in the USSR, and U.S. SST cancellation later had a dramatically dampening effect on Soviet SST supporters. But in the late 1960s, SST proponents could point to the reportedly frenetic activities of their future competitors to keep critics at bay. In the same way that military authorities of East and West needed each other, SST enthusiasts in the Soviet Union and the West were locked in symbiotic alliance against skeptics and budget-cutters.

In December 1964, Sir Giles Guthrie, Chairman of BOAC, predicted that the Soviets would be first to produce an SST. By this time the British were nervous. The cost-paring of the new Labour government, hostile to the Concorde, inspired rumors that the French had approached the Soviets to act as partners in case the British backed out. The French denied that a separate approach had been made to the Soviets; besides, the Soviet design could not meet international certification standards.[38]

In February 1965, Tupolev deputy Leonid Seliakov predicted in the Soviet press that, "A fundamental breakthrough will be made in civil aircraft between 1970 and 1975" involving "flight speeds up to 2,500 kilometers (1,550 miles) an hour." By 1975, Muscovites would be able to fly to Khabarovsk, 4,000 miles distant, in three instead of eight hours. Such future airliners would have shorter wingspans and longer fuselages—a veiled reference to the delta wing required for sustained supersonic flight. Seliakov also raised the possibility of "variable wings,"[39] a feature then limited to the F-111, which served as the basis for American SST designs. Variable-geometry wings would appear on Soviet aircraft in the later 1970s, but only on combat aircraft.

55

Seliakov's remarks were an overture to the formal introduction of the Soviet SST at the Paris air show, in June of 1965.

The Western Roots of the TU-144

Once the Soviets launched their SST venture in 1963, it quickly became obvious that they would have to borrow heavily from the West's design heritage. Myasishchev's failed M-50 was the only large Soviet supersonic aircraft that had flown by this time, though Tupolev medium bombers did provide some data. The TU-144's salient characteristic—its large delta wing—was almost unknown in Soviet practice, outside of a few experimental aircraft built in the late 1930s. Prejudice against tail-less delta wings had been institutionalized. TsAGI, the Central Institute of Aerohydrodynamics, Moscow, had issued an edict insisting on separate tail planes in every Soviet aircraft.

The failure of Myasishchev's big bombers in the 1950s and the spurt given to Soviet aircraft design in general by the Tushino triumph in 1961 lay behind Tupolev's 1961 decision to begin SST studies at the Experimental Design Bureau. The direction it took—in opposition to known TsAGI insistence upon retention of the separate tail plane—meant that its design was based on Western practice. The first thing that Tupolev OKB technicians would have done was to begin detailed analyses of successful Western supersonic designs, using Western data obtained by the scientific and technological collection apparatus of the KGB and the GRU (Soviet military intelligence).

It is no coincidence that the three Western nations that developed tail-less delta-winged combat aircraft in the 1950s were those that developed SST designs in the 1960s. Tail-less delta wings, originated in research by Dr. Alexander Lippisch in the late 1930s, first appeared in the rocket-powered Messerschmitt Comet fighter, 279 examples of which were produced in 1944-45 as a somewhat flawed Luftwaffe "Wunderwaffen."

Another common ancestor of both the Concorde and the TU-144 was the Hawker-Siddeley Vulcan, an eighty-five-ton, four-engine medium jet-bomber that first flew in 1952 and remained in production until 1964. Its combat career lasted until the Falkland Islands War. The Vulcan was the first delta jet-bomber. Its Olympus engines were developed into those fitted into the Concorde, their power more than doubled in the process. The Vulcan's early delta wing was much wider than those later designed for SSTs, which may account for its maximum cruising speed just under the speed of sound. The Vulcan is a significant early delta design of relatively large size.[40]

Smaller delta-winged fighters first explored supersonic dynamics in the later 1950s. In the United States, General Dynamics was developing the F-102 and F-106 delta-winged interceptors, which delivered true supersonic speeds with a wing area only one-fifth that of the Vulcan. The F-102 first flew in December 1954, and served the U.S. Air Force from 1955 to 1972. The F-106 was developed from it but featured more sophisticated aerodynamic analysis to minimize supersonic drag. It ultimately was capable of Mach 2.3 speed, almost twice the F-102's Mach 1.25.

In Europe, the Fairey Delta, which first flew in 1954, was capable of over 1,100 mph. The Saab Draken fighter and the French Mirage III, both of which first flew in 1955, attained Mach 2 performance.

But what really captured the imagination of the Soviet decision makers was the U.S. B-58 "Hustler," a supersonic intercontinental bomber. In the United States in the late 1950s, Convair had the first large aircraft capable of sustained supersonic cruise. Developing a supersonic aircraft of this size for the first time raised design problems applicable to an SST. The Draken, for example, weighed only seven tons at takeoff; the B-58 was in another magnitude at eighty tons, weighing about 40 percent as much as the first Soviet SST.

The B-58 was a state-of-the-art wonder in the 1950s. First flown in 1956, it entered service in 1960. It was capable of carrying ten tons of weaponry in a detachable streamlined pod for 5,000 miles at supersonic speed. However, the successful Soviet shoot-down of the U-2 in the year it entered service rendered the B-58 obsolete. It was designed as a high-flying, high-speed penetrator, but the USSR's new Surface-to-Air Missile (SAM) capability made it highly vulnerable and almost certainly ineffective for its highly focused mission. The powerful Soviet TU-22 interceptor was developed specifically to stop it. The B-58 could not be redesigned as a low-altitude bomber, since its fragile wing could not withstand the buffeting and stresses of low-level flight. It was slowly retired from the U.S. bomber inventory. Peak numbers in service were ninety-four in 1964, and the last two flew in 1970.[41]

Strategically, the B-58 was a victim of an unanticipated advance in military technology. Technically, it was a tour de force: the first aircraft capable of sustained supersonic flight. The U.S. Air Force deployed it as a record-breaking public-relations vehicle in a series of highly publicized speed flights. It was flown from Tokyo to London in eight hours, thirty-five minutes. In June 1961, a B-58 was flown to the Paris air show, setting a new transatlantic record and received the Bleriot Trophy for a new closed-course speed record. After its first low pass over the air show, the aircraft climbed into the clouds and was never seen again. A deep crater six miles to the northeast marked its final resting place. This was not the last time a large supersonic aircraft was to crash during its first outing at Paris.[42]

The Soviets were well aware of the B-58's potential, for both the SAM missiles and the TU-22 were specifically designed to counter it. Once its military potential had been neutralized, the speed and range of the B-58 surely spurred Soviet—and Western—thinking about the potential of a civilian SST.

In addition to the catalytic advent of the B-58, British and French movement forward to an SST also inspired Moscow. In Britain, the first official step toward the Concorde was the formation of the Supersonic Transport Aircraft Committee in 1956. Bristol Aircraft distinguished itself in early powerplant and aerodynamic research. Much work was required to correct the chief drawback of the delta wing—its inability to recover from low-speed stall—eventually countered by an ogival (or lazy-S) shape to the leading edge of the delta wing. In 1961, the year of the B-58's crash at Paris and the unveiling of the Soviet Union's first supersonic combat craft at Tushino, the Bristol 221 first took to the air as a flying SST test bed. The 221 was a Fairey FD-2 high-speed fighter refitted with a prototype Concorde wing.[43]

Politics inescapably impinged. Both European states were looking for an aircraft to counter America's near-monopoly of civil aviation, recently consolidated by the introduction of the Boeing 707 and Douglas DC-8. British politicians welcomed a large-scale collaboration with France as an indication of their country's seriousness in joining the Common Market. The French welcomed any movement to counterbalance Britain's transatlantic connection. Only Britain possessed engines potentially powerful enough for an SST: the Bristol-Siddeley Olympus fitted to the Vulcan bomber. In addition, the tremendous development cost for such a venture would be better shared by two countries. Anglo-French discussions, begun in June 1961, culminated in an intergovernmental agreement sixteen months later, in November 1962. These negotiations did not escape alert Soviet intelligence services, and their progress surely hardened resolve within the Soviet Union to pursue a similar project.

American SST work was suspended at this time, ironically owing to Soviet initiative. Soviet success in shooting down Gary Power's U-2 in May 1960 indicated that high-altitude penetrators of Soviet airspace would no longer enjoy an uninterrupted, risk-free life expectancy. The capability of Soviet surface-to-air missiles in destroying a high-altitude aircraft had a catalytic impact on the U.S. Air Force, and had come much earlier than expected. Air Force strategy against the Soviet Union had been built on high-altitude, high-speed penetrators. Now the Soviets showed they could cope effectively with such intruders. Entire weapons systems were dismantled or downgraded. The B-58 was phased out; development on its sucessor, the B-70, was halted.

The B-58 was at the edge of the technological frontier at this time; the B-70 was beyond it. The B-58, the fastest bomber in the world, could do one thing fantastically well: it could deliver a nuclear payload flying at twice the speed of sound over a long range. But this capability was limited. The B-58 was efficient only at a high altitude, where the less turbulent air did not threaten the tricky aerodynamics of its small delta wing. If one of its engines surged, the supersonic shock wave would "pop out" in front and turn the B-58 sideways into an unrecoverable spin. At lower altitudes its engines were inefficient and its wing fragile. For all its impressive speed and range, the B-58 was a fragile, tricky benchmark for large supersonic aircraft. Such was the supersonic state of the art in 1960–61.

The crash of a B-58 at the 1961 Paris air show, after a record-breaking crossing of the Atlantic, dramatized the frailties of large supersonic aircraft. Bombers, even ones embodying the then-unique capability of flying at Mach 2 speeds for two hours, were a long way from being supersonic airliners. The Soviet strategic advance meant that no more U.S. supersonic bombers would be built to absorb the development costs for a civilian SST. A U.S. SST would now have to pay its own way. Three separate U.S. SST projects evolved in the 1960s, but neither the companies developing them nor the U.S. taxpayers, then absorbed with another high-technology adventure in Vietnam, ultimately proved willing to foot the bill. Ironically, the Soviet advance in air defense eliminated the American SSTs that the Soviets could have studied to make their own designs more viable.

Soviet Procurement Practices

In the USSR, a decision to proceed with an SST was much simpler. There was no organized body of political opinion to appease or to be accountable to. Normally, by the time an important Soviet project enters the formal decision mechanism, its success is already assured by an elite consensus. Among the thousands that make decisions, support was building for a Soviet SST to further shrink the nation's unparalleled distances. For Aeroflot, responsible for servicing a network that stretched across eleven time zones and 130 degrees of latitude, an SST flagship represented the culmination of a long struggle to link Siberian development sites with European Russia, and to unify the country's transportation and communication networks. The Soviet elite found fascinating a transport concept that later was criticized in the West for its elitism and expense. Soviet aircraft work at this time was not heavily influenced by considerations of cost efficiency or fuel consumption. Resolving the many unknown technical complexities was the chief concern.

Soviet SST development departed from the normal Soviet aircraft procurement process in several important respects.[44] According to Khrushchev, the SST project was launched after the elder Tupolev presented the idea to him at the beach. Tupolev KB was chosen because it was the oldest, best, and most diversified design bureau though Halaby, after his 1963 visit to the USSR, knew of *two* Soviet SST design teams developing two SSTs. The only other KB that could have competed was Ilyushin, at this time absorbed with the protracted travails of the IL-62. Myasishchev's SST design studies were rejected. The Soviets focused on the TU-144 design at the expense of a more ambitious and parallel Mach 3 design project. After 1963, Tupolev became the center of a project that absorbed the entire Soviet aerospace sector. This was not unprecedented, following, rather, the pattern employed in developing the Great Leap Forward aircraft such as the ANT-20 *Maxim Gorky* in 1934, the TU-4 derivative of the B-29 in 1945–47, and Myasishchev's ambitious strategic bombers of the 1950s. Supersonic design had few precedents in Soviet practice, beyond a few fighters. What was unique in this case was that the Soviets would join the West at the technological frontier, rather than imitate. Hence, the mobilization of the entire resources of the industry under Tupolev's aegis.

Formally, the commission to build the aircraft would go through the Civil Air Fleet. Although no R & D cost figures have ever been cited by the Soviets, we do know that preliminary costs were calculated by trebling those for the IL-62 airliner, then the most costly aircraft developed in the sector. This "commissioning" meeting was chaired by Pyotr Dementiev, the Minister of Aircraft Production, later praised for his skillful coordination of the many factories and elements deployed to build the TU-144.

In the case of the TU-144, the decision had already been made by the political leadership to build a prestige SST aircraft of "state importance," so "permission to build" was pro forma.

Normally, this conclave would be followed by the *Skitsovy* or *Eskiznyi Proyekt* (Preliminary Design Meeting). This is a "paper on the table" conference in which Tupolev OKB would have laid out its studies made since 1961 on the subject, based on Western and Soviet data. It is normally an important session, "absorbing the whole of an arduous day" with outlines of proposed performance, quantities of materials required, man-hours, and time scale, or project schedule. Here, we might visualize the "Old Man" leading the Tupolev delegation personally, with detailed questions referred to his son Alexei, designated Chief Designer.

The atmosphere of this meeting is one of day-long "quick-fire cross-examination [with] no room for vagueness or waffle." In the case of the SST project, however, one can imagine that the cross-examination was dominated by the uncertainties of SST technology, which, in 1963, involved more questions than answers. Large delegations from the Ministry of Aviation Production, the Economics and Finance ministries, the Central Institute of Aerohydrodynamics, and the Central Institute of Aviation Engines would normally be involved. By 1963, early versions of the engine ultimately used for the TU-144—developed from the Kuznetsov NK-8 turbofans being readied for the IL-62 airliner—were already running on test beds.[45]

A Technical Project Conference (Tekhnichyeskii Proyekt) providing a more detailed engineering design, followed this by three to fifteen weeks. Preliminary wind-tunnel and aerodynamic data would be presented, especially on established Soviet supersonic designs such as the TU-22 and TU-26. Estimates of detailed weight breakdowns would be attempted, as well as schedules of airframe and systems components. Extremely exact tooling is required for a large supersonic airframe, and in 1963 the Soviets began to commission the manufacture of computer-controlled machine tools for this purpose. The Soviet plastics industry was asked to produce 10,000 separate parts. At this time, the Soviets began to order advanced electronic and navigation components from Britain. More obscurely, orders went out to the KGB and GRU to collect as much detailed technical information as possible on the Concorde being constructed in Toulouse and its engines being developed at Bristol, in the west of England.[46]

It is typical for Soviet authorities to force upon the design bureau an impossibly accelerated time scale, or project schedule. The normal Soviet time scale, from Technical Project Conference to first flight, is on the order of fifteen months. In the case of the TU-144, it was over five years. Part of this was due to the complexity of interlocking technical puzzles requiring solutions. New alloys needed to be developed, though the Soviets later announced that they would limit TU-144 speed to Mach 2.4, above which speed its aluminum alloys would simply melt from the heat created by air friction. This represented a compromise to concentrate for the moment on a Soviet aircraft that would compete with Concorde, and gave second priority to one that would compete with the Mach 3 American SST.

Great battles raged over aerodynamics. From 1964 to 1966, these arguments centered on the necessity of dispensing with the separate tail plane mandated by TsAGI. The TU-144, presented in model form in June 1965, featured the correct slim delta configuration. But TsAGI and the elder Tupolev initially insisted on grouping the four engines in a pod on the fuselage centerline, arguing that this cut drag by 10 percent. Skeptics in the West—and presumably, also in the USSR—pointed out that this increased the possibility of contagious engine failure. The 1967 scale models saw the engine grouping split into two smaller pods, and the distance between them grew with each new version of the aircraft.

Myasishchev's SST Designs

The flamboyant Myasishchev, nicknamed "artiste," or actor, by his Tupolev colleagues, played an unacknowledged role in developing many of the aerodynamic concepts behind the Soviet SST. Myasishchev's M-50 supersonic bomber, the final aircraft to appear as the climax of the July 1961 Tushino air show, was his last design to be realized in metal and fly. (It is now on display at the Soviet Air Force Museum in Monino.) Initially, Myasishchev wished to build the M-50 as a tail-less delta with a canard, or winglet, up front—the configuration adopted for the production version of the TU-144, which appeared in 1972. But after "long discussions" with TsAGI, he was forced to abandon this idea. Theoretical knowledge regarding delta wings was quite sparse in the 1950s, and there were fears regarding its stability and controllability. Myasishchev did provide the M-50 a changing angle of sweep for the leading edge of its wing, a precursor of the ogival shape that later appeared on the Concorde and TU-144 as a cure for stability problems.[47]

Myasishchev also developed other innovations: the small canard wing in the nose to counterbalance a large rear delta wing. He also investigated extensively the possibility of a nuclear-powered bomber. Much theoretical work was required before Tupolev could provide Khrushchev with its projected speed and range. Nuclear power promised to provide the requisite intercontinental range for a strategic bomber. Myasishchev also studied ideas developed by the Germans during the war for an Amerika bomber that would reach New York, such as a two-stage aircraft that would take off from dollies to save weight. Only a portion of the craft would sprint the final distance to the target. This idea was rejected: discarding part of the structure after only part of one flight was deemed too wasteful.[48]

Myasishchev's being kicked upstairs to TsAGI did not end venturesome experimentation. If anything, after he moved to TsAGI in 1960, Myasishchev intensified his theoretical work on large supersonic aircraft, produced at least two SST design studies, and claimed to have done much of the early theoretical work on the slim delta wing necessary for sustained supersonic flight. His contribution to the eventual TU-144 project may be substantial; in part, this may be rooted in the continued skepticism of Soviet designers regarding delta wings.[49]

A 1984 Soviet biography of Myasishchev, *Heavenly Aspirations,* nearly ignores Myasishchev's supersonic work, but provides an undated photograph of him, possibly at the Moscow Aviation Institute, pointing to a color rendering of an SST, with a large pronounced canard winglet behind the cockpit and a large wedge-shaped delta wing. The SST rendering overlaps a chart depicting the evolution of wings designed for rising speeds, leading from straight, to swept back, to three delta-wing profiles. A three-view drawing of a different and more detailed design, judged airworthy by aeronautical engineers, appears directly below.[50]

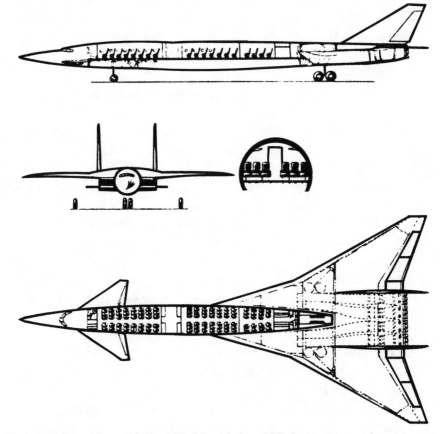

Pregnant Bat: a late (1963–64?) Myasishchev SST design proposal— probably his last. The large canard and double-delta wing reflect B-70 influence.

Although Myasishchev told *Komsomolskaya Pravda* before 1964 that he was engaged in SST "development work,"[51] this is the first evidence that he actually developed complete SST designs. Myasishchev may have had in mind a slightly slower SST than the Mach 2.2 TU-144; he predicted that SSTs in service by 1970 "would cruise at speeds approaching 2,000 kph," or about 1,250 mph. He personified the "We can do anything" spirit that informed the Soviet aircraft industry in the 1930s, once saying, "I set about to accomplish any task and will accomplish it—if the industry will provide me the necessary components."[52]

This illustrative evidence indicates that Myasishchev's SST work pushed beyond the purely theoretical and hints at a Soviet SST competition. These Myasishchev efforts must predate 1963. Khrushchev's story—that the TU-144 was commissioned from Tupolev during a conversation over sketches on the beach during a Black Sea holiday—masks unrevealed complexities. As usual, Khrushchev is highly selective in his recollections. The Tupolev SST design may have been the possibly preordained victor over competing entries. There was a more ambitious Mach 3 design study team whose work paralleled the Mach 2 design study that became the TU-144. Myasishchev's plan drawings indicate he had detailed on paper a flyable SST airliner. It is possible that Tupolev's chief rival in airliner design, Ilyushin, may have developed design studies, though it is likely these were subordinated to Tupolev in 1963 when the project was commissioned. No reference to SST work appears in a recent Soviet history of Ilyushin, though Ilyushin himself was observed picking up reams of Concorde data at Farnborough in 1961.

The salient evidence for an SST design competition—beyond the existence of the rendering and plan drawings themselves—is that Myasishchev is pointing to three series of numbers visible under the rendering, consistent with the design goals defining all Soviet aircraft design competitions: 2,500 kilometer/hour cruising speed; 5,000 kilometer range; 130 tons gross weight. Save for the range, these are identical to the design criteria prominently displayed by the Soviets at the time of the TU-144's announcement at the 1965 Paris air show.

Myasishchev projects only a 5,000-kilometer range for his design, whereas Tupolev projected 6,500. Myasishchev was still recovering from the pitfalls of overambitious designs. Following a seismic eruption by Khrushchev, his KB had been closed and his factory converted to helicopter production when it was learned that his supersonic bombers could not return from a bombing run on the continental United States, as hoped and claimed. Thereafter, discreet and modest claims were only seemly for a chastened Myasishchev.

Tupolev, however, had recently scored with the ultra long range TU-114D, and had apparently gambled on the hope that Soviet jet-engine makers could eventually match the range capability of the 114's German-developed turboprops. This triumph of hope over experience woefully miscarried. The TU-144 supersonically achieved slightly over half the claimed 6,500-kilometer range with its original Kuznetsov engines. As time passed, the 144's range and fuel efficiency deteriorated, as its "weight creep" upward overwhelmed what incremental power Soviet engineers were willing to extract from its fuel-thirsty engines.

The three Myasishchev SST plans reward careful analysis. Two features show a higher degree of sophistication than the prototype TU-144: the double-delta form of the wing and the very large fixed canard, with about eight times the area of the later 144's retractable canards. If these are products of the 1961–63 period when Tupolev was also engaged in design studies, this means the 144 production version was indebted to Myasishchev for both these features, which were softened and modified for the 1972 production version.

The later aircraft is an original, indeed exuberant, early version of an SST, as would be expected from Myasishchev. The fuselage had a pronounced area-rule profile and "sagging belly" that would not have survived much supersonic wind-tunnel work. The pronounced hump of the central wing gives it the aspect of a bat viewed head on. The twin tails recall the MIG-25, which first flew in 1965, while the outboard landing gear seems structurally suspect.

There is considerable dead space in the nose and belly of the aircraft as schematized and apparently a ballast tank to compensate for cg (center-of-gravity) shift in the tail of the fuselage. Evidence that these drawings were never realized in metal is provided by the complex path required for air to reach the inner engines. This air would have been subject to considerable "boundary layer" turbulence, since some of it was slowed by skin friction across the fuselage. Tupolev had endless problems regulating and controlling a longer, straighter intake on the 144, and these subtly double-curved passageways would have defeated the most ingenious of aerodynamicists trying to deliver a homogeneous wall of air subsonically to the engines from 0 to 1,500 mph. The pronounced rearward position of the engines and their isolation from the passenger compartment might have given it an advantage over the 144's deafening roar at cruise speeds.

The absence of Concorde influence—no droop snoot or ogival wing—is remarkable, given the Concorde's strong influence on the TU-144. This suggests that the Myasishchev SST was worked up before the Concorde's outline became public in 1963. The closest conceptual ancestor of this Myasishchev SST is the B-70 bomber, cancelled in 1960, which resembled it in fuselage and tail, but not in engine placement or wing plan. The last known Myasishchev creation was truly unique, and a preliminary examination of the plans suggests that it was airworthy.

By setting the distance from floor to overhead racks at six feet and extrapolating, it is possible to approximate the dimensions of this craft *vis à vis* its likely rival, the prototype TU-144. Its critical dimension—length—comes to approximately 196 feet, versus 180 for the TU-144 prototype. The seating shown provides for 101 passengers. The Tupolev was more space efficient, carrying the same passenger complement within dramatically smaller dimensions. On design criteria, the Tupolev seems the better design. If there was a design competition, the TU-144 would have been a better choice.

The Khrushchev Commission

In the normal course of events there would have been competition for the privilege of building Aeroflot's flagship, the supersonic airliner. Among Soviet designers, Sukhoi built a four-engined delta-winged bomber, with reported competition from Lavochin, for a later supersonic bomber competition. It is hard to imagine the Ilyushin KB failing to field a competing design proposal at a time when it was contesting Tupolev's supremacy in the civil-airliner sector. But Soviet sources affirm that the age, size, and experience of Tupolev KB made it the natural choice.

The "inevitability" of this choice was ensured by the patronage of Nikita Khrushchev. The Party Secretary had first met the "Old Man" in 1931, and regarded him as the dean of Soviet aircraft designers. Khrushchev especially respected Tupolev as one of the very few who had stood up to Stalin. When Stalin had reiterated his call for "one of the toughest problems facing our designers"—a strategic bomber that could reach targets in the United States and return to Soviet bases—Tupolev had the courage to tell him it couldn't be done. The task was "simply impossible to fulfill" owing to the "limits of contemporary knowledge." Khrushchev emphasizes that Tupolev was telling this to a man who had already jailed him for years on a manufactured pretext. But, "He understood his responsibilities and he understood his profession. He knew such a plane was impossible and he told Stalin so."[53]

In his memoirs, Khrushchev describes Tupolev as "a diplomat as well as a great scientist and scholar . . . head and shoulders above" other talented Soviet designers. He "never tried to force his ideas down my throat." Unlike most specialists, he didn't nourish grudges if his proposals were turned down. As far as Khrushchev was concerned, "The leader in the field is Comrade Andrei Nikolayevich Tupolev . . . one of a handful of men responsible for the birth and development of our civil and military aviation."[54]

This strong connection with the top goes far to explain Tupolev's return to prominence in the years following Stalin's death. Tupolev became a member of Khrushchev's entourage, accompanying him on Black Sea cruises and also abroad. His prominent role in endorsing Khrushchev's 1960 demobilization program was no accident.

Khrushchev, on his side, respected and needed the veteran designer. His memoirs reflect his sensitivity to the technocratic symbolism of aircraft and their major role in establishing Soviet international prestige. Khrushchev records his embarrassment in arriving for the 1955 Geneva Summit Conference in a modest twin-engine IL-14, when all the other delegations arrived in four-engined airliners: "Our own delegation found itself at a disadvantage from the very moment we landed at Geneva airport." Soviet civil airliners were an important backdrop to protocol and diplomatic prestige.[55]

The first State visit of a Soviet delegation to the United States, in September 1959, provided another opening for airliner one-upsmanship. Mikhail Kozlov and the elder Tupolev had already flown the huge, long-distance, high-capacity TU-114 to the United States three months before to test the route; "Aloysha"— Alexei Tupolev—the future Chief Designer of the TU-144, was in Khrushchev's retinue. On arriving in Washington, a potential disaster arose when it was found that the huge Soviet turboprop was too high off the ground for U.S. embarkation equipment, and the Soviet delegation had to descend via an emergency ladder. Khrushchev was secretly delighted:

> We had to leave the plane not in the formal, dignified way called for by protocol, but practically climbing down using our hands and our legs! We didn't let ourselves be embarrassed by this problem. Far from it. It was an embarrassment for the Americans. They hadn't known our plane was such a giant. We could see the wonder in their eyes as they looked at it. They'd never seen anything like it and they certainly didn't have anything like it themselves, nor would they have one for a long time.

Following this auspicious arrival, history records that this first visit was a great success. Khrushchev believed the Americans later postponed the signing of an air agreement to link the two superpower capitals because they did not have an aircraft that could match the TU-114's feat of being able to fly from Moscow to Washington nonstop.

Tupolev's capital, after supplying designs which bolstered the prestige and confidence of Soviet delegations overseas, was at its peak with Khrushchev. He frequently accompanied Khrushchev on his trips and had a vacation *dasha* only five minutes' walk from Khrushchev's summer home in the Crimea. He would walk over to visit Khrushchev, blueprints in a folder, to try out his latest and most visionary ideas on the Party Secretary.

One of these proposals was for a nuclear-powered bomber, which "greatly excited" Khrushchev because it promised unlimited range. However, its speed and altitude represented no advance over the subsonic TU-95, the original bomber version of the TU-114. It could climb only to 16,000 meters (over 52,000 feet) and would be vulnerable to anti-aircraft fire. Tupolev insisted, "An atomic-powered bomber is within the realm of possibility." Asked if one could be built for passenger use, Tupolev said the danger of radiation poisoning was too high; the flight deck could be insulated from contamination, but not a passenger compartment. Besides, building "special airfields" for such an aircraft would be too expensive. In 1959–60, the idea of a nuclear-powered aircraft surfaced in the Soviet press but was later abandoned. This exotic toy was too much even for the Central Committee.[58]

Tupolev's proximity to Khrushchev on the Black Sea gave him direct access to the Party Secretary, who then would carry the idea to the Politburo. It was in one of these seaside design seminars that the TU-144 had its birth. According to Khrushchev, Tupolev "brought the blueprints to me where I was vacationing on the Black Sea coast, and we gave him a go-ahead."[59] The alluring prospect of Soviet delegations arriving in a svelte supersonic airliner for the opening of the UN or an international conference must have danced like sugarplums in Khrushchev's imagination.

Brezhnev—The Kurator?

A few months before the Soviet SST was announced, Khrushchev was peaceably deposed, the only Soviet leader not to die in office. The conspirators moved on behalf of a Party bureaucracy upset at Khrushchev's reckless maneuvers and destabilization of Soviet institutions. The SST, however, was not cancelled as one of Nikita's "hare-brained schemes," for Khrushchev's successors were, if anything, even more caught up in technocratic intoxication. In fact, the available evidence suggests that its tempo was accelerated.

Although the formula of "collective leadership" cloaked for some time the dominant personalities in the new coalition, Leonid Brezhnev's appointment as First Secretary of the Central Committee foreshadowed his eventual emergence as kingpin.

One of the plums in Khrushchev's portfolio was the role of *Kurator:* sponsor or godfather of the SST. Soviet projects of "State importance"—the Baikal-Amur Magistral Railway to Siberian energy resource areas, the Kamaz truck plant, the automobile plant built in Togliattigrad—all enjoy a *kurator*, or coordinator at the very top. He squeezes resources from the rest of the sector and the overall Soviet economy to ensure that shortages of finances, engineering, talent, and raw material will not slow realization of high-profile projects associated with the Supreme Leadership's prestige. Even a superpower's concentrated resources, however, do not guarantee timely resolution of unprecedented technical problems.

It is difficult to identify a more likely candidate for the TU-144's godfather than Brezhnev himself. Here was a technocrat with unquestioned faith that technological breakthroughs could be mandated through simple perseverance and allocation of sufficient resources. In his memoirs, Brezhnev noted that he had inherited his father's "stubbornness, patience, and the habit, once having started something, of without fail carrying it through to its conclusion."[60] This may account for the fact that the SST project actually survived Brezhnev by three months. Brezhnev died on November 10, 1982; the first official intimation of the TU-144's end came in March 1983.

If Brezhnev was not the Soviet SST's actual godfather, his values certainly informed and fostered its development. Among his earliest acknowledged duties after Khrushchev's ouster was "development of astronautics."[61] Brezhnev had started his professional career as a metallurgical engineer. This exposed him to the excitement of rapid technical change in the 1930s. However, like other engineers who rise to high statesmanship, Brezhnev lacked strategic vision. He could not bring himself to abandon complex, costly projects once launched if they embodied the Faustian promise of technocratic breakthroughs. This is the major explanation of the twenty-three-year history of the Soviet SST project.

Brezhnev was a deeply religious man. His faith in technical progress—the one aspect of Marxist-Leninism with substance for him and his contemporaries—remained unswerving despite repeated disasters and costly reverses. In *Pages From His Life*, Brezhnev assigned a Stalinist quasireligious role to science and technology, "the life-giving well-spring of technical, economic and social progress, the growth of the people's spiritual culture."[62] Under Brezhnev and his successors, the "scientific-technical revolution" was the engine of progress. As high priest of Soviet scientific-technical progress, Brezhnev could not pull the plug on the SST program even after its impracticality was obvious. Only corrective, palliative surgery was permitted. This allowed the invalid a few added years of life. The hidden hand of the Central Committee can be seen in the massive financial and engineering resources focused on the SST in 1964–69. One aspect of this resource allocation may be tied to Brezhnev personally. Western visitors to the TU-144's assembly hall were invariably impressed with the quality of titanium work there, which several pronounced the most advanced titanium fabrication and application center in the world. This may reflect the eminence of a 1935 graduate of the Dneprodzerzhinsk Metallurgical Institute.

The TU-144 must have represented the ultimate toy for Brezhnev, an inveterate gadgeteer. He delighted in all manner of high-tech consumer toys. He used extensively a timed cigarette case that would deliver a cigarette every 45 seconds, and took a boyish delight in a fleet of forty-four exotic cars, many given to him by Western leaders on State visits. At its peak, Brezhnev's car collection included a Rolls-Royce limousine, a Cadillac provided him by Nixon, and a Citröen-Maserati from the French. On being offered a Mercedes-Benz sports coupe by his State hosts in Germany, he became so enthused that he jumped in the car, eluded his bodyguard, and tore down a mountain road to the Rhine so fast that he ripped out its sump on a pothole. Such a First Secretary would remain a strong patron of the SST.[63] This patronage by the Party's Supreme Leadership guaranteed the Soviet SST an early, high-profile introduction on the world stage.

3

SOVIET LEAKS
AND WESTERN
SPECULATIONS, 1965–1968

F*light International* speculated that the eleven-day 1965 Paris air show would "surely be the largest, most comprehensive, most ambitious, most bewildering and inassimilable aeronautical exhibition of all time." Breaking all precedent, the Soviets flew in ten civil aircraft at the last minute, which proved to be the stars of the show. This impressive coup was backstopped by an impressive sales effort featuring 100 Soviet representatives, brochures, color films, desk models, and giveaways including badges, lapel pins, calendars, and postcards. Aviaexport, the new Soviet air export agency, had been launched with a vengeance.

Debut: Paris, 1965

The Soviet sales chalet at the Paris air show was populated by a galaxy of Soviet celebrities, including Chief Designers Tupolev and Antonov. Cosmonaut Yuri Gagarin was on hand to sign autographs at the exhibit of Soviet space hardware. The original Soviet show stealer was the huge AN-22 transport. But on the third day of the show, this was eclipsed by a scale model flown in from Moscow: four feet long; it was the first tangible proof of the long-rumored Soviet SST.

Flight International had guessed that the TU-144 might be a giant transport or the SST. The somewhat imprecise model was surrounded by Soviet engineers, who provided tidbits of information to inquirers, which the elder Tupolev garnished with occasional flashes of sharp, biting humor. Technical replies often left "infuriating uncertainties and doubts"; only Tupolev and Antonov spoke "with the assurance and certitude of the Oracle."[1]

The model, however impressive, was enigmatic, with many details unclarified. A prominent board asserted design goals: cruising speed was Mach 2.3, or 2,500 kilometers per hour (1,500 mph); range was 6,500 kilometers (4,030 miles); gross weight was estimated at 130 tons (286,000 lbs), including 121 passengers. The Soviets claimed the SST had been "ordered by Aeroflot." Paris–New York flights were guaranteed nonstop. The impression was left that it would fly in 1968, a promise kept by a margin of a few hours. Several different engines were reportedly being developed, all with thrust reversers—a feature never seen on the completed aircraft. Undercarriage details were unknown because the model was presented in flying trim. Questions regarding details of the navigation system and autopilot were ducked.

As general as it was, it was plain that the model was not a clone of the Concorde: the semi-oval cross section and flat floor of the fuselage more closely approximated the U.S. SST, the Boeing 2707. British observers were skeptical regarding its projected weight of only 128 tons—rightfully so—and estimated correctly that each of its four engines must produce 40,000 lbs. thrust.[2]

The manner of the TU-144's presentation in Paris reflected conflicting goals. Previous leaks and hints from Soviet authorities had focused on its potential ability to cut its flight time across the USSR's unequalled distances by two-thirds, particularly the rapidly growing West-East axis of Siberian development expanding out to Khabarovsk. The high-profile debut in Paris, with a firmament of Soviet notables in attendance, introduced new elements into the equation. Like its older siblings the TU-104 and TU-114, the TU-144 was a symbol of Soviet prestige, a showcase of advanced technology. Its debut coincided with a Soviet export drive for a variety of aircraft. For the first time, references were made to possible international service; to Paris, London, and New York. Whether the TU-144 was intended primarily for domestic or international service remained unclear for some time. Propaganda imperatives took precedence over realistic consideration of its potential economic contribution or potential costs. Its role as an airliner serving the Soviet economy was eclipsed by the drive to play up a showcase of Soviet technology on a global scale.

The TU-144's older sisters had been sprung upon the world fully grown. It was a mark of growing Soviet confidence, or overconfidence, that the TU-144 was presented in a highly un- developed state, with many technical details still provisional. Whereas the 104 and 114 had initially appeared as flying pre- production prototypes, the 144 was represented by a Concorde- like scale model and a list of specifications that in reality were design goals. At least one of these—range—was never fulfilled.

The last-minute arrival of the massive Soviet exhibit and delegation at the 1965 Salon Aeronautique, and the arrival of the SST model only on its third day, reflected a decision to make as impressive a publicity splash as possible, in the manner of the now-disgraced Khrushchev. The Soviet SST project was still in a malleable, immature, unsettled state when first thrust into this spotlight.

It was in some senses a premature birth. Design features of the 1965 model—in particular, the engine placement—were in flux. Two additional TU-144 models circulated in Europe in 1967. No two of the three scale models were identical. Because details of their SST development were closely held, rarely detailed in the Soviet press or expanded upon by Soviet principals, the initially confusing differences among these scale models offers unique insights into the Soviet struggle to produce an unprecedented aircraft type at top speed. Soviet zeal for publicity to a degree outweighed instinctive secrecy. Unveiling of the Soviet SST was a boon to SST protagonists in the West, who used it to support their parallel projects. Western fascination with a Soviet SST had predated its debut by half a decade.

Soviet SST Leaks Useful in the West

The advent of a Soviet SST inspired SST protagonists in the West, and it was seized upon for various political and commercial purposes. Its appearance coincided with the first public revelations of true Concorde costs and by 1966, Britain's Labour government was taking a hard look at this high-tech adventure initiated by its Tory predecessors. Projected costs had ballooned to $1.4 billion, four times the November 1962 estimate.[3] Concorde supporters pointed to the TU-144 as evidence of the soundness of the concept.

In the United States, the TU-144 played a supporting role in Senate debates on an SST. Senator A. S. "Mike" Moroney, chairman of the Senate Aviation Subcommittee, later to distinguish himself by introducing a bill to ban the TU-144 from U.S. airspace, noted, "The Russians are trying their best to be first with a supersonic plane. I would hate to see us trail in the international field." Senator Henry "Scoop" Jackson—from Boeing—asked how fast the Russians were moving "in this direction" and was told that secrecy prevented the United States from discovering the degree of Soviet progress.[4]

Moroney continued to beat the drum for a U.S. SST, using suspect data. In September 1966, he argued that the Soviets might replace the British in the Concorde consortium. He asserted, "The Soviet engines fit the French airframe . . . the French are raving about the Soviet engines." Later events indicated that the French would indeed have raved had they installed NK-144 engines in the Concorde, though not in the way Senator Moroney intended. Moroney expressed concern that, "a Franco-Soviet combine might build a second-generation titanium superjet to rival the proposed design," though this was a speculation founded only on rumor. The idea, however, achieved a life of its own. In October 1966, Pyotr Dementiev, Soviet Minister of Aviation Production, visited Paris as part of a delegation drumming up trade with Europe. One Soviet official allowed that the USSR might indeed provide engines for French fuselages.[5]

SST advocates East and West found mutual publicity synergistic. In December 1966, Soviet Premier Alexei Kosygin visited the Concorde assembly bay at Sud-Aviation in Toulouse, commenting, "we have similar problems with our aircraft" and wished the French "every success in solving theirs." He inspected a Concorde fuselage in pale green (probably zinc chromate) still devoid of nose, wings, and tail. At the Toulouse city hall, he proposed to the crowd that their two nations share "our scientific efforts and unite them . . . we can advance much faster than if we go along separate paths."[6] This was the beginning of formal technical cooperation between French and Soviets. But the thrust of his speech went unheeded: it is much more satisfying to direct the thrust of an expensive national prestige program in a competitive direction. The East and West were engaged in a race to see which would first fly an SST.

Soviet progress received mixed reviews in the West. Gordon Bain, first director of the U.S. government's SST program, doubted that it was commercially competitive because of the uncertainty of Soviet warranties and parts supply. Joseph Califano, McNamara's aide, noted, "The Soviets have had virtually no success with their commercial airline ventures." The CIA reported, in August 1966, that the Soviets were contemplating a Mach 3 SST and predicted that the TU-144 would enter service one or two years ahead of the Concorde, but would not achieve its design objectives. The introduction at Paris was the debut of a "propaganda campaign" that might end with a first flight to celebrate the fiftieth anniversary of the revolution, in November 1967.[7]

In March 1967, the CIA reportedly predicted that the TU-144 would be flown to that year's Paris air show. Halaby, now Vice-President of Pan Am, predicted that the Soviets would flight-test the TU-144 during the 1967–68 winter and enter it in service three years later. A full-scale mockup had already been seen in the USSR. Its NK-144 engines had already logged 1,000 hours on the test beds. Other reports echoed the CIA story that the Soviets were racing to have their first test flight by November

1967. Reportedly, all the Soviets did on this important anniversary was to roll out the prototype.[8]

The most ambitious attempt to exploit the TU-144 was an article ascribed to Najeeb Halaby that appeared in *Look* magazine in 1967. Halaby had learned Russian while hoping to become naval attaché in Moscow during World War II. But as head of the FAA, he was sent twice to the Soviet Union to negotiate air service between the two superpowers.

Halaby made public earlier official concerns that the Soviets could create an SST at any time by installing a "passenger pod in one of their supersonic bombers and fly their leaders to a politically important spot." In 1961, some of Kennedy's advisers had been concerned that Khrushchev "might make such a spectacular flight from Moscow to New Delhi or Peking, or even London or Paris, to demonstrate their technological progress. We could have done the same thing." In fact, there had been a 1961 proposal to modify a B-58 as a "Special Air Mission" plane that would presumably have delivered JFK quickly to distant destinations. This configuration was not economic: only "a few seats" could be created within a bomber fuselage by forgoing the bomb bay and electronic components. But Convair did plan a airliner version of the B-58, utilizing its disposable pod. The B-58's skittishness in service must have ended this dubious proposal.[9]

By 1967, there was "much evidence" that the TU-144 would beat the Concorde into the air. NK-144 engines had spent "more than a thousand test-hours" at TsAGI, where a full-scale mockup that "passengers were trying" had also been seen. About thirty French aeronautical experts spent three weeks at TsAGI, Kharkov, and other sites in October 1965, and a number of Franco-Russian reciprocal visits had followed. But to the best of Halaby's knowledge, no American had visited the Soviet SST research, development, or manufacturing sites—nor had any Soviet visited Boeing or Lockheed, where U.S. SST development was sited.

Halaby optimistically believed that the 144's first flight was planned for the 1967–68 winter, with commercial service to follow in 1970. Halaby had spent much time conversing with Soviets disappointed with the "long-range" IL-62 airliner who "would like to recover with a resounding victory." It was likely Soviets would attempt to undersell the $16 million price of the Concorde.

British and French engineers who had recently inspected it reported that the Soviet SST was designed for a 143-ton takeoff gross weight, smaller than the Concorde.

Although propaganda was one of the reasons for producing the TU-144, the Soviets had real reasons for wanting an SST: Prestige routes from Moscow to Peking or Havana were very long. Halaby concluded that the SST promised to be "the greatest, the most efficient, most productive long-range transport in history, so they have a basic Communist communication need for it."[10]

Informative Scale Models, 1965–67

The fomenting behind-the-scenes evolution of the Soviet SST was reflected in the series of scale models that proliferated in 1967–68. Expo 1967, which opened in Montreal on April 27, 1967, was another opportunity for a splashy exposition of Soviet technical progress. The Soviets spent $15 million on their pavilion, versus $9 million spent by the Americans. A highlight of the Soviet exhibit was another scale model of the TU-144, which differed considerably in detail not only from the one shown at Paris in 1965 but the model that appeared in Paris a month later. Taken together, they provide the best clues to the 144's design evolution and the engineering debate behind the scenes.

The Montreal model reflected the rapid evolution of the design. The 1965 version had grouped the four engines together in a pod on the fuselage centerline, the most distinctive design difference from the Concorde. The Montreal version split them in front and joined them at the rear. Landing gear was also changed, with the reinforcing strut to the front rather than to the rear. The Paris model shown a month later went a step further and moved from an ogival wing to a double delta, a feature of the production TU-144 not to appear full size for another five years. It also featured engines on the wings, about halfway to the position finally adopted in 1972. The prototype of 1968 trailed these models in design concept.

In 1965, the Concorde had been eclipsed by the dramatic debut of the TU-144, challenged in Paris only by the bare specification sheet of a heavier Concorde. However, at the 1967 Salon Aeronautique, the tables were turned. The West clearly upstaged the East with a full-scale mockup of the Concorde, through which 50,000 people passed during the course of the air show.

After the publicity blitz of 1965, the Soviets were almost secretive at the 1967 Salon Aeronautique. The English-speaking press complained that the Soviet press conference had been held under "somewhat clandestine" conditions in the cavernous depths of the huge AN-22 transport, with only the French press invited.[11] But the British were soon to see the prototype itself.

Three months later, Sir John Stonehouse, Minister of Technology, led a high-powered British delegation to the Soviet Union, which inspected the TU-144 prototype taking shape in its final assembly hangar. The delegation reported that it had been shown more details than any previous group, and was told that the aircraft would fly in early 1968. Stonehouse found Tupolev's assembly facilities in Moscow almost primitive in comparison with Filton, but the "same unmistakeable pterodactyl shape" loomed in the hangar. The assemblers were "thick-set workers clambering all over the slender air-frame . . . peasants straight from the steppes." Inspired by the scene, Stonehouse seized a microphone and delivered an impromptu speech on international friendship, using an interpreter.[12]

Invited to inspect the prototype, Sir George Edwards, Chairman of the British Aircraft Corporation, delivered a bluff lecture to the Chief Designer on SST design: "There were so many things that were transparently not right about it that I said to young Tupolev, 'You'll have to change a lot of things. You've got the intakes and the engines in the wrong place, for one. You've got too unsophisticated a wing design, with no camber or twist, for two. And although your bypass engines will help you when it comes to airport noise (which I wouldn't have thought in Russia was very sensitive),' I said 'you'll lose a lot of efficiency when it comes to your cruise performance.' " When told the engines needed to be put "just about halfway across the wing," Tupolev responded, "Well, I know that, but we just can't get the control system to work with the engine-out case."

This struck a poignant note with Sir George, because the Concorde team was simultaneously wrestling with the same difficult problem. Both SSTs in 1967 were having theoretical problems recovering from a situation in which both of the engines on one side had quit. Tupolev appears to confirm that actual design work in 1967 was being devoted to the underwing engine location, not the configuration of the prototype the British visitors had been shown.[13]

In mid-1968, the Soviet propaganda tempo began to pick up as the time for the first flight of the TU-144 drew near. In July, the medal given to the USSR's top civil pilots was amended to include an image of the TU-144. SST lapel badges on sale at newsstands in major Soviet cities proclaimed, "We shall conquer time and space." A roll-out of the 144 was scheduled for October, with the first flight before the end of the year. The flight-testing schedule was foreshortened in prospect to a few months. Photos of the first assembled airframe began to appear in the West.[14]

The TU-144's first commercial flight was tentatively scheduled for March 1970, between Moscow and Osaka, Japan, for the opening ceremonies of the Expo '70 world's fair. Negotiations were underway with both India and Pakistan regarding SST service to those countries; a TU-144 would reportedly either be leased or sold to them under liberal credit conditions. M. M. Kulik, Deputy Minister of Civil Aviation, stated that Soviet designers were already at work on a second-generation SST that would replace the TU-144 by 1980.[15]

In August, Marshal Bugayev, the new Aeroflot chief, published in *Aviation and Cosmonautics*—the Soviet Air Force monthly—so glowing a report of the 144 that some Western experts concluded that the aircraft had already flown.[16] This mistaken impression was corrected by a delegation of senior Soviet engineers "closely associated with the project" present at a Soviet trade exposition in London. The original 144 scale model had been relegated to the permanent Moscow exhibit of Soviet economic achievements. But a new scale model, forty feet long, was the centerpiece of this Soviet trade fair in London. Mounted on a twelve-foot-high pole, the model could raise or lower its landing gear and lower its nose. Telephones surrounding the huge model stated that the aircraft would enter "worldwide service" in the early 1970s. The engine exhausts were lit in red to stimulate afterburners.

Encouraged by this heartening setting, Soviet officials provided rare insights into TU-144 technical snags. The prototype was still in its hangar at Zhukovsky Airfield, undergoing tests on its communication gear. Engines had not yet been installed in the airframe, but this would shortly follow. The two most serious development problems were internal aerodynamics: "problems with the air intakes"; and problems dealing with the heat of the skin, which rose in temperature to 150° C during cruise. These problems were not to go away. But the British concluded that TU-144 progress made it a more formidable competitor than the Boeing proposal.[17]

Economic Thinking Behind the TU-144

In 1968, Alexei Tupolev, now eighty years old, responded to an invitation by British aviation writer Bill Gunston to write an SST article for *Science Journal*. He began by drawing a comparison with the other superpower: "Air transport has a special significance in vast countries such as the Soviet Union and the United States." Here the spur to travel faster was greatest, because of the time saved on long distances. (He did not address the dramatic differences between the two superpower transport systems and the dominant role of air in the USSR.)

Tupolev reviewed the great leaps forward by Aeroflot in the previous decade. In 1956, the year his TU-104 jetliner was introduced, every Aeroflot flight was carried by piston-engined aircraft and the average speed of Aeroflot flights was 200 kph, or about 120 mph. By 1966, jets carried 85 percent of the traffic, turboprops the rest, and average speed had risen to 550 kph, or 350 mph. Since 1966, average speed had increased still further, partly from using even-faster aircraft and partly from eliminating fuel stops. In 1968, the average Aeroflot passenger saved over twenty-four hours compared with the best alternative road or water route. In carrying 53 million passengers in 1967, Aeroflot had saved the Soviet national economy 55 million man-days, equivalent to saving a year's work for 150,000 people.

These faster schedules generated additional traffic. In nine years—1956 to 1967—Aeroflot's passenger and freight volume had increased nine times. Cost per unit of traffic was cut in half, and income per unit rose 10 percent. Profitability more than doubled. The Soviet Union therefore had "a peculiar interest" in SSTs.[18]

Tupolev later told Gunston that the Soviet SST had been based on the costs of man-hours saved. Early Soviet SST thinking was dominated by consideration of the USSR's vast internal distances, unparalleled in the world. Since exploitation of western Siberian resources was one of the main emphases of the State plan, the SST became associated with Siberian development schemes. Eighty-five percent of the travel between Moscow and Siberia was by air, and the bulk of this, around 1960, was done by senior bureaucrats and planners. It was estimated that SSTs would cut flight time between Moscow and Siberia from eight to three hours. Multiplying each trip by five hours and calculating the time saved became an important economic tool for advancing the Soviet SST program internally. The Soviet SST obviously was not originally intended for the toiling masses, nor were its infrequent scheduled flights truly open to the public. It was conceived as a conveyance for the Soviet elite.[19]

Having constructed these elaborate rationales—including

trebling the development cost of the IL-86—to impress the State planners, the "Old Man" admitted, "We then spent more than this." Economic considerations did not loom large in the inception of the project. The Soviet leaders did as they did with any new aircraft: they defined the performance levels required, decided how many they needed to fill requirements (references to requirements for seventy-five SSTs probably echo early projections), and went ahead with the project. True costs were almost irrelevant. Materials and resources were brought to bear on this State prestige project.[20]

The technological challenges involved, unparalleled and unanticipated in their complexity, meant the aircraft was woefully uneconomic by the time it entered service. By the time it became available in numbers, commercial aviation conditions, even within the Soviet Union, had radically changed. The assumption of the Tupolev father and son that continuing acceleration of flight speeds was "the wave of the future" was overtaken by the advent of cheap mass flight via widebodied airliners. Continuing Aeroflot growth in activity overwhelmed Soviet aviation fuel supplies, leading to spot and seasonal shortages that were analogous to the fuel shortages in the West. This myopic vision was hardly restricted to the Soviets; the Tupolevs were merely expressing the views of their professional caste.

In the immediate aftermath of the TU-144's greatest triumph, its first flight—"as the world press marked with yard long headlines its epochal achievement"—its Chief Designer gave a long interview to *Tekhnika Molodezhi (Technology for Youth)*. Questions flowed and could not be cut off; the interview continued close to midnight. The 144 designers recognized that it was relatively easy to design a plane to carry passengers at supersonic speed. What was difficult was satisfying the requirements peculiar to civil aviation, the three pillars of which were efficiency, reliability, and comfort.

Cost assumptions behind Soviet SST development were naïve and simple minded, a straight-line extrapolation of earlier experience with the transition from piston to jet airliners. There was no anticipation of how technical complexity and costs could jump in geometrical, not arithmetic, progressions.[21]

The transition from Soviet piston-engined airliners such as the LI-2 and IL-14 in the mid-fifties to the TU-104 and IL-18 saw transportation costs double at first. But with development, jetliners twenty years later had halved the cost of the "piston veterans." As flight speeds now were doubling again, Tupolev naïvely assumed that the experience would repeat itself:

> Economists had calculated that the first stage of SST exploitation expenditures would double those of subsonic aircraft of equal flight weight. That does not imply that the work of hosts of scientists, designers, and production personnel was wasted. This is the unavoidable price of progress. Experts believe that in 10–15 years, owing to SST aerodynamic refinements and reduction of fuel consumption, their use cost would surpass subsonic jets by only 10–15 percent.[22]

The unprecedented complexity of the TU-144, which represented a near-trebling of cruising speeds, not a doubling, was not fully recognized. The "huge complex of literally hundreds of groups in areas of aerodynamics, durability, etc. . . . Each . . . contributed their share to the SST's perfection, but also to its cost." Landing-gear hydraulics, for example, had to be custom built and could not be ordered from available catalogs of mass-produced components. But the rough rule of doubled cost was woefully erroneous: wind-tunnel time was ten times—a whole magnitude—more than previous designs, not double, and this figure was released at an early stage in the 144's aerodynamic development.

Aeroflot's original economic rationale in 1963 was that the increased speeds of jetliners saved 24.9 hours per passenger. It was calculated that widespread use of the TU-144 would save thirty-six hours per passenger. Yet overall R & D costs started out at an estimate of three times those of the IL-62, the most complex Soviet airliner up to that time. Cost estimates did not take into account that high speeds would "unduly" elevate maintenance costs; the TU-144's engines were rated for only 250 hours between overhauls in the beginning.

The Chief Designer Recalls Design Challenges

Basking later in the success of the TU-144's first flights, Tupolev the younger provided a fascinating review of the technical puzzles that had impeded development of the prototype. Although Alexei Tupolev was more optimistic in 1969 than he was to be later, it was plain that the TU-144 had thoroughly tested his professional mettle. He confirmed that airliners were much more demanding to design than military aircraft, which weren't "such a problem." The real professional challenge was "to achieve civil-aviation qualities."

Western experts who knew both Tupolevs observe that Alexei did not inherit his father's occasional spark of genius, but did have a better grasp of the business and economic factors which predominated airliner design.[23] Alexei emphasized that the prime requirement for civil airliners was "economic efficiency," which he saw in terms of aerodynamic efficiency and airport logistics. Drag had been reduced "literally by bits." Reflecting the widespread technical search, even the surface paints were carefully analyzed. The final prototype exterior shape had been chosen only after study of over 100 variants.

Major design debates revolved around the use of glass. Air friction, which generated high temperatures, required that a visor be developed to protect the cockpit glass at high speeds. The traditional panoramic view from the cockpit had to be abandoned. As with the Concorde, a "droop snoop" was devised where the heat shield could be dropped for better forward vision during takeoffs and landings. Pressurizing the passenger compartment presented a similar challenge. Serious thought was given to eliminating windows altogether, in the interests of saving weight and simplifying pressurization. Unmentioned was the consideration that metal fatigue around window cutouts had caused the crashes of Britain's pioneer jetliner, the Comet. Window elimination was rejected on the grounds that it would make the passenger cabin even more tubelike and claustrophobic. Standard window cuts were made, which had to be reinforced, adding weight. Each passenger could see out, a "costly pleasure." Varying colors of upholstery also helped to break up the interior's tubelike effect.[24]

Alexei claimed that the prototype's landing-gear arrangement provided an advantage over the Concorde. It retracted forward instead of sideways, providing room for five abreast instead of four, and allowed larger angles of attack during takeoff and landing—critical for the delta wing. The battles over use of the delta wing were still echoing; once this wing type had been decided upon, it was researched solely for supersonic airliner purposes, not general applications. This focus had not simplified matters: "hundreds of scale models" had been evaluated "in the crucible of wind tunnels." Even these had not provided all the answers, so the analogue-144, a MIG fighter with a one-third scale replica of the proposed wing, was made and flown.

Although funding was no problem for the TU-144, its tremendous costs reflected the fact that it had no precedents in the civil or the military realm. The required "high efficiency, economy, and comfort" were not present in bomber designs, and its threefold leap in speed over subsonic airliners necessitated starting with a clean slate. Where a normal airliner could be designed using components from catalogs, the unique SST requirements meant ready-made subassemblies were unavailable. Everything had to be created anew, custom made. The Chief Designer hinted at the 144's high cost: it was "economically sound" only on long hauls, with over 100 passengers aboard—nearly full capacity. Civil airliners had to represent the state of the art for five years and remain in service for ten.[25]

In 1969, Chief Designer Tupolev foresaw the TU-144 entering Aeroflot service rapidly, the design task completed. Its path to mass production, he believed, should take no longer than did subsonic types such as the TU-134, TU-154, and IL-62. Likewise, piloting should prove no more difficult than a conventional subsonic airliner, since it was "saturated" with measuring and control instruments which could even land the 144 automatically. No "radical retraining" of Aeroflot crews would be required, thanks to the ability of the delta wing to land at relatively low speeds—this in spite of the limited cockpit vision and greater height from the ground. In serving Aeroflot lines—he made no reference to international service—Tupolev was confident that the 144 would prove "economic, comfortable, and profitable." And powerful: "This take-off with such sudden acceleration . . . women will probably love it; it sort of pushes you tightly back in the seat, and you feel the power of the plane and its terrific strength."

Alexei Tupolev exuded pride in his creation: "Design of any aircraft is an exciting affair. One obtains deep satisfaction seeing how a well-integrated design appears in blueprints. One enjoys it when design elements, in metal, begin to work as planned. So it was with the TU-144. Only the problems we had to solve proved to be much more complicated."[26] Unfortunately, the SST's problems were only beginning.

4

"KONKORDSKI": MYTHS AND REALITIES OF SST ESPIONAGE

The most durable legend associated with the TU-144 is that it was a "copy" of the Concorde. As we have seen with the Tupolev adaptations of the DC-3 and B-29, the Soviets were unable to perfectly reproduce U.S. aircraft, even when mandated to do so. Conversion to metric measurement alone was a Herculean task. Differences in Soviet metallurgy, the inferior output of Soviet engines, and the more robust Soviet airframe and landing-gear requirements resulted in Soviet "copies" with hardly a part interchangeable with their Western archetypes.

The Soviet SST was different in type. It resembled in outline its Western analogue, but it differed in every detail. And in kind. Previously, Tupolev had developed Soviet versions of the DC-3 or B-29 from purchased or complete captured aircraft on hand. But the TU-144 was developed concurrently with the Concorde, whose design details changed endlessly, especially prior to its first flight in early 1969. Anglo-French design approaches and solutions to technical problems were followed closely by Soviet engineers struggling to resolve the same conundrums. But the TU-144 design team—which probably tapped the resources of the entire Soviet aircraft industry—was not a slavish imitator and independently developed its own design solutions.

The "Konkordski" canard masks a more complex reality. The TU-144, like most advanced aircraft, did not depend solely on its Anglo-French "cousin" for inspiration. A well-informed U.S.

writer, Edgar Ulshamer, notes that the failure of Myasishchev's M-50 "Bounder" inspired a "hectic scramble by the Soviets to acquire whatever data they could on the B-70. Especially in the technologically difficult area of variable-geometry engine inlets, nacelles, and nozzles and other sophisticated design areas, the B-70 served as a model for Soviet SST designers."[1] As indicated earlier, the M-50 would have more closely resembled the B-70 had Myasishchev been allowed to develop the forward winglet and double delta wing he originally had in mind for his supersonic bomber. These B-70 features did surface, in subdued form, in the final version of the TU-144 after 1972.

In the first half of the 1960s, prior to the showing of the Concorde-like scale model at the 1965 Paris air show, the Soviet SST project was undefined, in a plastic state. We know now that the Soviets were developing two different proposals. The first was a Mach 2 aircraft that became the TU-144; the other was a Mach 3 SST similar to the American SST. In May 1966, Tupolev announced that Soviet SST efforts would focus on the more realizable Mach 2 aircraft, for reasons of durability and economics. Holding maximum speed at Mach 2.2 permitted the use of existing, readily available metal alloys. Higher speeds would generate skin temperatures requiring more exotic metallurgy.

The more ambitious Soviet Mach 3 project[2] was never shelved completely, but continued to inspire a series of design studies. Soviet authorities followed the Mach 3 Boeing SST with unusual interest, and lamented its cancellation in 1971. Occasional references to a second-generation SST appeared in the Soviet press. At the 1981 Paris air show, the Soviets exhibited a model of a Mach 3 HST (Hypersonic Transport).

Because in the beginning the Soviets were pursuing two separate and distinct projects, all of the resources of their scientific and technological search network were attuned early on to supersonic technology. Voracious Soviet curiosity extended to all levels.[3] Although the thousands of Soviet technicians working on the SST had no Western archetype on hand to study, the State espionage apparatus carried out detailed research on Western progress in supersonic transports.

Gumshoes and Runway Sweepings

The most colorful yarn connected with Soviet spying on the West's SSTs concerns a Soviet technical delegation who arrived at a Western aircraft assembly hall all shod with "gumshoes." The Soviets had donned adhesive soles in the hope of intercepting fragments of exotic alloys on their way to the trash can. Extracting these filings from their soles later, the Soviets forwarded them to Moscow for metallurgical analysis so that the alloys might be reconstituted. The story strains credulity, save for the fact that it can be sourced to Boeing, Lockheed, and Aerospatiale. In another variation of bizarre Soviet ingenuity—reported by chief test pilot André Turcat of Aerospatiale—the Soviet Chief of Aeroflot-Paris wined and dined a member of Le Bourget's runway cleaning crew, hoping to persuade him to pick up shreds of airplane tires from the tarmac of the Paris airport for similar purposes.[4]

The latter story has a date and names connected with it. The weakness of the gumshoe story is that the Soviets were probably in advance of the West in some branches of metallurgy by the late 1960s and early '70s, and they hardly needed help from the West in aircraft alloys. There is every indication that they would have had problems reproducing Western alloys even if they did get the formulas right, owing to the different mineral mix of the Soviet resource base. The "airport sweepings" report is more credible because the Soviets had continuous problems with the SST's small tires, which had to cope with high weights and high landing speeds. Regarding the gumshoe story, as the old Russian proverb puts it, "If not true, it's true enough." If the details seem bizarre, this caper nonetheless reflects general reality. The appetite of Soviet technocrats and the Soviet scientific-technical establishment for state-of-the-art secrets is institutionalized, too ingrained, and too well rewarded by the system to make such grotesque scheming implausible.

Soviet technical trawling in the West is the product of a long-established State-administered apparatus. In the early 1960s, tens of thousands of translators culled Western technical literature to spot the latest scientific and technological developments. By the early 1960s, scientific and technological collection had become the first priority of the KGB and GRU, and aerospace was the first-priority sector. By the early 1970s, the KGB alone had 500 full-time science and technology analysts. The volume of this Soviet research is difficult to grasp and sometimes seems to extend to material of no apparent value whatsoever. The technical institute VINITI subscribes to 3,500 journals from 130 countries and translates almost 10,000 articles a year. It was this flood of material from the West that probably inspired Tupolev senior to begin SST sketches in 1961. Western SST excitement incited the Soviets; in 1967 alone, the *British Technology Index* listed eighty-four SST articles.

In 1960–61, just before SST design sketching started at Tupolev, at least two far-reaching Soviet-sponsored espionage networks were launched to garner Western data on SSTs. One of these—possibly the more successful—was not discovered until 1977, and involved a network of high-level French technocrats: the Fabiew network.

Sergei Fabiew was the son of a White Russian emigré who had come to France via Yugoslavia. The GRU was able to recruit him by playing on his nostalgia for the Russian homeland he had never seen. In the course of three visits to Moscow, he was trained in espionage techniques. Fabiew may have had some connection to the spymaster Sergei Pavlov, since Aeroflot serves as a front for the GRU. When eventually confronted by French security services in 1977, Fabiew surrendered his communications codes. One French counterintelligence specialist was brought back from retirement to decipher the messages, and ruefully broke a "historic message" from Moscow congratulating Fabiew's network on stealing the entire technical documentation for the Concorde prototype.[5]

The second network was even more elaborate, at least twenty

operatives working in four European countries. In this case, Soviet intelligence services worked through the intermediary offices of the East German and Czech secret services, as is customary in Soviet espionage efforts in Europe, where subtlety and indirection are advisable. Through hard work and luck, the second network was detected early on and was rolled up by early 1965, even before the TU-144 had been officially announced. But it may have passed on some data of use to Moscow.[6]

Operation Brunnhilde

Societ SST espionage was an intricate and complex process. Much of the TU-144's technology paralleled that of the Concorde, but both aircraft were undergoing rapid design evolution when this industrial espionage occurred in the early 1960s. Both were moving targets in a process of dynamic development. If it is believed that the TU-144 is a copy of the Concorde, the question is, *Which* Konkordski is a copy of *which* Concorde? The TU-144 prototype was subtly transformed in its production version, later modified with major wing redesigns and later still with a different engine.

Operation Brunnhilde, a name which anticipated the noisy, temperamental nature of the TU-144, was the earliest and best-known Soviet-sponsored espionage campaign against the Concorde. Brunnhilde began, developed, and was almost completely rolled up before the public introduction of the 144 at the 1965 Paris air show. The export value of the Concorde was taken very seriously at the time: a British writer prophesied in 1969 that the future 9 billion pounds sterling SST market was "one of the most glittering prizes in business history."[7]

Brunnhilde was underway by late November 1961, months after Soviet exhibition of the supersonic aircraft at Tushino and the crash of the B-58 at Paris, and a full year before Britain and France announced their Concorde collaboration.[8] On November 21, 1961, in London, an East Bloc agent met the first British contact in the Soviet campaign to glean the technical secrets of the Concorde. The agent, Jean-Paul Soupert, a retired Swiss chemist living in Brussels, had been recruited by East German intelligence as a courier after he applied for a teaching job. Soupert's subsequent life-style, transcending the means of a pensioner, attracted the attention of the Belgian Sureté, who carefully shadowed him through most of 1962 and 1963. Because Soupert was the courier for the espionage ring on thirty missions, surveillance established that an international effort was being directed against the Concorde's engines in Bristol and its airframe in Toulouse.[9]

The Ministerium für Staats-Sicherheit in East Berlin—the "Statsi"—often fronts for the KGB in tricky assignments when a more European touch is useful. The interconnections of Brunnhilde revealed the Soviet hand behind the activities of several Eastern Bloc intelligence services. One tip from Soupert led to a Soviet diplomat in London who was expelled in February 1965. Another led to the Aeroflot chief in Paris, who was arrested and expelled for espionage in February 1965. He had recruited French Communist workers within Sud-Aviation's factory at Toulouse. Kingpin of the operation was Herbert Steinbrecher, age thirty-two in 1965, a Statsi officer trained as an engineer. When arrested in Paris in November 1964, Steinbrecher was en route to set up an engineering office in Toulouse. He had already worked in a French aircraft factory to learn French production processes and approaches to prototype testing.

Steinbrecher recruited two Britons working at Kodak, who seem to have been part of the effort against the Concorde and were tried at the Old Bailey in February 1965. The final strand from Soupert ran to a Catholic school near Toulouse, where two "Czech priests" were arrested in January 1966. Under cover as teaching brothers in a Roman Catholic order, they were preparing to penetrate the Concorde's assembly hall and technical documentation center. Their names, Krigorovsky and Sarati, to a Czech ear sound Polish and Hungarian, respectively. The two pseudo-ecclestiastics were sentenced in April 1967.

Soviet Espionage Against the Concorde's Engines

In Britain, the Soviets early targeted Bristol-Siddeley, engaged in doubling the power of Vulcan bomber engines to the more powerful and efficient Olympus 593 required for the Concorde. The 593 endowed the Concorde with its unique ability to cruise for three hours at supersonic speed. This intrigued the Soviets for, if it could be assimilated, it would endow the SST and Soviet supersonic bombers with long-elusive range.

Soviet approaches to Bristol-Siddeley took many forms. A Rumanian diplomat called at the firm's London offices, asking for publicity films of the engine-development process. A Soviet "journalist" lunching at the company's facilities suddenly startled his hosts by firing a battery of technically abstruse questions regarding high bypass-ratio jet engines. Specialists working at the engineering center in Filton were invited to visit the Soviet embassy in London, to meet with Soviet counterparts who just happened to be in the neighborhood; this ploy failing, the same specialists were invited on a Soviet Grand Tour, to give lectures and visit aircraft facilities. It was hoped that Soviet specialists would glean technical secrets in one-on-one discussions between peers.[10]

These invitations halted after a Soviet official at the London embassy was expelled for spying in January 1965, and the two Britons from Kodak were tried for espionage at the Old Bailey the following month. Soviet espionage was sensationalized by a London *Daily Express* front-page headline of November 1966: a "Concorde Spy Alert," had resulted in a "Security Watch on the Engine Tightened at Bristol and SCNEMA" in France. "Intense Russian interest" in the Olympus 593 had been observed since 1961, when Tupolev SST studies had commenced. East European surrogates played an active role: "Inquiries by certain Iron Curtain embassies about the availability of slides and records of the engine while under construction, running on the test bench, or during the flight tests are now known to have been made on behalf of the Russians." Senior Bristol-Siddeley ex-

97

ecutives had been offered grand tours of the USSR. Concorde makers were "keeping a close watch on the information potential rivals are seeking."[11] This high-profile publicity forced the Soviets to resort to more subtle approaches, at least in Britain.

Soviet SST Espionage Against France

Soviet attempts to gain data on the Concorde's airframe in France began later than engine-data collection in Britain, suggesting that engine secrets were a higher Soviet priority. It is questionable how much the Soviets learned of airframe secrets from Brunnhilde, though *Teknika Molodezhi* published an outline drawing of Concorde features in mid-1965. Because Soupert, courier of the stolen data, had been turned as a double agent as early as January 1964, the efficacy of this channel from the Soviet point of view was limited. French sources assert that the Soviets were fed doctored data to further scramble the SST's technical complexities.[12] Soviet émigré engineers who had worked on the TU-144 have testified as to the inscrutability of Western data received in the USSR, the difficulty of deciphering Western technical notation, and the problems of locating Soviet materiel that could meet more exacting Western specifications. Even successful delivery of secrets in the USSR did not guarantee they could be exploited.

Brunnhilde began to be rolled up. On November 28, 1964, Steinbrecher was arrested in Paris amidst the tourist traps of the Place Pigalle. In his pocket was a bag of bonbons; microfilm hidden inside the candy contained copies of confidential documents. Although Steinbrecher was only thirty-two, it was his twentieth visit to France in five years. Under questioning, he admitted recruiting two Britons to collect restricted Concorde data, and on the day after his arrest, their flats in London were searched. Steinbrecher was tried in secret on April 7, 1965, and sentenced to twelve years.[13]

Other dominoes began to fall. In February 1965, Sergei Pavlov, head of Aeroflot-Paris, was the first official of that organization to be arrested and expelled for espionage. He was found in a

Paris restaurant, carrying a napkin full of secrets on landing gear, aircraft brakes, and high-tech metallurgy.[14] It is likely that Pavlov worked for the GRU. Pavlov's apartment contained "reams" of secret data on Concorde; he had constructed agent pipelines extending down to Aerospatiale in Toulouse. President de Gaulle was reportedly so infuriated by Soviet perfidy against the prestige Concorde project that he insisted on personally signing Pavlov's expulsion papers.[15]

Sergei Pavlov originated the ingenious method of obtaining data on aircraft tire compounds, one of the TU-144's weaknesses. As previously stated, he recruited a member of the maintenance crew at Orly, plying him with magnificent meals in expensive restaurants. In return, Pavlov requested rubber debris from the runways. This presumably would be forwarded to Soviet labs for analysis, in the hope that Soviet aircraft tires would be more durable. Something went awry. When the TU-144 first appeared at Paris in 1971, its tires were changed at Prague before landing in Paris. After only two landings, the tires were threadbare again. This may have been a sting by French counterintelligence: informed of Pavlov's pitch by the airport cleaner, pains were taken to ensure that the rubber samples forwarded to Moscow were composed of compounds previously unknown to the world of industrial chemistry.[16]

French intelligence services pursued this cat-and-mouse game against Soviet technology collectors with élan. Pavlov was offered data on exotic Concorde alloys by a high Aerospatiale official. According to the Concorde's chief test pilot, the data transmitted to Moscow must have plunged Soviet metallurgists into despair. Pavlov was expelled from France and sentenced to a five-year prison term in absentia. Disgrace did not touch Pavlov; he rose to become Deputy Minister of Civil Aviation and would later negotiate Aeroflot landing rights with Western officials bemused by his former vocation as spymaster.[17] Pavlov's lowly accomplices were given prison terms of three to five years.[18] The two "Czech priests" were given eight and four years in a secret trial on April 27, 1967. This was Brunnhilde's last "performance."

The route whereby Concorde secrets were conveyed to Moscow

came to light in the various trials of the Brunnhilde principals. In 1960–64, Soupert carried microfilm on board the Ostend-Warsaw Express, hiding them in the first-class lavatory inside a tube of toothpaste or in a sponge hidden behind a heating grill. He would leave the train at Cologne, while the microfilm would roll eastward to be intercepted in Berlin by Statsi officers and then forwarded to Moscow.

Official Visits

On July 1, 1965, the Soviets signed an international agreement protecting intellectual property, and in 1976 they were granted U.S. patents to protect unique technical features of the TU-144: its five-across seating, engine nacelles, and two-position nose.[19] This solicitude for guarding TU-144 secrets did not diminish the Soviet appetite for Concorde information. Though Soviet agents did succeed in obtaining full data on the Concorde prototype, tightened Anglo-French security defeated their attempts to gain data on the updates and design changes to the finalized Concorde design, which first appeared in preproduction form in September 1971.

Because some of their industrial espionage channels had been blocked and uprooted, Soviet curiosity was forced out into the open and surfaced in visits of Soviet, French, and British aircraft delegations to each others' facilities. An era of growing détente and "peaceful competition" facilitated Soviet entrée, since the British and the French hoped to export their high-technology eastward.

Western missions to the USSR discovered that Soviet technical inquisitiveness knew no bounds. The maker of the simulator to train Concorde pilots was interrogated for a full day to see if the device could be adopted for the TU-144. The torrent of Soviet questions abruptly subsided when he asked for 144 performance data to enter into the French computer. A representative of SAVEM, maker of the Concorde's electronic flight control system and inertial navigators, was similarly besieged by Safromonov, an

Aeroflot representative. French technologists were intrigued by this incident: inertial navigators derived directly from ballistic-missile technology. Was Soviet compartmentalization of information so severe that the Ministry of Aviation Production was cut off from rocket research?[20]

The Soviets were equally insatiable abroad. In February 1967, a Soviet aviation delegation, headed by Dementiev and including both Tupolevs, visited Aerospatiale. The elder Tupolev was likened to a smiling crocodile, while the younger, in French eyes, resembled a recent graduate of a top-flight technical school, with fashionable clothes, unctuous speech, and a swiftly averted gaze. Confronting the Concorde prototype, the younger Tupolev drew forth from his pocket a measuring tape and instantaneously established the height and width of the engine inlets. With a sly smile, he announced, "You've enlarged it eight percent." Dufour, an Aerospatiale executive, purred, "No need to measure, Monsieur Tupolev. You need only peruse our technical bulletins." Lesser Soviets followed up on this initiative by taking numerous precise photos of the inlets, a TU-144 design imbroglio unresolved to the end.[21] The direct approach was a Tupolev tradition: in the 1930s the elder Tupolev, while visiting Caudron, startled his French hosts by opening drawers and cupboards to inspect blueprints during his honorary tour of inspection.[22]

André Turcat, the Concorde's chief test pilot, was an eyewitness to these Tupolev antics and concluded that the Soviets had targeted the Concorde's automatic mechanisms, air inlets, and metallurgical specifications. Of the informal Franco-Soviet technical exchange that set the stage for such visits, he judged that, "France gave much and received little. . . . Past a certain point, it was important to think of one's duty to France." At least one of a group of Soviet journalists touring the Aerospatiale plant on another occasion, a "TASS correspondent," proved to be a highly trained aeronautical engineer. Indirect probes via East European surrogates continued: in 1968, one Elias, a Czech, telephoned Aerospatiale requesting data on the Concorde's wing design and photos showing its fabrication.[23] At this time the Soviets were feverishly generating more complex contours for the TU-144 wing, to provide greater low- and medium-speed lift. The earliest version of the 144's wing had optimum performance at Mach 2 cruise only.

In one area, the Soviets were in advance of Western practice: titanium shaping and fabrication. To demonstrate this, in 1967 they provided their French visitors with a titanium samovar, an impressive showpiece of exacting workmanship and welding in this hard, strong metal. In his presentation speech, Dementiev recalled that Russians a century previously had given Napoleon III a samovar made of aluminum, then an exotic metal. Having established that there was a tradition of Russian pioneer work in metallurgy, the Soviets seemed interested in selling titanium-sheet and -forming technology to the French, but never were forthcoming with specifications.[24]

This ceremony should not signal Soviet indifference to advances in Western metallurgy. Soviet aviation engineers visiting southwest France in 1969 were drawn to the Messier foundry in Bidosse. Years later, their French escorts recalled the Soviets' fascination with the processes for making the light alloys for the Concorde's landing gear.[25] At this time the Soviets were redesigning the 144's landing gear to fit into a compact space between the two engines: complex, articulated structures with high-strength, lightweight metals were very much on their minds.

Most of the Soviet espionage successes on behalf of the TU-144 seem to have been registered in the early years, before Western industrialists recognized that state-of-the-art civil technology was a priority target. The unmasking of Operation Brunnhilde alerted Western industrialists to the espionage. In addition to press reports, the Direction et Surveillance du Territoire, the French internal security agency, in 1965 distributed a primer—*Espionage: A Reality*—to 9,000 French industrialists.[26]

Questions and probings of Soviet officials on visits after 1965 were not the only remaining source of Concorde data. The breakup of the Fabiew ring in 1977 indicated other leaks. As mentioned earlier, Fabiew, of Russian émigré background and Yugoslav citizenship, obtained information from well-paid officials in the French industrial establishment.[27] Whether more up-to-date material on the definitive production Concorde of the 1970s was sequestered was not revealed. It seems on balance unlikely, for in the 1970s the Soviets attempted to purchase technical fixes for the TU-144 through normal commercial channels, when all else had failed.

Soviet espionage against the Concorde was sufficiently notorious that the popular weekly *Paris-Match* could introduce the news of the 144's first flight with the words, "This Tupolev which flies thanks to spies" and include in the story the exploits of Steinbrecher, Soupert, Pavlov, and the two "Czech priests." This inspired a stinging riposte in its letters column from V. Smirnov, Director of the Soviet Information Bureau in Paris, who recalled historic Tupolev exploits and noted that *Paris-Match* had conceded the TU-144 resembled no other SST.[28] As the 144 took to the air for the first time, Soviet attempts to address its technical problems through Western borrowings took on new forms.

5
1969: YEAR OF WONDER

The historic first flight of an SST on December 31, 1968, saw the semisecrecy of the project displaced by a flood of exuberant publicity. Promises made at Paris in mid-1965 that it would fly in 1968 were redeemed, but just barely. It was a closely run thing: the last days of 1968 shrouded Moscow with fog, but the final day of the year dawned clear and sharp: ideal conditions for a tricky test flight.

First Flight, First Sight

December 31, 1968, developed into a sunny and quite cold day—around zero—at Zhukovsky Airfield in the Moscow suburbs. The first flight of the TU-144 was a long-anticipated event among the assemblers and technical crew, even though the exact date of the event was kept secret from the world. As was Soviet practice with space shots, they did not publicize it until after the event. If there were some hideous accident, it might be possible to shield the fact from the rest of the world and then Soviet prestige could remain untarnished. But time was running out. Probably this deadline had been fixed by the Supreme Leadership and this was the last day possible. An earlier attempt three days before had been aborted by fog.

Airport personnel chose good vantage points to see it off: balconies and rooftops of hangars and buildings were crowded with people. Film crews arrived to capture the atmosphere of this historic moment. Some boarded escort aircraft that would precede it into the air. Other cameramen boarded the 144 itself to film its first crews while in flight. Their footage was collected into a color film, *Take-Off*, which was widely distributed in 1969. The "Old Man," newly turned eighty, arrived by limousine in a heavy coat and fur cap to witness the 120th, and last, inaugural flight of an aircraft bearing his name. He was met by a delegation and his son, the Chief Designer.

The TU-144 itself was pulled out of its hangar by a bright red ZIL-150 truck, then down the runway by a second, more exotically designed Tatra 6×6 tractor.

The flight crew of four arrived, wearing visored helmets, high boots, and leather jackets. The Chief Pilot was Edward Elyan, forty-two, born in Baku. Elyan had "given a start in life to one dozen aircraft types." A graduate of the aircraft construction faculty of the Moscow Aviation Institute, he had begun his test-pilot career in 1951 and had been the Chief Test Pilot for the first Soviet jetliner, the TU-104. He had logged many hours in SST simulators and the modified MIG-21 "analogue," which carried a smaller version of its wing. As is Soviet custom, he would interact directly with the designers during the flight-testing phase.[2]

Joining Elyan were Mikhail Kozlov, the copilot also with many hours on the simulators and the analogue, and Flight Engineers Benderov and Seliverstov. Benderov as Chief Flight Engineer was responsible for the entire flight-test program. (Kozlov and Benderov were to perish in the fiery midair breakup of an early production example of the TU-144 in 1973.) Waving, the quartet climbed a steep yellow ladder into the gutted—and as yet unpressurized—interior of Prototype 00068. Here, pressurized flight suits, special hatchways, and ejection seats awaited them, fitted for test flights at great expense. The normal interior would be installed much later.[3]

Today the SST's birdlike configuration is a familiar caricature. In 1968, it was startlingly new and fresh. Photographic coverage had been severely limited, which magnified the impact of the TU-144's flying debut. *Izvestia* commented on the aircraft's exotic appearance, a reminder that the now-familiar profile broke much new ground at the time. To 1968 Soviet eyes, the TU-144 seemed unbelievably rakish: "very long and sharp nosed with the unusually rectangular engine block carried below. It had no stabilizer at all. . . . It appears as though the aircraft has spread its bird wings and lowered its head."[4]

Izvestia rhapsodized on the shrinkage of the globe the 144 had brought about: Moscow to New Delhi was now possible in two hours, twenty minutes. Khabarovsk, on the Pacific at 100 degrees latitude east of Moscow in the Soviet Far East, could now be reached in three hours, twenty minutes. A passenger flying the TU-144 from Moscow at noon would land in Montreal at nine the previous morning, "outdistancing sound and the sun."

The NK-144 engines, which ultimately developed half a million horsepower, started up with a roar. "Permission to take off" was granted and the 144 rolled down the snowy concrete runway, past the gathered crowds of onlookers. It gathered speed toward the point where eminent specialists had estimated it would first leave the ground. Flocks of birds scattered.

After a twenty-five-second roll, an SST took to the air for the first time. The flight lasted twenty-eight minutes, during which its landing gear was never retracted. Hundreds of recording instruments were switched on in the air, thousands of measurements taken, and the telemetry sent back to earth to be "recorded on thousands of kilometers of tape." Escort aircraft, including the MIG-144 analogue, flew alongside, some recording the historic event on film, others enhancing the photogenic character of the occasion. Tape recorders monitored the pilots' voices: "Whatever happens their comrades on the ground must know what took place." The "Old Man" exulted, "We've been first for thirty-five years; we remain the first."[5]

Returning to earth following the historic flight, Elyan exuberantly embraced both Tupolevs in succession, father and son. Once again, the Soviet Union could celebrate an epoch-making achievement to follow up on its ventures into space. Coming from behind, the 144 had beat the Concorde into the air by more than two months, a superb technical achievement by any standard.

Izvestia celebrated the magnitude of this great leap forward in speed. Progress seemed to be literally accelerating: previous advances in locomotive, automobile, and aircraft had seen transport speeds jump by 10 to 15 percent increments. But the first jetliners of the previous decade raised speeds 250 to 300 percent. Now the TU-144 almost trebled the jetliners' speed again, from 800 or 900 kph to 2,500 khr, or from 500 or 540 mph to 1,500 mph.

This great speed mandated a radical "refashioning" of every element: aerodynamics, construction, materials, technology, and most subsystems. (In the West, Concorde constructors claimed that only the seats were untouched by the supersonic revolution.) Frontiers previously explored only by specialist aircraft—the speed of the supersonic interceptor, the capacity and reliability of the airliner, and the range of a bomber—were now combined in a craft that would be available to the general public. Much was made of its quadrupling of vital subsystems; even a double failure could not affect its safety. Pilots leaving its landing gear up or deviating from the landing path would be warned by lights, instrument panels, and earphone voices. It would take an entire book to describe the TU-144's central control system. It processed flight information and flew the aircraft about 90 percent of the time. It could also calculate the best trajectory, the wind velocity, make turns, report on position, and calculate fuel reserves.

A few favored Westerners—American astronauts and British and French cabinet-level delegations—had seen the prototype under construction. The TU-144's public debut was given at Shermetyevo Airport, in Moscow, on May 21, 1969, to compensate for the fact that the TU-144 would not fly to the Paris air show, as had been widely hoped. This event was clearly aimed at a world, rather than a Soviet, audience. Selected Western diplomats, the military, and the Western press corps were given an opportunity to inspect the aircraft on the ground. The Soviets reportedly charged those taking pictures $500 each.

Those visiting the interior found it impressive in its "surface features." Instead of the Robber Baron Gothic decor of the early TU-104s—heavy seats, dark wood, and somber colors—the 144's interior was light and spacious, with ample leg room and a very modern look throughout. For the first time, the Soviets were seen to have made a serious attempt to cut weight in interior fittings: the previous cast-iron plumbing fixtures were banished at last. The only criticism was that the seats were too narrow: "A normal Soviet woman would never fit them."[6] This may have been a result of the drive to increase payload by fitting five seats across the narrow cross section.

After standing inspection, the TU-144 took off, made two slow passes over the airfield, and departed on a ninety-minute flight with no passengers aboard. Westerners would wait eight-and-a-half years to ride the TU-144. Deputy Minister of Aviation Alexander Kobsaryev explained that the TU-144's flight-testing program was "too intense and complicated at the moment to be interrupted," though the French weekly magazine *Air et Cosmos* estimated that the aircraft had not yet been in the air more than twelve hours.[7]

The TU-144's absence from the Paris air show disappointed experts who anticipated comparing the Soviet and Anglo-French SSTs side-by-side. Two Concordes—one French, one British—arrived simultaneously to symbolize the smooth partnership of the technocracies. Both provided a low-speed handling exhibition. Soviets at the show repeatedly attempted to visit the Concordes without success, but French observers hoped that reciprocal rights to inspect might ultimately be negotiated.[8]

Kobsaryev announced that mass production of the TU-144 had begun and that export orders would be accepted in 1971. The head of Aviaexport, Boris Sachenko, hoped aircraft would be ready for sale abroad in two years' time.[9]

In view of the fact that TASS had announced a temporary halt to the testing on January 30, when only seven flights had occurred, the "intensity" of the flight-testing program appeared hollow. The Soviets plainly needed the TU-144 at Paris to crown an otherwise lackluster collection of previously shown aircraft types. Loginov, Soviet Minister of Civil Aviation, visiting the Paris Show, granted a detailed interview to *Air et Cosmos* that conspicuously avoided all references to the TU-144.[10]

The Solitary Prototype

Something had happened. Reports persisted that the Soviets had lost or had severely damaged a second prototype in a "heavy landing" early in the testing program. This suggestion had been repeatedly denied by Soviet civil-aviation authorities as early as February–April 1969.[11] Soviet statements indicate that only one prototype flew "through 1969," but this does not account for two others reportedly built.[12] Whether there was a "heavy landing" in late January or early February will probably never be known, but it's plain that the 144's testing schedule was not too intense to permit a flight to Paris. The Soviets coveted the prestige that would have accrued from SST representation there. What is known is that the first aircraft, registered 68001, was the only one shown in photographs and seen in visits to Eastern Europe and the West up to 1973.

The Concorde had two prototypes and two preproduction models—four in all. Western delegations visiting Tupolev before 1969 were told of three prototypes, one of which was slated for static testing; this would be consistent with Tupolev practice. International indexes record 68003,[13] a second prototype, while Gunston states that the second prototype may have first flown in 1971,[14] although it was never seen. Dependency on a single prototype may have resulted from a great compression of the flight-testing cycle and precipitate haste to move into production. The provisional prototype, technically frozen earlier to get into the air earlier, was passé: Tupolev was already concentrating efforts and resources on the final production version.

Uniquely, a single prototype—number 681001—would carry the entire Soviet SST flight-testing program for over three and a half years. This is contrary to usual Soviet and Tupolev practice. Normally, two or three prototypes are simultaneously put through their paces. Though the TU-144 was designed for an operational life of 30,000 hours, or ten years, unanticipated faults at any time could have led to the destruction of the early prototype. At least two prototypes were built: did the Soviets cover their bets by painting the same number on two aircraft? If one crashed, the Soviets could produce the other as proof that no problem had occurred. This switching game would explain the otherwise miraculous recovery of a severely damaged prototype in Warsaw in 1971 while returning from the Paris Air Show.

An accident early in the testing program would certainly have frustrated Tupolev's plans to fly the TU-144 to Paris in 1969. Compensation for the Soviet SST no-show at Paris was provided by the announcement made during the Salon Aeronautique that the TU-144 had made its first supersonic flight to a height of 110,000 feet only thirty minutes after takeoff. A "slight tremble" was recorded as the aircraft passed the sound barrier. Another record could be chalked up for the Soviet SST.

Soviets Probe SST Export Sales

The 1969 Paris air show did provide further indirect entrée to the secrets of the Soviet SST. In return for a tour of the new Boeing 747 jet, Soviet officials, through Aviaexport, invited a small but select American team of experts to inspect the TU-144 on its home ground. On July 28, a delegation from Pan Am, Boeing, and TWA flew to Moscow on a "fact-finding" expedition. Pan Am President Najeeb Halaby, Director of Research Scott Flower, and Chief Engineer John Borger were accompanied by Warren Spannuth, TWA Director of Aircraft Development, and Maynard Pennell, who had directed Boeing's SST project.[15] The small group of Americans were met by a galaxy of talent from the Soviet aircraft industry, possible compensation for the international recognition forgone the previous month by failing to fly the 144 to Paris. Minister of Aviation Production Dementiev and Minister of Civil Aviation Loginov met the Americans at the aircraft, at the head of a delegation of forty, including the

Tupolevs, father and son. The 144 had not been absent from Paris because the Soviets were ashamed of it.

Westerners had inspected the TU-144 before, but none who were so expert, thorough, or publicly forthcoming. Halaby, an SST enthusiast, has indicated that a ninety-minute inspection of the 144, followed by a ninety-minute briefing led by Dementiev and Loginov, left the U.S. specialists "very, very impressed." Halaby believed the TU-144 was ahead of the Concorde in development, based on its flight-test progress. It had already broken the sound barrier and reached 900 mph, while the Concorde would not go supersonic for another six months.

The Soviets allowed the Americans to peer "into every nook and cranny" of the TU-144, and they openly discussed their desire to enter it in world markets. No questions were barred; there was a forthright exchange of technical comments. The Soviets, according to Halaby, "couldn't have been more outgoing." He was impressed by the amount of titanium employed and by the advanced instrumentation of the cockpit, presided over by Edward Elyan.[16]

Other members of the delegation characterized the meeting as a Soviet fishing expedition to test American commercial interest in the TU-144. Revelation was selective: "They didn't show us an awful lot, but what they did show us looked pretty good." The delegation agreed that the 144 was the USSR's "best shot" for breaking into the international air market. Spannuth of TWA stated that the Soviets were "serious about selling the TU-144 overseas; I got the idea that they're going to be very aggressive on their own time scale."

To these experts, the 144 appeared "the product of basically sound engineering and quality workmanship," ahead of the Concorde in its development. The Soviets' technical openness was not, however, matched by a willingness to discuss issues affecting commercial viability; performance, potential operating costs, engine design, and other parameters were treated as State secrets. This was no way to lure Western customers. The Soviets did discuss the possibility of lengthening the 144's fuselage to improve its economics. Export sales might be possible within eighteen months, with overseas delivery in 1973 or 1974. Cost was undetermined, but would undercut the Concorde.[17]

The 144's ease of maintenance and operating costs were judged to be an improvement over previous Soviet airliners. It was believed to be quieter than Concorde, if noisier than conventional jets. Borger remarked that the TU-144 looked better than any Soviet craft he had previously seen, but held off on judgment until technical data were "in hand." It had seen less wind-tunnel testing than the Concorde, but it was impressive enough to "ultimately dilute the SST market."[18]

Comparisons with the Concorde

In response to British questions, the consensus of the U.S. delegation was that the TU-144 could "pose a threat to the Concorde where world sales are concerned, but . . . it is unlikely to match the Anglo-French aircraft either in performance or operating costs." Maynard Pennell, former head of the Boeing SST program, believed the 144 was "probably less sophisticated than Concorde today . . . it may be as good in low speed or supersonic flight. . . . By U.S. standards, its economics probably will be quite poor." The 144, he believed, did not match the Concorde's range, but it might be able to fly more passengers shorter ranges as a medium-range SST.

The experts noted that the estimated first service had slipped two years, to 1972, for routes inside the USSR, "where stringent international requirements would not apply." The Soviets admitted they could not provide "normal technical data" to U.S. airlines until late 1971.

The aircraft as configured could not meet FAA certification requirements. There were too few emergency-escape doors and there was little evidence of the fire, flying-object, and other passenger-cabin precautions common in the West. No strain gauges were visible nor was there water ballast to help determine different fuel-weight variations. Most test instruments were shrouded, so that the type of data collected could not be seen. No inspection panels or access doors were open, but the cockpit was inspected.

There was a considerable gap between the TU-144 and the Concorde in flight experience. Americans were told the 144 had accumulated twenty hours in flight. "Not far into a development program," growled Pennell.[19] Two Concorde prototypes had accumulated 100 hours in sixty flights, starting two months later. The 144 program was curtailed mysteriously in spring 1969, however it had flown higher—twenty minutes at 45,000 feet.[20]

Compared to the Concorde technically, the TU-144 was a "little less advanced." There were small but important differences in the wing. Based on wind-tunnel tests, the British and French determined lift-drag improvements to be gained by more dramatic twisting of the wing; the 144 wing was "essentially flat" and conceptually cruder. These small differences were to drive the Soviets into a series of wing redesigns over the next eight years. There was a tendency to overrate the 144: Pennell believed—erroneously—that the 144 was built entirely of titanium, which would enable it to withstand very high speeds, indeed.

Soviet technical prowess was offset by rigidity of approach and hostility to error. Whereas U.S. makers would provide data with a 1 to 2 percent chance of error, or even 4 to 5 percent, the Soviets insisted that everything be all correct. Technical expressions were not always translatable: the U.S. group left Moscow with the impression that the outer engines had provision for reverse thrust, which was not true, and never did find out if the 144's fuel had been chemically heated to minimize explosion and burning in case of accident.[21]

The TU-144 strongly resembled the Concorde configuration of three years earlier, including since-superseded small windows, but it had a wider fuselage and a flat floor. Workmanship was excellent. Engine nacelles were much longer than in the Concorde. It was believed this was to place the inlets in front of the nose wheels, but more likely it was to provide additional room for the crude Soviet intake system. In 1969, there were no blow-in or pressure-relief doors, though this was to change by 1971. Tires

113

were unusually small to fit inside the flat wing. They usually lacked tread, reflecting the limitations of undersized tires in coping with high weight and landing speeds.[22]

Speculation that the 144 could be a presence in world markets (encouraged by the Soviets) ascribed capabilities to the TU-144 it was never to have. In the heady perspectives of 1969, however, it fell to the *Wall Street Journal*, mouthpiece of capitalism, to paint the rosiest picture of the 144's prospects. The *Journal* noted that the Soviets had agreed to give Japan Air Lines air rights across Siberia by March 1970, apparently to coincide with a Soviet SST flight to Osaka to open the World's Fair. TU-144 purchases had been introduced as part of the deal. Sonic booms would not be a problem; only polar bears were affected.[23] Pennell had the impression that the Soviets were prepared to bargain flying rights across the USSR as a sales tool. It was believed that the Soviets would undercut the Concorde's price, whatever it was.[24]

Although the TU-144 prototype was known to be experiencing problems and putting on weight with a subsequent loss of range, the *Journal* believed that the lack of an American SST might give the Soviets a commanding commercial lead. "So seen from Moscow, prospects for quite a bit of prestige and not a little much-needed hard currency must seem bright if the Russians can continue to set the pace." It was even possible that U.S. airlines would consider operating a Soviet aircraft—but only if the American SST remained stillborn and the Concorde did not work out. "If the Russians can rise to the demands of selling and servicing such an expensive and sophisticated piece of hardware over-seas—a good many "ifs" to be sure—some U.S. lines might take the plunge." TWA Vice-President Robert Rummel was monitoring TU-144 progress "to the extent the Russians permit" to know "what we should do about it."

The Soviets did their best to boost the prospects of Aeroflot and its future flagship. In April, Leonid Zholudev, First Deputy Minister of Civil Aviation, indicated that Aeroflot might soon join IADA, the international air organization.[25] In June, a press conference to celebrate the beginning of Moscow–NY air service provided a platform for futuristic hopes and SST hype. Vladimir Samorovkov, Aeroflot manager for the United States, speculated that U.S.-USSR SST flights might begin the next year, 1970, cutting New York–Moscow time from eleven to five hours. But he predicted Moscow–Tokyo SST service would start earlier, in 1970, when 144s would replace present IL-62 equipment.[26]

In October, Halaby of Pan Am asserted that he would buy TU-144s if there was no other way to meet the competition. "Suppose it developed better than the Concorde or is put into service quicker? We simply could not tolerate Aeroflot crossing to New York in three hours with the Tupolev while we were taking seven hours to do it."[27] In November, Soviet officials addressed the Aviation Writers Association and the Wings Society, touting the technical prowess of the TU-144.[28] In 1969, while the American SST was dying and the Concorde was suffering from overruns, the Soviet SST looked attractive—from a distance.

6
UNRESOLVED PROBLEMS: THE SOVIETS AT THE TECHNOLOGICAL FRONTIER

The Soviets grossly underrated the difficulties involved in developing a supersonic airliner. To some degree they were misled by the ease with which the TU-104 had been developed from jet bombers in two or three years. But the root of the problem was that the technical sophistication of airliners was growing at a geometric rate. One of the most complex designs of the 1930s, Kurt Tank's FW-200 four-engine Kondor had taken little more than a year from the first design sketch to first flight. The first jetliners took roughly three to four years.

But even subsonic airliner designs undertaken by the Soviets in the 1960s stumbled, subject to long development schedules and protracted modifications. The IL-62 first flew in January 1963, saw its first service in 1967 and was followed by the improved IL-62M in 1970. The IL-86 widebody airliner was first announced in 1971, first flew in 1976, and entered Aeroflot service in December 1980, too late to provide its long-promised support of the Moscow Olympics. The YAK-42 trijet was announced in 1973 and first flew in March 1975, but is still not in service. Its three small jets provided good liftoff from short airstrips, but burned too much fuel while doing so. By the late 1970s, even Aeroflot was beginning to focus on fuel consumption.[1]

These lengthening development schedules for Soviet subsonic airliners reflected the general complexity of commercial aviation

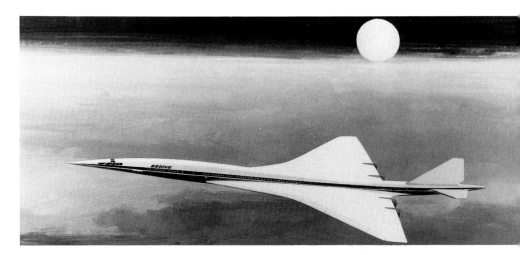

A later Boeing rendering shows a wing quite similar to the Concorde and the prototype 144; its general layout was picked up in certain Tupolev design sketches. Boeing later moved on to an overambitious variable-geometry wing, which doomed the American SST project to overcomplexity. Public funding for the Boeing 2702 SST was cut off in May 1971. *(Boeing)*

Nose of the prototype being constructed in the Zhukovskii factory, Moscow, probably mid-1967. The object at lower left might be part of the otherwise-elusive second prototype, never seen subsequently. *(Novosti)*

Father and son—the two Tupolevs—at a staged design conference in the Soviet film *Take-Off* (1969). The two informative design drawings on the wall behind were apparently never published.

Prototype being towed out of hangar for maiden flight. The elaborate publicity preparations and Soviet conservatism raise the possibility that re- hearsal flights might have been carried out. *(Take-Off)*

The flight crew—Edward Elyan, copilot Mikail Kozlov, flight test director V. N. Benderov, and engineer Y. Seliverstov—just before the 38-minute flight. Kozlov and Benderov would perish in the crash of the second production 144 in Paris, June 1973. *(Take-Off)*

Showing signs of haste—the rudder is unpainted—the prototype maneuvers on the apron prior to first takeoff. *(TASS)*

The MIG-144 analog, fitted with a scaled-down version of the ogival wing to serve as a flying test bed, escorts the prototype to its first landing.

Official TASS portrait of the prototype, 1969.

Prototype at Soviet airfield. This camera angle captures dramatically the ogival leading edge of the wing and the crude joining of trailing edge and fuselage. *(Ruffle)*

Main landing gear and six-foot engine inlets. The landing gear redesign again required small tires to fit between the engine ducts. The massive engines, whose design was now over a decade old, produced the requisite power at the cost of great weight, size, and fuel consumption. *(Ruffle)*

This early shot of a production TU-144 captures the features that distinguished it from the prototype: the front canards or winglets, the double-delta leading edge, and the further outward movement of the two engine nacelles, which have now swallowed the landing gear.

77102 demonstrating over the 1973 Paris Air Show.

First-class compart-
ment, May 1973, a
sign that the Soviet
SST was still in-
tended for world
service. Domestic
Aeroflot is "class-
less."

Kuznetsov, head
of the Design
Bureau responsible
for the original
NK-144 engines.

technology. For supersonic airliners, complexities were compounded as designers in many cases were asked to work in areas where previous experience was largely inapplicable and much was almost completely unknown. At the beginning of the 1960s, supersonic flight was an experience limited to a cadre of fit young fighter-pilots flying in pressurized suits. To fly at these speeds while maintaining acceptable levels of comfort proved the ultimate technological challenge of the SST, a problem which the Soviets never completely solved. A passenger commented to Sir George Edwards of BAC (British Aircraft Corporation) that the Concorde felt the same at supersonic speeds as other airliners and was told "that was the hard part." The Soviets, in contrast, never succeeded in taking their SST past comfort levels suitable for a combat crew.

Engines

The first technical challenge of the SST was its power requirement, roughly twice that of the Boeing 747, then the largest of commercial aircraft. Powerplant state of the art at the beginning of the 1960s is suggested by the B-58's GE-J79 turbojets, developing 15,600 lbs. of thrust, each with afterburners and variable inlet ducts.[2]

The Olympus engines adopted for the Concorde were originally employed in the Vulcan bomber, where their power was gradually raised from 11,000 lbs. of thrust in 1955 to 20,000 lbs. by the late 1960s. Further intensive development of these powerplants for maximum efficiency and range in the Concorde saw their thrust doubled again to 38,000 lbs.—and 39,000 for "contingencies."

In the Soviet Union, the most powerful engine in use at the beginning of the 1960s was the NK-8, which developed slightly over 23,000 lbs. of thrust. According to its chief designer, the TU-144 design was developed first and the engine chosen for it later. But there really were no competitors for the NK-8, which became the NK-144. Because Soviet engines were not notably fuel efficient, the solution was sheer size. The TU-144's engines were over seventeen feet long and nearly six feet in diameter. As Alexei Tupolev boasted, "so huge that a man can easily walk through them."[3]

In contrast, the Concorde's engines were twelve and a half feet long, with a forty-seven-and-a-half-inch diameter. The Soviet engines were not noticeably heavier, weighing 6,283 lbs. without jet pipe but with afterburner, while Concorde engines weighed 6,780 lbs. without exhaust.[4]

The two major problems of the SST engines were dealing with the high operating temperature (a product of the high temperature of the entering air and fuel) and controlling the engine and its complex afterburning equipment.[5] Methods to raise power inevitably raised internal operating temperatures to 1,000 to 1,100°F. The Soviet cooling solution was to run a huge oil passage through the center of the engine.[6]

Compressor-blade metallurgy was most critical. This was the hottest component of the engine, now asked to deal with still-higher temperatures. The method used in the West to cast turbines was the "lost wax" shell-mold process. The great challenge was to control the grain size; the mold must be very durable. The first stage was to develop "equiaxe" metal grains, which would resemble a pepper-and-salt mixture in X-ray analysis. The second stage was to make blades with "directionally solidified" blades, which had a single grain of metal from end to end. The third step was "single crystal" metallurgy, in which the grain has no boundaries at all.

The Soviets may have mastered the first step of this process in turbine-blade metallurgy, which put them two stages behind the West's state of the art.[7] General Electric is the leader in "film cooling" of the turbine blades, in which a set of holes is drilled in the leading edge of the blade to provide "showerhead cooling." The volume of air circulating within the blade keeps its temperature below the melting point.

Air quality at entry to the engine ideally should be quiet and consistent. The engine doesn't like "pressure holes", it prefers uniform, still air moving at all the same speed. The inlet at supersonic speeds has to go through a series of shocks. Air bounces around inside the inlet door and has to "bleed" through blow-out doors. The B-1 uses a series of baffles to smooth out this air flow. The B-58, the first multi-engine supersonic, would "pop" the air shock out in front of the aircraft if one engine surged. The airplane then would be forced sideways and crash. But if the shock was retained inside the lip of the engine nacelle, control could be maintained.[8]

Soviet engine design did not possess the subtleties of the West's. Sheer size took care of the power problem, though the less exact control processes cut into efficiency, hence range. In 1976, The Soviets offered Lucas Aerospace a 17 million pounds sterling contract to make the NK-144 more fuel efficient, but this was ultimately turned down on military grounds, since the NK-144 also powered the "Backfire" bomber.[9]

Internal Aerodynamics

One area where Concorde and TU-144 designs diverged was in the development of the engine inlet ducts. A jet engine cannot accept air at above the speed of sound, and to run with maximum efficiency, it should have air at a consistent speed and pressure across its intake. The major technical challenge here is to slow down the air once the SST is in supersonic regime. As the speed rises, so must the air be progressively slowed down, so as not to overwhelm the engine intakes. This is done through a system of variably controlled internal airfoils. It is not enough to develop a ducting system efficient for one speed; rather, it must handle the entire spectrum of deceleration, from about 600 to 1,500 mph. Thus a consistent wall of air arrives at the engine intake in an ideally unturbulent state and at slightly subsonic speed.

This design goal proved one of the true technical challenges of the SST. Half of the Concorde's wind-tunnel time, in fact, was devoted to resolving this internal-aerodynamics problem. The design solution developed by Bristol at Filton was to fit two aerodynamic ramps that, in fact, functioned like two variably shaped wings. These two internal ramps were complemented by two smaller air doors, which either admitted or expelled air according to the prevailing speed and the requirements of the engine.

All four of these independent internal aerodynamic elements were coordinated by computers. This computerized system is so sensitive that it can adjust ramp position to compensate for changes in air temperature and pressure during flight. The internal-aerodynamic system, operating within the eleven-foot-long intake duct of the Concorde's engines, not only slows down air, but compresses it and raises its temperature about 200°C. Internal components of the Concorde's engines therefore required special alloys.[10]

The Soviet approach to the internal-aerodynamics problem initially was much cruder: the inlet ducts were much longer. In fact, seen from the side, the much longer engine ducts were the most dramatic visible difference that distinguished the TU-144 from the Concorde. Overall length of the duct was seventy-five feet, of which an estimated thirty feet was devoted to the inlet. According to a cutaway drawing published in *Teknika Molodezhi* early in 1969, internal aerodynamics of the TU-144 were regulated by a single aerodynamic panel that moved down from the top of the duct. This was complemented by airflow dump doors midway from the inlet to the engines. Variable inlets and control systems were installed later, during the early part of the flight program, and modifications could be noted on later aircraft as the inlet cutouts were moved.[11]

In the end, in September 1977, the Soviets approached the Concorde consortium for help in making their inlet doors, setting up a computer regimen to coordinate ramp and movement, and possibly to obtain access to the advanced electronic and ducting systems that accounted for so much of the Concorde's superior fuel efficiency. The Anglo-French partners rejected the Soviet request on the grounds that the technology was incorporated in the latest Western fighter-bomber, the British-West German-Italian Tornado.[12]

The Soviet request to improve the TU-144 was probably sincere, in view of dogged Soviet development of the aircraft that continued well after 1977. The additional possibility of a broader application to Soviet combat aircraft is also likely. The stubborn development of the TU-144 that followed its second fatal crash in 1977, and withdrawal from Aeroflot service, derived some of its impetus from technical spinoffs of the project which would have accelerated development of the "Backfire" bomber, among others.

Airframe

One of the most daunting technical challenges for Soviet engineers was heat buildup. Their previous experience with supersonic speeds involved fighters and interceptors required to produce supersonic speeds in bursts of a few minutes to reach a target. A proper SST, however, was a "supercruiser" that would maintain 1,200 to 1,300 mph for two or three hours. At these speeds, air friction quickly heats up the airframe—over 300°F. above the surrounding air at Mach 2, well over 800°F. at Mach 3. This heating is not distributed evenly over the airframe, but is concentrated on the nose and leading edges of the wings. To some degree, it is mitigated by the high altitude at which SSTs fly: at 50,000 to 60,000 feet, the air temperature is about –60°F. (–55°C). Even so, aluminum quickly fatigues in the endless cycle of heating and cooling, shrinking and expanding involved in SST flight. Therefore, Tupolev engineers endowed the 144 with a remarkably high proportion of titanium, which made up 18 percent of its total weight.

The heat problem was aggravated by the continuous contraction and swelling produced by this wide range of operating temperatures. This phenomenon is present in all aircraft, but SSTs experience it in extreme form. The Concorde, for example, expands nine inches overall in the course of a normal flight and all components swell slightly, with a one-inch gap opening up between the flight engineer's panel and the bulkhead behind it. The Concorde's floor, which does not expand, rides on rollers.[13] The TU-144, whose range is perhaps 60 to 70 percent that of the

Concorde, does not suffer from this effect to such degree, but the Soviet design solution in part was to fit huge air-conditioning units, which were deafening enough to threaten passenger comfort. Soviet approaches to the expansion-contraction problem were never revealed.

The heat problem mandated not only an unprecedented ductility in the airframe, but also new specifications for delicate components such as hydraulic fluids, greases, and electric wiring. Fuel had to be modified with special additives to retain stable characteristics through a very wide and rapidly fluctuating temperature range, from −40°F. typically encountered in a Russian winter startup to the 1100°F. encountered in the engines. To the degree that the fuel was used as a cooling medium to suck heat away from the skin, as was done for Concorde, this required stability at high temperatures for long periods of time. Gaskets and seals around doors and windows had to be flexible and effective, while electronic components had to be adapted or shielded from the high skin temperature. This challenge doubtless inspired whole new branches of Soviet technology.

External Aerodynamics

Foremost among the many unknowns were supersonic aerodynamics. Air behaves very differently at speeds above sound, and the SST would have to contend with these conditions for hours, instead of the minutes experienced by Soviet interceptors. The "insidious compressibility" of air produced dynamics that were "totally unrecognizable" in the sustained supersonic regime. In addition to lifting force and friction, wave resistance appeared as a new enemy.[14]

Wave resistance required the Soviets to rethink two areas. The first was wing shape. Typical Soviet configurations of the 1950s featured swept-back V-wings, some approaching the delta configuration but always retaining the separate tail, which remained a TsAGI shibboleth. Although Soviet fascination with Western technical innovation knows no bounds, attenuated behind-the-scenes struggles in the mid-1960s over the delta reflects strong Soviet resistance to imported, untried design solutions. The delta wing may have been reluctantly adopted because the Soviets had no alternative.

The M-50/52 had demonstrated the drawbacks of more ordinary wings for supercruise. Soviet resistance to the delta raises the possibility that they wished their SST to be as distinctive as possible. That the TU-144 ended up resembling the Concorde as closely as it did does not mean that the Soviets did not assiduously investigate alternate solutions that turned out to be blind alleys. Well-known Soviet lust for Western state-of-the-art technology must be balanced against an inherent bias against unnecessary risk-taking in design. "Not invented here" is as powerful an argument in Moscow as elsewhere, even while the Soviets were making relative innovations in combat craft.

It seems to have taken the Soviets even longer to adopt the Concorde solution for compensating for the nine-foot shift in center of lift occurring at the transition into supersonic speed. The Concorde handled this through surplus fuel-tank capacity: large quantities of fuel were rapidly pumped forward by powerful, quick-reaction pumps to restabilize the center of gravity. When first seen by Western eyes, the 144's fuel-pumping system appeared to be an afterthought, with parts of its piping still external to the fuselage in the airflow, a blatant transgression against clean aerodynamics. The delta wing and the high-speed fuel pumping system were both essential elements of a synergistic system permitting the required two different control settings for the subsonic and supersonic modes.

But the delta wing was the salient characteristic of the SST. Once committed to it, the Soviets recognized a new type of rear stabilizer and control surfaces (elevons) as "big, serious, extremely urgent" needs. Theoretical imbroglios such as this prompted a Soviet-style pragmatic experiment. In 1964–66, while battles over adoption of a delta wing still raged, MIG was asked to graft a scaled-down delta wing to a fighter as an "analogue" to test the concept. The wing, 30 percent the size of that planned for the SST prototype, was fitted to a MIG-21. This technique aped the British, who had used a smaller BAC aircraft to test a delta wing for the Concorde in 1964.[15] The success of this transplant crumbled the last resistance of the conservatives. According to Soviet media, MIG OKB, "a collective of world renown," produced a hybrid that proved "successful and timesaving." Reflecting the involvement of all major Soviet design bureaus in the project, MIG reportedly interacted with the "aerodynamicists, structural engineers, and designers" of other KBs, including Tupolev, Ilyushin, and Antonov, conveying lessons learned applicable to the SST.

The exact shape of the wing was important. The Soviets did not opt for an exact delta with straight leading edges, as seen in Western designs of the 1950s, like the B-58. Tellingly, the profile was ogival, with two very shallow S curves defining the leading edges. This was the shape of a Gothic cathedral vault or the onion dome of Russian Orthodox cathedrals. It was also the latest in Western thinking, the shape developed by Concorde engineers. *Red Star* described the TU-144 wing as "slender, with a sharp edge [Soviet pilots joked they could shave with it] and a little curved in the forward part."[16] This was a great leap forward from the double sweepback wing as seen on the transient supersonic Soviet designs of the 1950s. Soviet designers kept changing the SST wing shape until 1977.

The MIG Analogue

Central to the SST's evolution in the mid-1960s was MIG test pilot Oleg Gudkov. Because Soviet practice depends more on flight testing than on well-considered blueprints, with many fixes occurring on patched-up prototypes, Soviet test pilots play an even more important role in developing new types than they do in the West. They are played up as heroes in Soviet propaganda. Chief Designer Tupolev paid tribute to these few "brave men," paladins of Soviet technocracy. There is substance behind the ballyhoo. The TU-144 alone claimed the lives of six Soviet pilots and technicians between 1973 and 1978, while seriously injuring three more. Its chief test pilot wore medals indicating survival of three crashes before being extricated from the second fatal crash of the TU-144 in 1978.[17]

As a pivotal member of this hypercompetent fraternity, Oleg Gudkov was known for his meticulous attention to detail and his ability to communicate flight problems to engineers. *Red Star* stressed he "could obtain valuable information in the most difficult situations"; for once, the Soviet press may have been guilty of understatement. His in-flight comments were recorded and full debriefings followed each flight. Reportedly, Gudkov dedicated himself to testing the analogue like "a soldier intoxicated by battle."[18] On his first visit to the MIG assembly area, workers regarded him with "obvious curiosity." He touched the wing, among the first to find it "beautiful and a little strange."

Gudkov characteristically asked for a change in the instruments on first sight of the cockpit: essential instruments and gauges on the left, secondary ones on the right, his invariable practice before "complicated tests." The analogue's maiden flight established that the plane overreacted to control inputs and bucked, but Gudkov "calmed the skittish, tail-less creature and managed to ease her snugly onto the strip."

Delta wings were a novelty in Soviet experience. Though Gudkov was thoroughly familiar with the MIG-21, on which the analogue was based, the delta hybrid was completely different in its handling characteristics. Its elevon rudders had to substitute for both conventional rudder and elevators. In the air the elevators were excessively responsive to the joystick. After engineers recalibrated the controls, it became more obedient. A serendipitous discovery was that a delta wing created an exaggerated ground effect—a cushion of air—that enabled the TU-144 to land and take off at the same speed as the TU-104, with one-third its top speed. The analogue's wing was innocent of trailing or leading edge flaps, so this was welcome news.

The elder Tupolev is said to have "sighed with relief" on learning of the delta wing's first successful flight. Work could now proceed on the TU-144 without further hindrance. But problems remained. Gudkov found the delta occasionally heavy

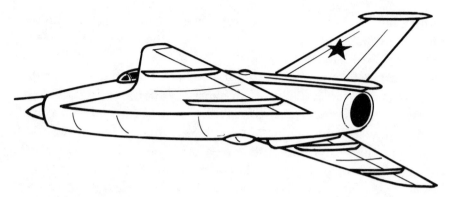

The MIG analogue, a modified MIG-25, was developed in 1965–68 to test the delta wing dynamics. Two wing shapes were in fact tried. This is the final version, as flown as escort to the TU-144 on its first flight, 31 December 1968.

handling and sometimes "unpleasant." The designers were slow and meticulous in developing this innovation. After Gudkov had tried it in a series of dives and attacks, it was flown in a formation with a conventional MIG-21 for comparison. Finally, the analogue was flown by Elyan and Kozlov, the future two Chief Test Pilots for the TU-144 itself. Kozlov, after his first ride, did not catch his breath but immediately went into conference with Gudkov and Volk, the two MIG analogue chief testers. He told Gudkov he found its handling nice and light, though it sat "like a bobsled in the air." It took some time to get used to. When the elder Tupolev was told that the analogue handled well, he replied with elation, "Now we will send up the big one."[19]

The exact timing of the analogue flights is not known, but Soviet sources reported that the first roll-out of the TU-144 prototype took place in 1967.[20] This may have been planned to celebrate the fiftieth anniversary of the Revolution. It may have been abortive; Soviet media did not refer to this event in November 1967. Perhaps like the groundhog that does not see its shadow, the TU-144 returned to its hangar to be completed and await a better day. Later, it was escorted on its first flight by its MIG-based cousin.

Soviet R & D Strategy: A Special Case

Not only did the TU-144 embody unique technology, but its technology was conceived and assembled in a manner that diverged from normal Soviet practice. The 144 development followed the pattern of mass development introduced by Tupolev forty years before. That the TU-144 was not solely the product of Tupolev KB, but instead involved the resources of the entire Soviet aerospace industry, was revealed in a front-page article in *Izvestia* the day following its historic first flight. Hundreds of plants took part in equipping the TU-144, as well as scores of scientific research institutes and design offices and thousands of workers, engineers, and scientists. In this latter-day application of mass development—probably the last—all pooled their talents. Ilyushin was involved with the airframe, while the prototype's wings were flown to the Tupolev assembly hall near Moscow from the Antonov factory in the Ukraine, where they had been assembled.[21]

This extensive support network had been growing from 1963 on. Computer-operated machine tools had been imported and installed, and special test stands fabricated. New alloys, fuels, and specialized fluids had been developed, as well as new techniques for fabricating and rolling special titanium-alloy sheets. The Soviet chemical industry contributed 10,000 new small plastic parts to each TU-144.

Tupolev had been nominated the lead KB because it was the "oldest" and "most experienced." But Dementiev's Ministry of Aviation Industry was singled out for praise in coordinating assembly work and deliveries of subcomponents. This was no small task, for the normal Soviet practice of working from catalogs of available equipment was useless in assembling an aircraft whose specifications invariably exceeded the known state of the art.

Soviet media noted that the "volume of research on this machine [was] ten times that of creating other machines." Basic research and verification required computer analysis and wind-tunnel studies, an "avalanche of the most laborious scientific and engineering tasks." TsAGI under Myasishchev must have tested over 100 different variants proposed, and Myasishchev played no passive role in SST designing and conceptualization. This was not publicized in the hour of the TU-144's greatest triumph, suggesting that Myasishchev's unredeemed promises regarding the M-4 and M-50/52 had made him something of a pariah to his colleagues, who may have perceived him as a dangerous dabbler. His studies probably preceded those of Tupolev in 1961, but he was firmly kept on the sidelines in a project with an abundance of concrete problems to resolve. Exuberant visionaries were suspect.

7
WINGS OF
GREAT HOPES

Foreign designers started working on the Concorde one and a half years before we began. When they built the first prototype, they thought that the airliner would soon be placed into operation. But life shows that loud advertising and haste lead to nothing good. A test flight is one thing, and regular commercial flight is quite another.—Andrei Nikolayevich Tupolev, Pravda, May 8, 1971 (seventeen days before boarding the prototype on its first flight to the West)

The period 1969–71 saw a continuation of the exuberant sales and diplomatic drive by the Soviets for the TU-144, and its appearance was welcomed in the West by SST proponents in the United States, France, and Britain.

In the FAA report on SSTs dated the last day of 1969—a year to the day after the TU-144's first flight—the Soviet aircraft was considered a formidable commercial competitor. This contrasted with more negative evaluations by the British, who made it plain they did not consider it a serious sales rival. The FAA believed the TU-144 could penetrate world markets, posing a potential threat to the American SST. It had a 200 mph faster cruising speed than the Concorde, though its payload of 120 passengers was less than the Concorde's 128. Japan, Holland, Pakistan, and India had all expressed commercial interest. The Soviets might use a number of incentives to increase its commercial appeal, such as favorable financing and the use of Soviet airspace.

TASS reported in October 1969 that 250 hours of flight-testing had been completed. Aeroflot announced plans for one craft to fly to Japan the next year to participate in Expo 70. According to *Aviation Week*, 144s would be flying the New York–Moscow route no later than 1971, two years in the future.

A table of comparative statistics at the end of the FAA report indicated that the 144 was marginally smaller than the Concorde in all dimensions, except wingspan:

Concorde	TU-144
385,000 lbs. maximum takeoff weight	330,000 lbs. maximum takeoff weight
193 feet long	188.5 feet long
38 feet high	34.5 feet high
72-foot wingspan	83 foot, 10-inch wingspan

The 144 was marginally more powerful, with 38,500 lbs of thrust, instead of 38,300.

These global perspectives were lightened by a touch of farce. A Berwick, Louisiana, aircraft dealer, Doyle Berry, claimed that he had negotiated an oral contract for the Western hemisphere sales rights for the TU-144 and that a formal contract would soon be forthcoming from the USSR.[1] Nothing further was heard from him again.

However, the TU-144 proved useful ammunition for American SST proponents. At a meeting of SST supporters at the Aero Club in Washington, Neil Armstrong, who had been the first man on the moon and had seen the TU-144 the previous spring, said, brandishing a TU-144 scale model, that it was "a fine looking aircraft—as good as the best kind of products we're putting out." These views were seconded by Robert Holtz, editor of *Aviation Week*. Congress was pressured to appropriate $290 million for an SST.

The invisible hand of the lobbyists occasionally surfaced. On March 8, 1971, the *New York Times* carried a full-page ad from

"American Labor and Industry for the SST," predicting that the TU-144 would commence Moscow–Calcutta service on October 23, 1971. The *Washington Post* ran a long piece in March 1971, the week the House cut off funds for the SST. The Soviet Ministry of Civil Aviation had announced that Soviet pilots "will start mastering" the 144 during the year. Moscow observers asserted that Soviets did not have to worry about the ecological or economic problems that threatened to abort Western SSTs. But "traditional Soviet marketing disabilities" would undercut Soviet SST sales to the West. Warnings that the Soviets would export TU-144s echoed from untraceable sources.

Aviaexport ran ads for the 144 in *Aviation Week* and *Jane's*, scorned by Western experts as a wish-fulfillment fantasy. The Soviet Aviation Ministry had no precise guarantee of its share of the resource pie, it was pointed out, but could ask for more money if the United States entered the SST race. The pleas of Halaby and Armstrong were exploited by their Soviet counterparts. Most rumors of 144 flights to Khabarovsk, Calcutta, Karachi, or New Delhi usually could be traced to Paris or Washington.

Most Moscow observers of the 144 believed it could not be economically flown less than 2,000 miles. Soviet economists responded that its costs would not exceed those of subsonic flight. Yet a U.S. study of the Concorde estimated that its seat-mile costs were 40 percent more than subsonic flights, and this was before the first run-up in fuel costs that occurred in late 1972. The Soviet government, therefore, would subsidize the operating costs of its SST at a rate even higher than normal Aeroflot flights.[2]

On the eve of the 144's first appearance in the West at the Paris Air Show, Jacques Mourisset, the astute editor of *Air et Cosmos,* commented on the confusion caused by the Soviets' conflicting needs for secrecy and publicity. There were many contradictions in the Soviet record. Entry in service meant something different in the USSR. The U.S. *Aviation Daily* had announced entry for the USSR as scheduled in 1972, with 1973 for international routes. Yet Marshal Bugayev of Aeroflot had set

1975 as the date, while his predecessor, Loginov, had said that a long period of "operational experimentation" would lead to long-distance mail routes in 1982–83.

The same imprecision persisted in Aviaexport publicity, possibly reflecting the rapidity of 144 development and Soviet studies of a larger Mach 3 SST parallel to the more advanced development work on the Mach 2 prototype. The number of passengers had now changed from 98 to 120, but Aviaexport said it must carry 130 to 150 passengers. Range was usually stated to be 6,500 miles, but the same publicity also gave 4,560 miles. Dimensions were even more protean. Specified wing span fluctuated from 179 to 188 feet. Length grew from 55 to 58 meters (179 to 188 feet), and weight from 130 to 150 tons.[3]

First Visit to the West

The Soviet decision to bring the TU-144 to the West for the 1971 Paris Salon Aeronautique involved some risk, especially since propaganda stops were planned at Prague on the way out and at Warsaw and East Berlin on return. The TU-144 at this stage was still a raw test aircraft with about 100 hours in the air. Yet the history of the Soviet space and nuclear programs reflects a willingness to accept risk and low safety factors in the cause of "scientific progress" and State prestige.

Some clues as to Soviet motivations were provided by Alexei Tupolev, the Chief Designer, in an interview given to *Leninskoye Znamya (Leninist Banner)* on the eve of the 144's first trip to the West. Tupolev began with the standard official picture of a careful test program calmly proceeding: "We are satisfied with the prototype. . . . No changes would be made save for finishing touches and the regulation of certain units." Following these bromides, however, he signaled that the final version of the TU-144 "will differ somewhat." Certain unspecified changes were required in the design: "Such a complex, expensive craft as the TU-144 cannot immediately be mass produced." Several models had to be made and carefully checked in flight.

What was driving the program, in addition to national prestige, was the lure of hard currency earnings: "The world market for supersonic passenger planes is extremely large." When the finishing touches were applied, it would be "up to the market" itself to determine how many SSTs could be built and sold[4]— a curiously capitalist comment for a Leninist publication.

In retrospect, Tupolev's soothing evocation of an on-schedule test program contrasts somewhat with the risks involved in taking the 144 to Paris. There, its worn tires, its rough-and-ready appearance, and the admission that it had been flown only 150 hours revealed it as a hard-working test aircraft—in spite of its mockup interior. The passenger cabin was apparently still unpressurized. An emergency landing on the return leg dramatized its marginal reliability.

However, the need to show the Red flag, and to confront the Concorde now making its second appearance at Paris, took precedence over the caution of the engineers and technicians. If the TU-144 was to maintain credibility as an airliner for world markets, Soviet prestige required its presence at the world's premier air show, nearly two and a half years following its record-making first flight. Its huge smokeless engines, primitive flight deck, undeveloped wing, and other details provided a feast for analysts and the curious. If its finish left much to be desired, the Soviets had already hinted that this was a provisional test vehicle, with a more definitive version waiting in the wings.

Western curiosity was relieved by the 144's first visit to the West, in May–June 1971. The Soviets were not slow to exploit the political prestige of their SST's first international outing. En route to Paris, the 144 stopped in Prague for a Congress of Communist Party Chiefs. Czech crowds reportedly "mobbed" the airport. Their comments indicated Soviet technological prowess to some degree counterbalanced the effect of Soviet political-military intervention two and a half years before. On its way to Paris, the 144 carefully skirted West German airspace.[5]

In a news conference at the 1971 Paris air show, Pyotr Dementiev, Soviet Minister of Aviation Production, disposed of the alleged lead of the TU-144, pushing its entry into service forward to late 1973 or early 1974. This meant that the two SSTs were now neck and neck for the start of commercial service. The 144 shown at Paris was the only one now flying, though Dementiev said that two more would take to the air during 1971, without revealing that these were to be the radically improved production type. This schedule also slipped. After Dementiev, Alexei Tupolev dismissed questions about price and performance as "premature." "It's still in the stage of testing and perfecting. There are a lot of facts, of parameters, to explore."[6] This point was underscored by the admission of Soviet officials at Paris that the true maximum range of the 144 as presented was only around 2000 miles, instead of the 3700 officially claimed.

Among the real advantages of having the TU-144 in the West was that members of its accompanying entourage occasionally let slip such glimpses into reality behind the propaganda screen. A leading light of the Soviet delegation was "courtly" eighty-three-year-old Andrei Tupolev, "whose penetrating wit and historical perspective were always worthy of attention."[7] This was Tupolev's last visit to the West; he was to die in December 1972, just after the introduction of the TU-144 production version. The "Old Man" was at least spared by death before his SST's limitations became too public.

The 1971 Paris air show was not only the 144's first visit to the West, it was also the first opportunity to compare the Concorde and 144 side by side. Its arrival had been eagerly awaited by Western experts. The SST competition had just been dramatically narrowed. Two days before the TU-144 landed in Paris—on May 27—a final Senate vote had killed the last hope for the overambitious, Boeing-built, Mach 3 variable-geometry U.S. SST.

Because of sensitivity to environmental issues in the West, the salient impression created by "Konkordski" during its Free World debut was the absence of smoke and low level of noise coming from its engines; its turbofans were quieter in subsonic operation than the turbojets fitted to the Concorde. Concorde officials conceded that the Soviet craft was quieter and cleaner. Western experts overestimated its engines. Henri Ziegler, head of the French aerospace industry, estimated that the TU-144's engines were "at least a year and a half ahead" of the Concorde's, while a Rolls-Royce engineer said the noise occurred only because the Western engines were more powerful.

John Swihart, chief engineer of the just-cancelled Boeing SST project, believed the Soviets could sell the TU-144 in the West at "the right price and the right guarantees." Use of parachutes in landing indicated that the Soviets had abandoned reverse thrust.[8] The TU-144 sent to Paris was the original prototype, now thirty months old.[9] There was no evidence for the Soviet claim that the 144 was in mass production.[10] *Flight International* estimated that it must represent an investment of 500,000 pounds sterling, if its costs were the same as Concorde's.

Western experts were irritated by the exaggerated security precautions required by the Soviets. The TU-144 at Le Bourget was protected by armed guards, its "interior securely barred from the eyes of Western journalists," in dramatic contrast to the open, public presentation of the Concorde. *Flight International* grumbled: "Once again the Russians steal the show [exploiting] the advantage of proceeding with a project in complete secrecy and revealing it with a flourish when and where it suits [them] . . . getting all the headlines."[11]

Members of the Soviet delegation put other aspects of the Soviet program into perspective. Only one TU-144, the prototype, was currently flying and 100 test flights had been made, data hard to reconcile with the 1973 entry date announced by Aviation Minister Dementiev.[12]

Similar in Outline, Different in Detail

Aviation Week scrutinized most closely the issue of similarities between the Concorde and its alleged Soviet clone. The first opportunity to examine the two SSTs almost side by side led experts to conclude that they had "evolved from separate design approaches which have produced two basically different configurations . . . different nose designs, different fuselage cross

sections and different wing profiles." Landing-gear design dictated by engine placement also differed.[13]

Design and development approaches were also quite distinct.
The TU-144 at Paris, the original prototype showing the wear of
thirty months of flight testing, was finished rather roughly. The
pipe to transfer fuel to the rear tank was external to the fuselage,
a drag-inducing add-on. The crude, unstreamlined joining of
engine nozzles to fuselage indicated that the prototype was basically a flying laboratory. Swihart noted: "Rivets showing, tires
worn, that's what you expect of a test airplane."[14] The Concorde,
more refined "in almost all aspects of its design," showed better
attention to detail and general workmanship, reflecting the Western practice of resolving design problems before building actual
aircraft. The Soviets instead get designs into flight testing as soon
as possible, and make running changes to the design as indicated
by flight tests and wind-tunnel studies.[15]

Divergences in design included the wing, nose, fuselage, tail,
and crew escape systems. The Soviet supersonic's wing was
primitive compared to the Concorde's elegant camber and twist.
(Subsequent 144 wing designs more closely approximated Concorde sophistication.) Wing placement also differed. The 144's
wings were mounted low on a fuselage with a flat bottom resembling the discarded Boeing 2707 design. Concorde wings were
mounted higher on an oval cross-section fuselage. Boeing's Swihart believed the Soviet "flat floor" provided better directional
stability and lift. The 144's tail fin was much larger, probably to
provide extra stability in advance of precise data on directional
stability that would come from advanced wind-tunnel testing.
While the Concorde had floor escape hatches and parachutes for
its crew, the 144 featured ejection seats.[16]

The "droop snoot" of the TU-144 closely resembled the design
of the Boeing 2707. It dropped to a single position for both
takeoff and landing, in contrast to the two positions of the
Concorde, which in addition was equipped with a retractable
windshield visor.[17]

A walk around the two aircraft, plan drawings published by *Air
et Cosmos*[18] and photographs, confirmed the two's resemblance

only in general outline: examination of nearly every design detail revealed differences. The most dramatic visual difference was the length of engine nacelles. Although these helped make the Soviet engines quieter, the drag it caused was considerable.

Swihart pointed out that the large ducts of the TU-144 and engine position permitted the fitting of even-larger engines if required. Reports of new 144 engines were shortly to proliferate, while the Concorde's installation signified a commitment to the extant Olympus 593. Likewise, the Concorde's fuselage made no provision for a stretch version.

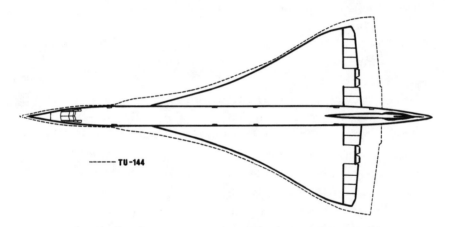

------- TU-144

A comparison of the Concorde and TU-144 (shown here) prototypes (1962–72) shows the larger wing area of the Soviet design.

Soviet test equipment was confined to a small compartment on the right side of the cabin, while the Concorde's main cabin was dominated by flight-test equipment. Several consoles had to be removed to install the twenty-four seats for demonstration flights at Paris. A Soviet official stated that much Soviet flight data was transmitted directly to the ground, but the dramatic gap between East and West test equipment was obvious. The production version of the TU-144 employed the same seats as the TU-154 airliner, but had no provision for an emergency oxygen system. The Soviets must have been confident about commercial use of the TU-144, for they negotiated with the Franco-American firm ICS/TEAM regarding an on-board entertainment system.[19]

Other Expert Opinions

Other Western experts hastened to subject the Soviet SST to critical, close-up scrutiny. All recognized that this was a test-bed workhorse, whose presentation was fairly rough by the standards of the Salon Aeronautique. The first impression on approaching the 144 was that all twenty-four tires in the main landing gear were equally worn down to the cord, with tread showing. The Soviets were forced to use a large number of small tires because the landing-gear design required retraction into the thickest part of the wing, in the split between the engine ducts.

The design decision to concentrate all four engines on the centerline under the fuselage required a complex and draginducing landing-gear operation. The retraction mechanism was characterized dryly by *Air et Cosmos* as "unexpected . . . highly original." Each twelve-wheel landing-gear unit on retracting turned and moved perpendicular to the airflow. When a full 180-degree turn had been described, the strut folded again to the front. *Interavia* wondered whether this arrangement resulted from the backwardness of Soviet tire, wheel, or brake design or from a requirement to land on poor surfaces.[20]

Soldat und Technik asserted that difficulties with the landing gear had already interrupted the "careful pace" of the 144's flight-testing. *Air et Cosmos* observed that the high angle of attack required for landing led to a lack of clearance. The rear of the engine nacelles brushed the ground on landing, with the engine blast scorching the runway surface. The "Konkordski," like the Concorde, was frequently likened to a giant bird, but the Soviet subspecies dragged its tail feathers on landing.[21]

The rough, high-speed landings resulted from the unrefined wing design. Neil Armstrong, *Apollo 11* commander and senior NASA administrator, had been given a tour of the TU-144 prototype in September 1970. Armstrong described its wing as "a highly contoured double delta . . . with variable camber twist on its leading edge." Experts in Paris, however, agreed that the wing still had a long way to go. The underwing was practically flat, compared to the complexity of the Concorde's. The Soviets had not yet established the ideal compromise shape that could best serve the conflicting requirements of takeoff and landing, subsonic maneuver and acceleration, and supersonic cruise. The wing was optimized for supersonic speed. This meant that uncertain low-speed lift at this stage in its development caused some hard, fast landings. The Concorde prototype could land twelve mph slower.[22] Canards, which appeared on the TU-144 production version of 1972, provided additional lift and cut landing speed at the price of additional drag and complexity. The canards may have been a quick fix to compensate for the crude wing design, unsettled at least until 1977.

The NK-144 engines were already identified as another troublesome point, with consumption and reliability so bad that the Soviets had begun a search for an alternative design. Western experts noted that the generous size of the housings would permit alternate installations. The Soviets announced that the 144 required only two engines for "normal flight" and could land with only one operating. This safety feature was shortly to be confirmed in a "white knuckle" segment of its return trip. Armstrong had pointed out the high drag of the engine installation and expected the Soviets to revise the engine, nozzle, inlet, and aft fuselage configurations. Other experts called attention to the lack of neatness in the aft engine fairing, with its high drag potential.[23]

Air et Cosmos noted past Soviet indeterminancy on engine location. The provisional location of all four powerplants under the fuselage were abandoned in the second scale model, shown at Paris in 1967, and the definitive location of the 144 engines well out on the wings was the most dramatic and visible change on the production model introduced in 1972. A general atmosphere of improvisation enveloped the 144. Armstrong, in late 1970, had described thrust reversers exhausting through wing slots opened for this purpose on landing. But no reversers could be seen on the prototype at Paris in 1971 and subsequent models made use of three landing parachutes.

A special additive had been added to TU-144 fuel to stabilize it at high temperatures. Turbine temperatures needed to be elevated fourteen degrees, providing a considerable uplift in power. The operating mode for the engine was reported to be "boost and coast" to prevent overheating—intermittent maximum power at the cost of high consumption. *Aircraft* wondered why such a "confusing and impractical" approach was necessary in a country with extensive supersonic experience with the MIG-23 and several bombers.[24]

The answer, of course, was that the 144 was a giant leap forward technically, requiring twice or four times the power exacted from previous Soviet engine types. Crude solutions such as near-continuous afterburning produced high power quickly, with a host of engineering fixes required *ex post facto*. At this point it is likely that the engine could only run well at its "supercruise" setting.

To the thoughtful observer, the unmatched TU-144 wing and engine designs reflects the rawness of the design in 1971. The engine was efficient only at subsonic speed and the wings fully functional in supersonic mode. This resulted from the telescoping of the 1965–68 crash development and the Soviet practice of working out design problems with test-bed aircraft rather than on paper or in theory. The final version of the 144 would therefore represent a much more dramatic jump in development than that of the Concorde.

Mishap and Mystery

The prototype's return home after the Salon Aeronautique was marred by a mishap at variance with its stately flying demonstration in Paris on June 5. Leaving Paris on June eighth, the 144 visited two Eastern European capitals to exhibit the latest Soviet technology. The TU-144 remained in East Berlin several days for the DDR's Party Congress and then, on June seventeenth, it flew to Warsaw for a preview the next day for the benefit of Polish dignitaries and the public.

According to reports circulating in Warsaw, the two left engines quit twenty minutes before touchdown. The pilot sounded "pretty frantic" when he contacted the Warsaw control tower. Soviet officials later confirmed that the 144 had to make an emergency landing on a 7,500-foot runway, short of the 9,600 feet required when the 144 was fully loaded. Fire equipment stood ready.

Polish mechanics who later inspected the aircraft reported "a crack at least three-quarters of an inch wide in the mounting between no. 1 and 2 engines."[25] Other reports specified two six-foot-long cracks in the housing. This suggested severe airborne vibration. The local Aeroflot spokesman denied that any trouble or damage had occurred; the plane would return to Moscow the next day. So it did, with the problem apparently repaired, and it was photographed in Moscow on June nineteenth. No further explanation of the incident was provided.[26] The Polish aviation magazine *Skrzydlata Polska* (July 23 1971) played the Delphic oracle, noting "in the highly improbable event of damage to two engines, the 144 could reach a reserve air field" and land on one engine. The rapidity of the Warsaw turnaround was not compatible with the severity of the reported damage, leading us to suspect the Soviets may have switched prototypes.

Supersonic record-breaking flights for political effect continued. On September 6, 1971, the prototype conveyed its Chief Designer from Moscow to Sofia, Bulgaria, to make the first supersonic flight between two capitals. The return trip of 1,900 kilometers (1,200 miles) was covered in seventy-one minutes at an average speed of just under 1,000 mph. Western journals noted its short range, which cut the fuel load required, and augmented its performance. Alexei Tupolev gave Zhivkov and other Bulgarian leaders a full briefing in his dual capacity as Chief Designer and Chairman of the Soviet-Bulgarian Friendship Society.[27]

The Soviet press predicted that the TU-144 would enter service during 1973, probably to mark the fiftieth anniversary of Aeroflot. The Civil Aviation Ministry began part-time training in supersonic flight theory for candidate TU-144 pilots. Formal ground training for the aircraft was scheduled to begin in early 1972.[28] Alexander Aksenov, Deputy Minister of Civil Aviation, said the "commercial" version would carry up to 150 passengers, 30 more than the prototype—a possible reference to the stillborn Mach 3 second-generation Soviet SST. But there was a great gulf fixed between service on Soviet and satellite routes and entry into international commercial service. Certification required close scrutiny and monitoring by the FAA for the United States, by ARB for Britain, and by SGAC for France.

Chief Designer Alexei Tupolev had asserted in Paris that two and a half years of prototype flights had necessitated "virtually no design changes."[29] Yet the Soviets had not yet submitted a single dossier concerning the TU-144 to any Western company or any of the three Western bodies as a prelude to certification. *Air et Cosmos* predicted that a second "international" version, requiring four to five years for certification, could not appear before the late 1970s. This would explain the gap between the aircraft shown at the Salon Aeronautique and the ambitious TU-144 specifications restated: a 130-ton weight and 6,500-kilometer, or 4,000-mile, range.[30]

Both the Concorde and the TU-144 were invited by U.S. Transportation Secretary John Volpe to attend the Transpo '72 exhibition in Washington in mid-1972. The Soviets accepted and said they would send an official delegation. The Soviets never reserved any space, but were said to have selected the flight crews that would bring the TU-144 across the Atlantic for the first time. In fact, the 144 never flew to the United States, confirming suspicions regarding its meager range. *Interavia* expressed it delicately: "Washington is thought too distant a destination for an aircraft still in the prototype stage."[31]

The 144 did attend the Hannover air show in May 1972, as a static exhibit. German authorities would not permit it to make any demonstration flights, for safety reasons. Its pilot Edward Elyan noted that three TU-144s were now flying. The production version predicted earlier was near. The Soviets had originally announced that a 180-passenger "version with improved takeoff and climb and increased passenger comfort" would appear at Hannover, revealing "major design changes" in the engine intakes and vertical fin. In "forthcoming international and transatlantic flights," the electrical systems operator would serve as navigator. The promised "first production prototype" was not ready for Hannover, however, and only surfaced later in 1972.[32]

Soviet interest in a second-generation SST remainly lively, even as the first-generation 144 approached production. The French were approached in early 1972 to learn if they had any interest in codevelopment of a Mach 3 craft. Henri Ziegler, head of the French aerospace sector, visited the USSR in January 1972, and on his return indicated that the Soviets might be part of a joint group treating SST problems.[33] Part of the French motivation was to develop the Soviets as a potential market; the Soviets were glad to gain additional entrée to Concorde technology.

8
REDESIGN AND DISASTER, 1972–1973

On December 23, 1972, Andrei Nikolayevich Tupolev died at the age of eighty-four, having lived just long enough to see the final version of the SST, whose design he had initiated over a decade before, enter mass production at Voronezh. Right up until his death, he had retained his faith in the future of his last project: the year before, he had predicted that even if there were a hitch in the 144's production program, "it would be short-lived."[1]

The Czarevich: Accession of Alexei Tupolev

The elder Tupolev held concentrated power unique for a Soviet private citizen, especially a non-Party member. His obituary was signed by Brezhnev, followed by all members of the Politburo, then Minister of Defense Grechko, Minister of Civil Aviation Bugayev, then Deputy Ministers of Defense and leaders of the Soviet aircraft industry. This crystallized his position "near the apex of a military-industrial-scientific-political structure." A consummate individualist became an ultimate Soviet insider. Colonel-General Tupolev, as a member of the armed forces, had direct access to the Minister of Defense. Academician Tupolev enjoyed contact with the academic and research elite. Engineer and scientist Tupolev could deploy his own research facilities and design bureau. Industrialist Tupolev controlled his own plants. As deputy to the Supreme Soviet after 1950, Tupolev could address the governmental power structure.[2]

Seventy-three Soviet dignitaries signed his obituary and tributes to his work were published all over the world. But no successor was immediately announced to fill the vacancy. It is a peculiarity of the Soviet system that all major posts are held until death by the incumbent: retirement sees the disappearance of power and many perquisites. In the case of a General Designer, this includes direct access to chief Party leaders, bypassing the Minister of Aviation. But it was unlikely that any successor would enjoy the overlapping of positions the elder Tupolev had enjoyed.

There were many highly experienced designers associated with the KB to succeed the patriarch, but most of them were now quite old. Arkhangelski, Bazenkov, and Myasishchev, the surviving chief lieutenants of Tupolev, were in their seventies. There was a general trend for a new generation to take over from the pioneering founders. Novozhilov, forty-eight, replaced Ilyushin; Tishchenko, thirty-eight, replaced Mil. But there was no direct indication of who had replaced Andrei Tupolev until September 1973, when Alexei Andreyevich Tupolev, among other general designers, signed the obituary of Tumansky, the engine designer. He had not been among the signatories of his father's obituary, so there must have been an awkward interregnum of several months in 1973, a fateful year for the TU-144.

Alexei had been carefully groomed by his father as heir apparent, and the passing of the torch from father to son was well cultivated in the Soviet media. *Izvestia*, for example, on August 30, 1969, published a feature, "Valuable Legacy," which dwelt on the intergenerational continuity of the Tupolev design heritage being passed on. But this form of dynastic politics increased grumbling among young Soviet designers, who complained that Tupolev had become a bureau of "fathers and sons," a place where a patron or well-connected relative was necessary to secure a permanent position on the staff after internship in dramatic contrast to the atmosphere of the 1930s.

This exercise in primogeniture was not entirely smooth. The

145

1969 propaganda film, *Bilët*, or *Take-off*, celebrating the first flight of the 144, presents the "Old Man" as in charge of all meetings. The son's role as chief designer was decidedly secondary. Other designers of his generation had arguably better credentials. Yeger, sixty at this time, had published several books on transport design and was generally regarded as more experienced. He left Tupolev for the Moscow Aviation Institute.

The Czarevich, now forty-seven, was well prepared. Alexei had been born in Moscow on May 20, 1925, and had gone to work at Tupolev KB in 1942, at the age of seventeen. He graduated from the Moscow Aviation Construction Institute in 1949, becoming a Doctor of Technical Sciences in 1964 and joining its teaching staff as a professor the following year. He began independent design work in 1957 and became a Chief Designer— in collaboration with his father—when the 144 project was approved in 1963. He was awarded a USSR State Prize in 1967, presumably for his work in developing the 144 and other supersonic designs. His specialty was supersonic aircraft planning and testing, or systems engineer. He was nominated, but not elected, as corresponding member of the Soviet Academy of Sciences in 1968, but was elected a full member in April 1979. He was made a Hero of Socialist Labor in 1972 and became a Deputy to the Supreme Soviet, ninth convocation. Unlike his father, he joined the Party, in 1959.[3] Alexei finally attained election to the Supreme Soviet in 1984, together with Antonov and Novozhikov, head of Ilyushin KB.[4]

Alexei probably had a finer sense of economics than his father. A master of press conferences, he was a skilled deflector of unwelcome questions, answering instead queries that had not been asked. He generally did not reveal his serviceable command of English, which probably gave him time to redirect the discussion. A query regarding the 144's fuel consumption, for example, would be countered by pointing out that there was no fuel shortage inside the Soviet Union, or by holding forth on the unique nature of the aircraft's fuel. Some of his statements were misleading and imprecise, such as when he said the 144 was "10 percent quieter than the Concorde." Its external noise was less, owing to its quieter engines, but the internal cacophony of the passenger cabin was revealed only in 1977.

In the early years of the 144 project, Alexei shared his father's optimism about the future. In 1969, speaking on "Aviation in the Year 2000" to the Science Society of Moscow, he predicted that the volume of air shipment would increase fifty times by the end of the century. The future knew no bounds: "giant stratospheric liners" would convey 1,000 passengers each up to 6,000 mph. These large-scale crowds would be unloaded in five minutes by outfitting each liner with eight to twelve doors. In the more distant future, nuclear-powered airliners might be possible. These remarks were widely quoted later, though not his suggestion that stewardesses be replaced with robots.[5]

Alexei was adept at illuminating important questions with futuristic visions. When asked by the Paris Communist daily L'Humanité in 1971 the question, "Why? Why go faster than sound?" he could only cite the inexorable trend of technical progress. He betrayed no sense that the price might be out of proportion with the gain. He "was certain . . . that the establishment of supersonic speed will be rapid and painless."

Alexei shared the contemporary faith of the Concorde's sponsors that "a huge world market" existed for SSTs: two models would hardly saturate it. Of course, the superiority of the Soviet planned system made "the entire process of the creation of the aircraft, from the first designs and up to mass production . . . more rapid . . . since it does not depend on economic circumstances. . . ." However, this distance from economic reality was a mixed blessing: the monolith of Soviet planning could go terribly awry if its aim was not prophetically accurate and on target.

Privately, on occasion and in small groups of Western counterparts, Alexei would drop the mask. On board the 144 prototype at the 1971 Paris air show, just after the Senate had voted 49 to 47 not to underwrite an American SST, he complained bitterly to his American guests. He had just been quoted in L'Humanité: "The logic of technical development will inevitably lead American industry to build a supersonic civil aircraft." It was an unkind cut for the United States to drop out of SST development. The United States and developers of SST designs such as Boeing and Lockheed had misled the Soviets. "First you went ahead and built wide bodies. Then you started SSTs and we had to go ahead and build an SST. Now that we are building it, spending money which could better be used to help our people in other areas, you back out of it."[6]

Tupolev's outburst must have revealed his true feelings, which indicate that his role as Chief Designer of the TU-144 must have been strange, indeed. It was a tacit admission that the Soviet aircraft industry felt constrained to follow the West into any new field without independent analysis of the cost or implications. It confirms what is only hinted elsewhere—that by 1971, Alexei had come to doubt the cost-effectiveness of the project and had become critical of focusing Soviet aerospace resources on a project whose payoff was becoming more remote. It was as though the Soviets' ceaseless aping of Western technical advances had caught them in an infernal machine of their own making.

Other comments by Alexei Tupolev hint that Aeroflot had lost its earlier enthusiasm for its putative flagship: "At the moment it is difficult to name a precise time when the TU-144 will be handed over to Aeroflot." But as late as 1976, the Chief Designer put on a bold front: his "very pesky, excitable new babes" had a 4,000-mile range; ten were needed to serve Soviet long-range routes. He looked forward, he told an American reporter, to flying Moscow-New York in 3½ hours.[7]

The growing technical difficulties of the 144, and the inability of Soviet engineers to solve them, forced Tupolev to live on two levels. Officially, as the 144 was launched into "regular service" on "the eve of Great October," to celebrate the sixtieth anniversary of the Bolshevik takeover, he would tout the TU-144's reliability, established in the course of many experiments and checks. "Its powerful engines with a combined thrust of half a million horsepower—"he said, "do not exceed in noise level the most rigorous domestic and international standards."[8]

Debut of the production TU-144 at Paris, May 1973, days before it crashed, with nose and flaps down but canards retracted. *(Schoenmaker)*

Aftermath, Goussainville, France, on Sunday afternoon, June 3, 1973, six miles north of Le Bourget. Eight villagers were killed in addition to the five Soviet crew members. Over sixty buildings were damaged. TU-144 technology does not appear to be a factor; the root of the tragedy seems to lie in miscommunications resulting from rivalry between the two SSTs. *(Photosource)*

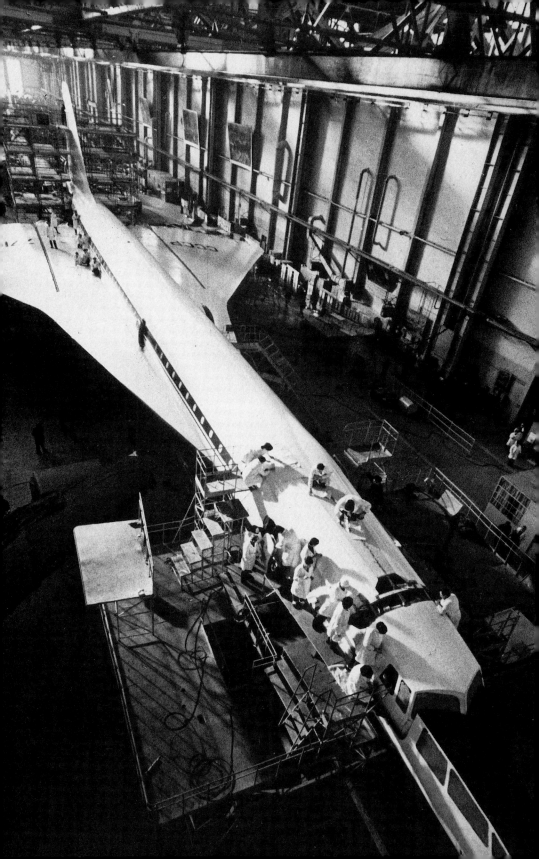

Left, 77103 in final assembly, Voronezh, early 1973. Ivanova's high shots capture the Faustian energy of the cavernous assembly bay. Fitters in surgical-style uniforms toil in the cool hangar; the structure on the left is probably a warming shed. *(APN)*

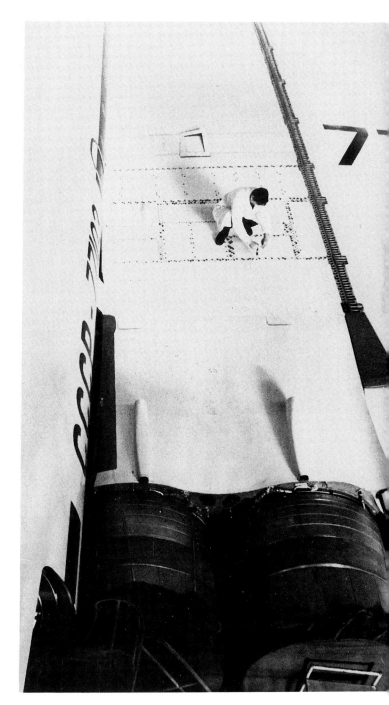

Right, winter 1972–73: a technician attends to the rear-wing paneling of 77102, fated to crash in Paris. The shrouded outlets convey the bulk of the huge NK-144 engines. *(APN)*

Testing rig for main landing gear of production TU-144. (*APN*)

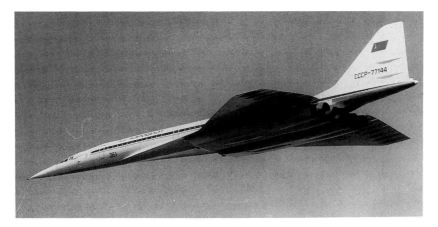

A low-level pass at the 1975 Paris air show reveals the doubler plate on the aft fuselage. *(Schoenmaker)*

Boris Pavlovich Bugayev, embattled Minister of Civil Aviation, at the time of the TU-144's first scheduled passenger flight in November 1977. An early SST enthusiast, Bugayev had become skeptical regarding the 144's fitness as an airliner because of faults revealed in route trials. *(NASM)*

Catalyst to the 1970s wave of Soviet bomber development, the B-1 was regarded as a penetrator against which the USSR had no defense. *(DOD)*

The Sukhoi T-101 was early evidence of revived Soviet interest in supersonic bombers, and first flew about 1972. It may have been briefly capable of Mach 3 speeds, and the large fixed canard and other features show the influence of the B-70. *(Ruffle)*

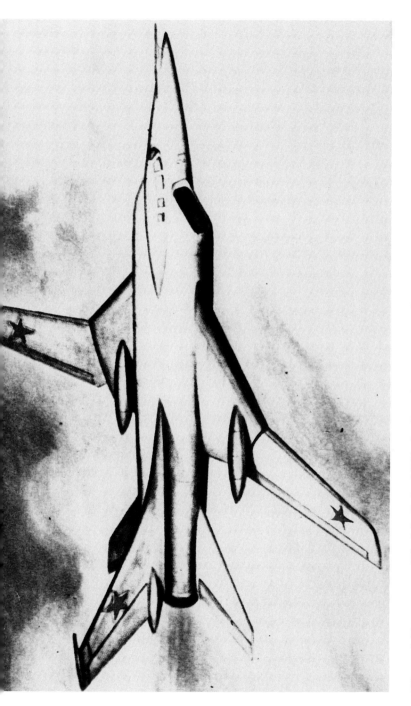

The variable-geometry "Backfire". In 1975, the British government blocked Lucas Aerospace from selling the Soviets digital fuel controls for the TU-144 on the grounds that the technology could convert the "Backfire" from an intermediate to intercontinental bomber. *(DOD)*

The TU-160 "Blackjack", the USSR's latest strategic bomber, is a beneficiary of TU-144 experience, as this Department of Defense rendering indicates. Wing root, landing gear, and engine inlets all show SST influence.

True enough, regarding noise outside the cabin, but the noise inside the cabin during cruise, which Westerners were shortly to experience for the first time, was something else. Tupolev's comments at the Paris show the previous June were probably a more accurate reflection of his true feelings: he was happy to limit the 144 to carrying freight; passengers were too much bother, suggesting that he had about given up on ways to end the noise and vibration problems.

Later, Alexei Tupolev was the first to give overdue official notice that the TU-144 program had run its course. On Aeroflot Day 1983, he again paired the 144 with the Concorde: "Operating them is economically inexpedient at present . . . however, the question of supersonic aircraft has not been taken off the agenda . . . more is being done on making them more economical."[9] Alexei inherited something of his father's empire, but ironically, Tupolev was to be drawn away from the civil designs that his father favored into a succession of military designs. Even the Tupolev dynasty could not prevail against State policy.

The changing of Tupolev leadership from generation to generation anticipated a new phase in the SST design. At Paris in 1971, Soviet authorities mentioned that a more definitive and larger version of the 144 was being readied. Originally slated to appear at Hannover, the new model TU-144, with "improved takeoff and landing and climb and increased passenger comfort," was not announced until October 1972, and did not appear in the West until May 1973.

The Production Version of the TU-144

The long-awaited definitive version of the TU-144 made its first flight in early August 1972. On September 20, three days before the fiftieth birthday of the Tupolev KB, which saw the "Old Man" given a third gold Hammer and Sickle Medal, it made a high-speed flight from Moscow to Tashkent. Announcement of this feat three weeks later constituted the debut of the finalized TU-144. The 2,980-kilometer (1,848-mile), from Moscow to

Tashkent was covered in 110 minutes at an average speed of 1,680 mph and an altitude of 17,000 to 18,000 meters (55,000 to 59,000 feet).

Accompanying photos provided an appetizing feast for Western analysts. This version of the 144 represented a radical revision of the prototype; in the West it surely would have been assigned a new model number. But it was common Soviet practice to put an airplane into the air with a much thinner layer of theoretical studies and wind-tunnel work behind it, and make running changes based on experience gained in the air. Though in outline the new aircraft resembled the prototype, almost every detail was changed—in some cases radically. It was a completely new aircraft.

The new design was a dramatic departure from the normal Soviet practice of introducing incremental, running changes in development. More than three years' experience of running the prototype, plus five years of analysis since the prototype design had been frozen in 1965–66, resulted in an accumulation of changes.

The sum of the changes was to modify design elements, distancing it from the Concorde. The four engines were split into two nacelles and moved from the fuselage centerline outboard to under the wing, midway between its original position and the midwing position of the Concorde. Whereas Concorde's nacelles were completely outboard of its landing gear, this 144's engines now absorbed them. The wing exchanged its ogival profile for a more angular double-delta outline. Whereas the prototype's wing was relatively undeveloped, optimized only for supersonic cruise, this version featured extensive sculpting to increase low-speed lift. The oval section and flat bottom of the prototype were now circular in section.

The intent seems to have been to surpass the Concorde in all its performance parameters. As seen at Paris in 1971, both TU-144 and Concorde were roughly the same size, but with dramatically different proportions. The prototype 144 was shorter than the production Concorde (191 feet vs. 204 feet), but wider

(90.7-foot wingspan vs. 83.1-foot wingspan). It was—in spite of official statements that its weight was 130 tons—heavier at 197.5 tons to the Concorde's 193.[10]

The production TU-144 went upscale in all dimensions. At 215.5 feet, the TU-144 was now 5 percent longer than the Concorde, could carry 140 passengers to the Concorde's 128 or the 144 prototype's complement of 120. As had been hinted at Paris, it had thirty-four windows to the prototype's twenty-five. Wingspan was increased to 94.5 feet, 12 percent more than the Concorde's. Its maximum payload was 18 percent greater than the Concorde's at 33,000 pounds. When empty, it was 7 percent heavier than the Concorde at 93.5 tons. The production Concorde

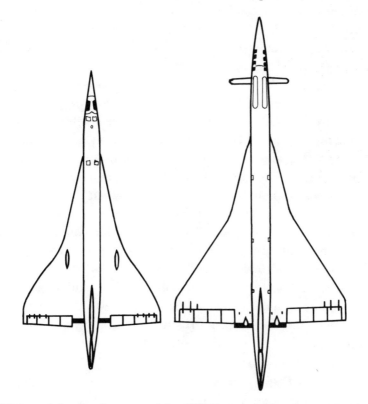

Highlights of the development of the SST from prototype to production included growth in wing area, lengthening of the fuselage to accommodate 140 passengers, and the addition of canard winglets.

surpassed the production TU-144 in only one statistic: its maximum takeoff weight was 200 tons, compared to the TU-144's 198. This may reflect Western ability to devote a greater proportion of its bulk to fuel. Although the production TU-144 was said to have more power, this and its increased weight probably cut more deeply into its greatest deficiency: an operational range of just over 2,000 miles.[11]

Structurally, a new species had been created. Everything had been changed in detail. Western experts, scrutinizing Soviet photographs, charted the changes from nose to tail. The "droop snoot" was longer, and its windows had been moved from its top to the side, recalling Lockheed design studies. Behind the cockpit was the most visible addition: two "canards," or winglets, that extended out behind the cockpit at low speeds like ears. Their purpose was to increase low speed lift 20 percent and end the high-speed hard landing problem.

Repositioning the engines forced a radical redesign of the landing gear. Undercarriage geometry was completely changed, in the interest of softer landings. The nose gear retracted forward into the fuselage instead of backward into a ventral spine between the engines. The shorter main landing gear now retracted into the engine nacelles instead of into the wings. The engines had been moved outboard about ten feet, farther out than the arrangement on the scale model shown at Paris in 1967. In addition, the engine inlets were now square, not rectangular, and the nacelles were canted and splayed. Blow-in doors were moved from the bottoms to the sides of the nacelles. The wing was now much more complex, with variable camber, twist, and negative dihedral incorporated. Trailing edge droop was believed to be greater than the Concorde's. Inside, photos of the flight deck revealed a much more workmanlike area.[12]

The Changing Future

As much as the TU-144 had changed, it had not changed as fast as its context. Even as the Soviets moved toward production, propelled by the momentum of Soviet institutions and the patronage of the Soviet state, worldwide trends made its future seem less certain. Not even the Soviet Union, in its isolation and semi-autarchy, could indefinitely ignore these changes.

The TU-144 had been conceived and commissioned in the exuberant technocratic romanticism of 1961–63. A decade later, the future had changed. International air traffic had trebled in passenger-miles during the 1960s, but now all indications were that future growth would be driven by the mass, not the elite, market. The USSR was not insulated from this development. At the beginning of the 1970s, Ilyushin, Tupolev's most credible rival, commenced development of the IL-86, the Soviet wide-bodied airliner. Where the TU-144 had originated in the dreams of technocrats and was shepherded by Khrushchev, the IL-86 was inspired by the Soviet equivalent of commercial reality. General Novozhilov, head of Ilyushin, introducing the IL-86, stated that it would be 25 percent cheaper to operate per passenger-mile than existing transports. It may have been the first Soviet consumer-driven airplane design: its characteristics had been determined by a poll of 7,000 Aeroflot travelers and a "prolonged study of traveling habits of Soviet citizens."[13]

In the West, SSTs had become a *cause célèbre*, with mass action directed against peripheral issues regarding smoke, noise, and various forms of "environmental impact." To some degree, this was a spectacle in which the two sides vied with one another in thundering irrelevancies. The true criterion of commercial air travel is economic: can the plane make money? In March 1973, both the Joint Economic Committee of the Senate and NASA delivered reports that concluded neither SST would be economically successful. They carried too small a payload for too short a range to be attractive to airlines.[14]

In the early 1970s, as the Concorde and TU-144 were positioning themselves for entry into commercial service and a SST market that many leaders believed was "extremely large," economic forces intervened to change civil aviation decisively. An OPEC embargo in 1973 caused temporary fuel shortages in the

West. Soon, fuel costs, as a proportion of airline operating costs, trebled. This put a premium on fuel-efficient aircraft. Aeroflot was not to be affected until the end of the 1970s, when the acceleration of Soviet air travel overwhelmed the supply of aviation fuel.[15]

An additional hurdle confronted the TU-144 if it wished to enter true world service. Even if its Achilles' heel of insufficient range could be solved so that it could cross the Atlantic, the TU-144 still faced the awesome task of certification. Three large Western organizations—FAA in the United States, ARB in Britain, and SGAC in France—held the key to world air routes. Together, they had established the FAUSST committee to set SST standards. The Concorde had been designed with these in mind from its inception. But as of late 1972, the Soviets had not submitted a single document to support an application for certification, a process which at any rate would absorb four to five years. The TU-144 could not appear on world routes until 1977 at the earliest if the process were initiated immediately. The lack of a first-class section on the last 144s produced seemed to confirm suspicions that the Soviets had given up on service outside the USSR and its satellites.[16]

By early 1973, as the production TU-144 was being readied for its first visit to the West, a number of decisive events had occurred that were to affect its future. U.S. officials had declared the SST concept essentially uneconomic. A fuel shortage had begun that underscored this judgment. Public acceptance of SSTs and certification for the TU-144 still seemed a thing of the remote future. But the worst blow was yet to come.

Catastrophe and Inquest

The plane is very beautiful and inspires respect and admiration just by its looks. It also provides information about our country—Mikhail Kozlov, pilot of the TU-144 at Paris, 1973

On Sunday, June 3, 1973, at 3:29 in the afternoon of the last day of the Paris air show, the second-production TU-144, the first to appear in the West, blew apart in the air in front of 300,000 spectators, including a significant portion of the world's aviation experts. Six Soviet crew members and eight French citizens on the ground, many of them schoolchildren, were killed. Sixty people were injured, many suffering burns and amputated limbs. Twenty-eight were hospitalized; 109 dwellings were damaged, 14 of which—including a village school—were destroyed. The conflagration recalled the *Hindenburg* thirty-six years before: it, too, blew apart in the air, a state-of-art air transport embodying the hopes of a totalitarian technocracy, which died a fiery public death.

The one mitigating factor was that the exploding aircraft carried a light load of fuel; otherwise the disaster might have been immeasurably worse. The TU-144 explosion followed a number of Soviet space disasters and was one in a series of public failures of Soviet high technology. The Concorde project, already foundering because of economic difficulties and public opposition, was tainted through association, though its defenders were quick to point out the differences between the two aircraft and their test programs.

The debut of the production TU-144 had been carefully rehearsed by the Soviets. The radically revised production version of the 144, unlike the prototype, had been seen by few non-Soviets previously. Its appearance at Paris was a much-anticipated opportunity to view the definitive commercial version of the Soviet SST in the metal for the first time. Previous Western analysis had been largely based on Soviet-provided photographs.

The Soviets had been full of confidence, aiming at international air routes and projecting even more grandiose versions of the 144. A Soviet press conference on board the first production model, 77101, in April on the eve of the Salon Aeronautique, established an intoxicating atmosphere. One participant reported that, "Professional aviation writers following today's press review were beside themselves searching for superlatives to describe the major changes in the Tupolev," which promised "to be the most startling attraction at the 30th Paris air show." Soviet officials were full of bravura, outlining attainments beyond the aircraft's capabilities. Kazakov, Deputy Minister of the Air Industry, referred to Paris–New York three-hour flights carrying 140 passengers. A 180-passenger TU-144 was said to be in an "advanced design stage."[17]

Victor Louis, the KGB-connected Soviet journalist, provided a Soviet view of the 144 in the *New York Times*. He stated that the 144 was already in mass production and would enter regular flight in the course of 1973. The TU-144 was insulated from the sales problems of the Concorde because the USSR's uniquely vast expanses guaranteed domestic demand. If the Concorde were scrapped, the USSR would persevere in SST development, "even if only for the sake of her long Siberian and Central Asian routes." The 144 seemed to have a dazzling future: a production run of twenty had already begun. Aeroflot would absorb half of these on internal routes. The balance would likely be picked up by the Czechs and East Germans for their international routes. The Chief Designer, Alexei Tupolev, projected a limitless tech-notopia for future air travel. He anticipated a fiftyfold increase in air passengers by the year 2000, as well as planes that would fly 10,000 kpm carrying 1,600 passengers. These monsters would stand sixty-six feet high and have twelve doors to disgorge their hordes of passengers complement. In-flight films would be restricted to cartoons because flight times would be drastically foreshortened.[18]

The production model's introduction at Paris had been auspicious enough. A one-hour, fifty-seven-minute flight from Moscow brought the craft in for a carefully-chaperoned static exhibition, though there were complaints of excessive Soviet security. Very few were permitted to enter the interior of the carefully guarded aircraft, though the TU-144 crew went along for a flight on the Concorde during the first days of the show. The 144's interior still included a first-class compartment, which indicated that the Soviets had not abandoned hope for export sales. Pilot Kozlov indicated that 77102 had already flown 230 hours.[19]

The fatal flight followed a spectacular ten-minute demonstration by the Concorde, which the TU-144's crew witnessed as passive spectators while waiting for takeoff. According to some reports, the TU-144 crew was under pressure from Moscow to stage a spectacular flying display. The ensuing exhibition featured the 144 swaying from side to side, with steep banks and turns at very low altitude. Mikhail Kozlov, its pilot, had told colleagues two days before, "We have a few tricks. We have more power than the Concorde."[20] After these passes, described by one onlooker as "spectacular" and "over-done," the 144 indulged in a low-speed exhibition of the superior low-speed handling provided by the canards. This was described as a low-speed "worm-burner" skim over the grass at minimum altitude.

Immediately following this low-speed pass, and with canards and landing gear still extended in low-speed trim, Kozlov swung the 144 into a steep climb with all afterburners lit. The 144 climbed to about 3,000 feet and then experienced what appeared to be a full classic stall, wobbling on three separate axes, slewing to the left and then diving steeply. Some witnesses said that two pieces separated from the craft at this point, possibly the canards, which led some to conclude that the winglets' debris had pierced the wings or possibly entered the engines. But most believe that the canards were still out and did not break off.

Other onlookers suggested that the fatal stall was induced by fuel starvation owing to the steep climb and relatively empty fuel tanks. The steep dive that followed indicated that the 144 was in mortal peril, for there was only 3,000 feet to recover—and the 144 was a large and heavy craft.

Kozlov came close to leveling out the 144 after an almost-perpendicular drop of several seconds, but the recovery was too abrupt, with the right wing breaking off at the root and the subsequent quick roll breaking off the other wing. Two engines were quickly engulfed in flames. Several explosions rocked the stricken craft, and it tumbled to the earth in incandescent lumps of titanium and steel. Many expert witnesses agreed that the 144 had been taken beyond the limits of its flight envelope. It had no "G-leveling" device that prevented it from being maneuvered beyond the strength of its robust airframe. The explosive dis-integration was the result of a desperate, foredoomed attempt at recovery.

The effect on the small village of Goussainville was that of a bomb attack. Huge chunks of incandescent metal and clouds of burning fuel rained down from the overcast skies, while the aircraft's oil collected in large, burning pools in the streets, igniting several houses. The TU-144's nose landed in a field, while the cockpit with four of the crew inside embedded itself in a ruined house. One engine came to rest in a garden and part of one wing crashed in the courtyard of the town hall. A boy playing in front of his home was decapitated by a piece of flying debris.[21]

The 100-ton airliner's impact left impressions both apocalyptic and surreal. Because the airframe broke apart in four or five main sections, the devastation extended over a considerable area, unlike the single-impact pattern of many crashes. Ruined pieces of milled titanium and honeycomb sheet lay at rest amidst the shards of disrupted domesticity. Parts of one burned-out engine straddled a garden, while a fuel tank lay in the roof beams of a cottage. Glossy English-language brochures extolling the TU-144's comfort and safety features festooned tree limbs and powerlines.[22] Amidst collapsed tile roofs, fragments of wings and fuselage alloy sheeting covered the ground. A blizzard of shred-ded insulation and paper littered the green wheat fields for miles around. Seats, parachutes, shredded clothing, and fragments of carpeting dangled from telephone wires.[23]

The Soviets arrived on the scene almost at once via helicopter, but not quick enough to halt ghoulish souvenir hunters. Ambu-lances picked up the survivors while loudspeaker trucks broad-cast appeals for RH-negative blood and announced that house-holders would be compensated by the government for damages to their property.[23] The Soviets later contributed the laughably small sum of 20,000 francs to cover damages (estimated to be roughly one-fifteenth those sustained). The mass funeral for the French victims of the disaster was attended by thousands. The tragedy, the first involving French householders killed by Paris air show aeronautics, inspired a grass-roots movement to bar flying demonstrations in settled areas. In an emotional debate in the French National Assembly on June 16, Deputies called for an end to "dramatics marking the route of progress."[24]

The Soviet media were initially mute, but the crash report "spread like wildfire" through Shermetyevo Airport in Moscow.[25] The front page of *Pravda* on June 5 carried a black-bordered announcement treating the crew as heroes and bestowing upon them posthumous decorations. The heroes were buried later at a well-attended funeral at Moscow's oldest cemetery. According to a GRU defector, the highest Soviet leaders took an intense personal interest in the crash. GRU films showing the 144's final seconds were rushed to Moscow by courier aircraft for viewing by the Politburo early in the morning of June 4. The GRU, which reportedly had twenty films of the crash, was begged by KGB Chief Andropov for just one reel, which was refused.[26]

A group of U.S. aviation writers who left Paris for Moscow the evening after the crash found their Soviet hosts canceling the agreed-upon agenda to launch an ad hoc inquest into the crash. Photos taken by the journalists were given to Soviet authorities and never seen again.[27]

In Paris, after the shock had subsided, machinery to investigate the crash was set in motion. According to international guidelines, the nation in which the crash occurs administers the inquest. But the French and Soviets had by now been cooperating in SST technical questions for some months and the French were hoping to get Soviet air rights for the Concorde. The Soviets were consistently aggressive behind the scenes. They initially proposed an independent inquiry, which the French vetoed, and it was agreed to establish a joint commission. The Soviets proposed a Soviet president, which the French refused. The Soviets then insisted that the military of both countries carry out the investigation, which was agreed upon. The Soviets were initially hostile and suspicious when the French reconstructed the 144 wreckage on the floor of a Le Bourget hangar, being unfamiliar with this technique. Some of the 144 wreckage was almost immediately flown back to the USSR in the AN-22 freighter at the show.[28]

This joint commission sifted through the wreckage for months, from July to October 1973. Soviet delegates included Vassili Kazakov, Deputy Minister of Aviation Production, Chief Designer Tupolev, and Kuznetsov, maker of the 144's engines, and five others.[29] Its report was completed, but never released, about a year later. The Soviets reportedly refused to agree to allow much in the way of hard conclusions to appear, but those connected with the commission let slip some of the most likely explanations for the disaster.

A Quest for Causes

The 144 had only gotten into trouble after its official maneuvers for the public demonstration were completed. The commission first investigated various technical explanations for the crash, such as problems with the flying control mixer box that controlled the elevons. The London *Daily Telegraph* published a report on October 24, 1973, that a wrench may have been left near the flying control mixer box, at the base of the control column, blocking it. It predicted correctly that the French would not publish a full inquest report: only a brief statement was later issued.

Within the joint commission, Franco-Soviet experts surmised that the crew in the cockpit, which had low visibility once the visor was up, had tried to land on the wrong runway. The laborious search for technical causes may have been beside the point. The root of the disaster lay in the circuslike rivalry between the two SSTs. The French curtailed the carefully rehearsed Soviet SST flight demonstration at the last moment, which forced Kozlov and crew to improvise a landing. On going around again and not in touch with the control tower, the TU-144 found itself on a collision course with a Mirage fighter. The nose was pulled down in an avoidance maneuver, throwing the copilot on the controls. The copilot had been given a TV camera, and this possibly fell into the funnel-shaped control-stick well in the cockpit floor. Removing this absorbed valuable seconds that necessitated a violent, last-ditch recovery, which saw the starboard wing fail. This scenario of a blocked control column was simulated in Moscow and the trajectory of the aircraft followed exactly the path of the 144 had taken.[30]

André Turcat, chief test pilot of the Concorde, had seen to it that the TU-144 crew received a ride aboard the Concorde the previous weekend. He had been invited by Benderov, the Chief Engineer in charge of the 144 flight-testing program, to ride aboard the 144 during the fatal demonstration flight. He refused, on the grounds that he preferred a longer duration cruise rather than a short demo flight, and this was scheduled for Moscow the next month.

Turcat's testimony establishes key events that led to the disaster. Michel Tauriac, a French TV journalist, tried to board the 144 to film from the plane in flight, but was barred by Benderov, who agreed to take the camera and film on his behalf. Turcat confirms that radar imagery revealed the "sudden proximity" of a Mirage III fighter in the 144's flight path, precipitating the first of its abrupt maneuvers. He believed it probable that the TV camera was wrenched from Benderov's hands and fell into the control-stick cone in the floor, blocking the controls.[31]

It was typical of the age that onlookers, journalists, experts, the mixed commission, and governments themselves should seek the cause of the crash in some technical failure. The Soviets, with perhaps two 144s in the air at this point and another five on the production line, grounded them all for about six months until they were satisfied the crash was not rooted in a technical fault. The most assiduous sifting through the smoldering wreckage immediately following the event, and the search for auguries among shattered 144 fragments laid out on the French hangar floor, could provide no conclusive answers. Eyewitnesses speculated that the canards had disintegrated, that the afterburners had stalled, that fatigue cracks had been spotted on the wings. A technological showcase, after all, would certainly be brought down by some technical failing.

Having gone through the evidence several times and heard the views of several experts and eyewitnesses, however, this writer is convinced that technical factors were peripheral to the fate of 77102. The precipitating factor in the disaster was political. The 144, whatever its failings as an airliner, was basically airworthy, even in the risky conditions of 77102's last moments. It was flying low and slow over a huge crowd in congested flying conditions that put it on a collision course with a French Mirage fighter. Its safety margin, however, was probably greater than that of the Concorde, which did not have canards to cut down landing and maneuvering speeds.

The TV camera that apparently fouled the controls symbolizes the dangerous intrusion of publicity, but the one event that made the crash unavoidable was the decision to cut short 77102's demonstration flight, practiced at least six times in the USSR. This left a disoriented pilot and crew above a strange airfield, in an aircraft with notoriously poor cockpit visibility. It is understandable that Kozlov attempted to land on the wrong runway. What seems less excusable was that a second aircraft in the area forced a series of violent evasion maneuvers which even the robust 144 airframe could not withstand. Their boorish pressuring in the joint commission nonwithstanding, it is hard to establish much Soviet responsibility for the crash. Errors may have been made in the demanding flying conditions over a crowded air show, but the sloppy air control of the airport, the straying fighter, and the truncation of the 144 flight routine were the precipitating, critical events. The managers of the air show appear to be chiefly responsible for the disaster.

The straying Mirage indicates poor air traffic control, lax technique. Shortening of 77102's flight to five minutes and expansion of the Concorde's exhibition which immediately preceded it to ten minutes reflect a more pervasive, disturbing reality. The prestige contest between the two SSTs had reached such a pitch that the French introduced risky, last-minute, unconsidered jugglings of the program. The manipulated schedule and circus atmosphere of the final hours of the salon ended in the surrealistic near-obliteration of Goussainville.

While the Soviets suffered an enormous loss in prestige, they could always retreat to using their SST only on internal routes. In the West, where public opinion really is a powerful factor, the crash hurt the SST cause in general at a time when its cost and perceived environmental impacts had already generated a host of enemies. Political pressure to move the air show away from Paris to a less densely settled region was overcome only with difficulty. If French responsibility for the loss of 77102 is as heavy as this analysis indicates, Soviet official silence regarding the causes of the crash may have been to the West's advantage. Drives for State prestige, spectacle, and publicity proved stronger than French safety procedures.

9
FALLING
BEHIND, 1973–1975

Soviet authorities were unprepared for the disaster. Prearranged visits by foreign experts to the production line took place immediately after the crash: the Soviets were too shocked to cancel invitations. While the macabre events in Paris overshadowed the situation, it now became obvious how deeply the Soviets had committed themselves to the commercial success of their SST project. Aspects of their production technology awed many Americans, who had seen the world's best. Coming immediately after the disaster, this first detailed inspection of the TU-144 assembly line would have caused those suspicious of SSTs to question the Soviets' commitment to a folly of immense proportions. The visitors were aircraft engineers and writers, however, who shared the technocratic vision of the Soviets and were impressed with their commitment, advanced techniques, and determination to succeed.

Visit to Voronezh and Soviet Production Technology

In the wake of the catastrophic crash at the Paris air show, a delegation of American aviation writers visited the TU-144's final assembly plant in Voronezh for the first time. Matters proceeded as if no crash had occurred. The writers were astounded to discover "full-series production" of the 144, with no fewer than five aircraft taking shape in the final assembly area. Subassemblies for a dozen more were arriving from subcontractors. Mikhail S. Mikhailov, Deputy Director of the Ministry of Aviation Production, indicated that Aeroflot had placed an initial order for thirty TU-144s, with total orders anticipated of between sixty to seventy-five.

Mikhailov outlined an ambitious three-level route expansion plan. First, passenger service was planned from Moscow to Novosibirsk, Irkutsk, and Khabarovsk in 1975, where "high-priority industrial traffic" supported burgeoning Siberian oil and gas development. Five other routes were also planned: to these three cities from Leningrad, and to Tashkent and Alma-Ata from Moscow. These routes would be developed in 6,500-kilometer (4,036-mile) stages. They would, it was calculated, absorb three years' production. After internal Soviet requirements were met, routes to Europe would be added in 1978–79. A third phase would add flights to the United States, Singapore, and Tokyo.

To deal with this anticipated demand, the six-story-high final assembly area was being doubled to house up to ten TU-144s simultaneously. Current production rate of one aircraft every six weeks was expected to double to one aircraft every three weeks during 1974. *Aviation Week* exclaimed, "The fact that the TU-144 was in full production, backed by a massive, sophisticated manufacturing facility, came as a surprise." Previous Soviet statements led Western experts to believe that only a pilot assembly of 144s was underway, one aircraft at a time. Pyotr Dementiev, Minister of Aviation Production, assured *Aviation Week* that the recent crash would not impede TU-144 production. The accident would be thoroughly investigated. Needed modifications would be incorporated into the design: "It simply pushes us to expedite the work ahead."

According to the Soviets, the equivalent of ten TU-144s had already been built: two original prototypes and three preproduction aircraft plus a variety of static test devices and full-scale subsystem test rigs that were the equivalent of five more aircraft.

While Aeroflot was developing a maintenance and training

facility at Domodevo Airport near Moscow, the Voronezh plant fabricated all major structural parts: fuselage, wings, nacelles, landing gear, and control surfaces. Subcontractors delivered engines, avionics, and other subsystems.

Voronezh officials proudly pointed out that the TU-144 incorporated more titanium "than any other aircraft in production anywhere in the world." Titanium comprised 18 percent of its weight, employed where strength was critical or kinetic and engine heat was a problem. Nacelles, wing root torque boxes, fuselage structure at the wing roots, elevons, and rudder control surfaces were major applications. Chemical milling was used on 1,500 titanium parts. It had not proved necessary to use titanium for the wing surfaces, since aluminum alloy was found sufficient to handle aerodynamic heating up to 150°C. In fact, it was estimated that this alloy could accommodate speeds up to Mach 2.6.

TU-144 production was a severe test of Soviet production engineering. The most challenging assignment was fabricating the integrally milled wings because of the "wide variety and complexity of the aerodynamic shapes involved." The trailing edges of the wings over the four-engine exhausts were a challenging compound-curve-forming problem. This part of the wing later betrayed signs of erosion and heat fatigue. Beyond the special demands of working titanium, each TU-144 required around two million contact welds and 576 kilometers of electric wiring.

Soviet design and development practices differed radically from those prevailing in the West. American designers tested subcomponents to destruction; Soviet designers established the goal of 30,000 service hours for each airframe and designed and tested individual components to meet this standard. This standard controlled material selection and manufacturing methods. Fatigue tests were conducted on all titanium parts for 30,000 hours. An extensive program of lifetime ground-testing of all major subsystems was also underway but not yet complete.

For the first time, details on manufacturing methods for the TU-144 were revealed. The aircraft employed 1,120 separate titanium castings. Medium-strength vanadium-alloyed titanium was preferred to higher strength alloys because of its greater resistance to corrosion. A special high-strength aluminum alloy had also been developed. The Research Institute for Aircraft Manufacturing Methods, Moscow (NEAT) had developed new titanium-manufacturing processes to reduce the corrosive effects of oxygen and hydrogen remaining in the finished parts. NEAT was one of twelve special aerospace institutes conducting fundamental R & D in the USSR and was said to hold foreign patents in several "major segments of the technical spectrum."

The Soviets believed they were "ahead of the world" in their understanding of hydrogen in titanium production. The huge size of the titanium sheets employed in TU-144 assembly impressed Western experts: they were thirty feet long and up to six inches thick. Some of these were milled to form the fuselage walls.

The visitors found it "difficult to get any meaningful cost figures on either production or operation of Soviet aircraft," but they did learn that the Soviets had cut the production costs of titanium parts to one-third its original expense. The battery of four huge milling machines, hogging out 30-by-15-foot sections of titanium plate, five to six inches thick, for wings and fuselage, was impressive, as were the platoons of pistol-packing female plant guards.

The editor of *Aviation Week* noted of plant manager Boris Danilov that "energy exudes from every ounce of his stocky frame up to the bristles of his brush-cut hair." Of the program, "There can be no doubt that we witnessed a tremendous high-energy program, using the most modern methods and materials to produce in quantity what must certainly be the most technically advanced transport being built anywhere in the world today. We believe that any group of Western aircraft engineers exposed to the same views would reach the same conclusion. Most of them will have had that opportunity before the end of the summer." This hope was not fulfilled.

Then came the "paradox of Voronezh," or rather, the paradox of the Soviet system. After a brief three-hour tour of this technological wonderland, the Western visitors were "transposed to

Tolstoy's Russia" during a drive through the surrounding countryside. Small villages of log cabins were served by a single well and bucket. Dusty unpaved roads wound past fields where hay was cut with hand scythes and forked onto horsedrawn carts. *Babuskas* in black dresses, with white kerchiefs on their heads "framing toil-worn leathery faces," cropped the earth with grub hoes. It was hard to believe that only a few miles distant a supersonic transport was entering mass production. This was grist for unresolved thoughts of Western visitors witnessing both countries. Concentration of national resources on showcase projects had little effect on the lives of most Soviet citizens.[1]

Shaky Progress June 1973–75

During the four years from its first flight to its Paris crash, the TU-144 basked in the spotlight of world publicity as an incarnation of Soviet technological prowess and prestige. But during the four years following the June 1973 crash, it was relegated to a fitful obscurity recalling the earlier years of secret, forced-draft development. Sometimes, however, months of obscurity would be punctuated by sudden flares of publicity, apparently designed to keep the Soviet SST before the eye of the public and keep the project alive as a viable, high-priority program. Because its public appearances were irregular, the TU-144's development gave the impression of being troubled, though the tragedy in Paris had little to do with any defect in its design.

Public resistance to the Concorde peaked in the West in 1973–77, for reasons that now appear largely spurious. In the context of escalating fuel prices after December 1973, it is tempting to see analogous factors working against the TU-144 in the Soviet Union. But there were no mass protests against its assumed noise and environmental damage at any of Moscow's airports nor were the central Asian inhabitants of Alma-Ata seen to picket against its landings there. The Soviet intelligentsia was quite aware of the various "scientific" or environmental objections raised against the TU-144 in the West, for these were published in the Soviet press. The celebrated 1977 incident, when thousands of New Yorkers drove their cars to Kennedy Airport to protest the environmental scourge of Concorde landings, was publicized in detail by *Pravda*. But no anxious Soviet citizens are known to have picketed the Voronezh assembly hall or demonstrated in Red Square to protest possible environmental damage by the TU-144. The more substantial issue of focusing substantial national resources to such an economically questionable project hardly surfaced in Soviet print at all; occasionally, though, grumbles could be heard from discerning Soviet officials behind the scenes. Indeed, it is conceivable that Chief Designer Tupolev raised the issue of the ionosphere and other "environmental impacts" to divert attention from more substantial, and continuing, TU-144 operational shortcomings.

Escalating developmental and operating costs, making SSTs increasingly irrelevant in the West by the mid-1970s, were prompting influential Soviets originally supportive of the SST to wonder if Soviet resources could have been spent more rationally, allocated to projects more directly beneficial to the Soviet economy. The TU-144's R & D costs, like the Concorde's, were largely unrecoverable unless some of the SST's technology could be spun off into either military or civil applications. But, strategic evolution conspired against a spinoff. Strategic bombers were coming back into vogue, but were now subsonic terrain-huggers that had little in common with the high-speed, high-altitude SST designed a decade before.

The spiraling cost of fuel after 1973–74 saw Western civil air operations cut 20–25 percent. Because the USSR, however, was the world's largest oil producer, these trends only indirectly affected their SST. Aeroflot fuel economy programs were not introduced until mid-1977, by which time the TU-144's fate had been largely sealed. Soviet aviation fuel was not necessarily in critical short supply, but distributing it across Aeroflot's far-flung network, and the necessarily heavily seasonal nature of Aeroflot fuel demand peaking each August, were defeating the Soviet supply and distribution system. Underlying these dynamics was

Aeroflot's explosive growth, and demand for fuel, which overwhelmed the growth in aviation fuel supply. Soviet household use of kerosene was already declining. During Aeroflot's peak activity in August, Moscow could divert export kerosene to airports; therefore widespread fuel shortages did not hit Aeroflot until 1977–78.

Deepening Soviet concern about fuel efficiency had only a minor effect upon the SST program, for by the mid-1970s it was apparent that the TU-144 itself was destined to be only a marginal, symbolic presence in Aeroflot. If the plans articulated in 1973 to put seventy-five SSTs in production had matured, matters might have been different.

Why, then was the TU-144 encountering such stiff bureaucratic opposition by the mid-1970s? Although the high-profile destruction of the TU-144 at Paris damaged the Soviets, and the SST cause in general, the conclusions that emerged from the joint Franco-Soviet investigating commission a year later exonerated the TU-144 itself. The mounting hostility had to be rooted in the 144's continuing operating deficiencies, as revealed in the test program. While the TU-144 continued to founder, the Concorde began to test, and then to serve, its first international commercial routes. The TU-144, which originally symbolized their overtaking of the West, now was an embarrassing reminder of Soviet technical ineptitude. The Soviet spotlight swung to illuminate the IL-86, a widebody airliner more emblematic of the future and the pragmatic needs of the national airline.

Aftermath of the Crash

The incandescent destruction of the TU-144 may have impacted more on French than on Soviet politics. In view of the large number of deaths, there was public clamor to move the Salon Aeronautique to a more remote airport, far from densely settled areas—a suggestion vociferously opposed by the show's organizers and the French aerospace industry. At the next show in 1975, more stringent rules were imposed on demonstration flights, and those of high-performance craft and heavy transports in particular. Test flights of the TU-144 on the occasion of the craft's last two visits to the West, in 1975 and 1977, were singularly meek and nonspectacular.

The report of the Franco-Soviet inquest, completed over a year after the tragedy in mid-1974, was singularly opaque, remarkable more for what it omitted than what it included. The public announcement asserted a series of negatives: the crash was "not the result of any structural defect" and the cause of the crash "remains undetermined." Franco-Soviet agreement was unanimous that "there was no abnormality either in the airliner's design or the general functioning of the aircraft and its systems." The French acquiesced in a technical acquittal of the Soviets' TU-144, which was in both their interests.[2]

Exploiting the tragedy, a self-styled group for the "Liberation of Rudolph Hess" claimed they had blown up the TU-144 to publicize the fate of Spandau's last prisoner. This was rejected by Hess's son, who admitted to no previous knowledge of this new Paris-based group.[3] This was not the unfortunate former Deputy Führer's first connection with Tupolev: the plane that he had flown to Scotland in May 1941 was a Bf-110, whose close resemblance to the TU-2 reportedly led to the elder Tupolev's arrest in 1937.

Western Critiques of the SST

Beyond the TU-144's travails, 1973 was not a propitious year for SSTs. In the months preceding the crash, analysis by highly respected bodies repeatedly attacked SST economic viability. NASA told a House subcommittee in Washington that neither the Concorde nor the TU-144 would be "economically successful." NASA judged that current SST technology was restricted to "too small a payload for too short a range to satisfy completely its potential airline customers." Senator Proxmire responded that NASA's request for $28 million to continue SST research therefore seemed "very frivolous."[4]

In April 1973, British Ministry of Aviation analysts completed a report pointing out that the TU-144 was no true commercial competitor of the Concorde. Because it used inefficient turbofans with near-permanent afterburner boost, it did not possess the Concorde's capability of crossing the Atlantic supersonically with an economically viable number of passengers. Its true supersonic range was 1,000 miles short of the Concorde's; it was only a medium-range SST. Undeveloped, it had spent only 700 hours in the air compared with the Concorde's 1,500.

This British analysis regarding the operating economics of both SSTs—undertaken just before the first oil embargo—provided a chilling view of the future of both SSTs. The Concorde's purchase price per seat was said to be ten times that of a modern subsonic airliner; operating cost per passenger-mile would be twice as much. Concorde fuel consumption was estimated at three times that of a normal subsonic airliner. Cost weighed heavily upon commercial decisions to buy the Concorde and it undercut even more heavily the prospects of the heavier and thirstier TU-144.

Moreover, the Soviet SST was hampered by Aeroflot's poor reputation for providing spares and overseas repair facilities, which for the TU-144 were centralized in Moscow even on internal routes. The British conclusion was that, "In these circumstances the purchase of such an advanced and expensive aircraft as Charger (NATO's designation for the TU-144) might well be considered an unjustifiable risk."[5] This conclusion presumably enjoyed an extensive circulation behind the scenes, and the spiraling cost of aviation fuel that shortly followed endowed it with additional authority.

A quadrupling in oil prices, which began in December 1973, made SSTs seem an even more ruinous economic proposition. While the arguments of environmental activists against the SST in the West received some notice in the Soviet press, the more substantial economic critiques were ignored.

Less a Competitor, More a Curiosity

By early 1974, the TU-144 had irretrievably fallen behind in the race for commercialization. In the Soviet Union, there was almost-irresistible political pressure from the Central Committee to show some concrete results from the multibillion ruble program before the end of the Ninth Five-Year Plan, ending the last day of 1975.

There was some shaky progress. In early May 1974, nearly a year after the crash, the TU-144's re-entry into "route testing" was celebrated by splashy coverage in *Pravda* and *Komsomolskaya Pravda*. A new and intensive test schedule was highlighted. Chief Designer Tupolev stressed that up to 2,000 test flights would be required for such a revolutionary design as the TU-144. Twenty flights had been carried out that month, sometimes two or three per day. Chief Test Pilot Edward Elyan dismissed the 1973 crash as "one of those fateful things, but now everything had been carefully reanalyzed." Tupolev emphasized progress: the 144 now had a reinforced undercarriage, and a redesigned engine section to ease maintenance. At a time when the Concorde was believed to be on the verge of cancellation, this resurfacing of the Soviet SST seemed to reaffirm Soviet faith in the concept. Publicity of this sort was usually associated with entry into service.[6]

However, the TU-144 did not fly to the British aircraft show at Farnborough that June, to the great disappointment of its organizers,[7] and its reappearance at Paris the following year was circumspect and low key. By 1975, the TU-144 was over-shadowed by other Soviet designs more indicative of the future, such as the Yak-42 and IL-86 widebody airliner.

Experts examining the TU-144 at Paris in 1975 found a hard-working test-bed aircraft. Its hydraulically dampered tail bumper, for example, had been hit hard. Reinforcing patches under the wings around the landing gear and trapezoidal doubler plates just outboard of the engine nacelles were notable for their crudity—"absolutely saturated with rivets." Their aerodynamic fairing left much to be desired, crudely painted over, with putty apparently applied by thumb. Tupolev claimed a 5,000-kilometer (3,100-mile) range and suggested that the 144 would focus on serving internal routes, fourteen of which were 3,000 to 6,000 kilometers (1,860 to 4,020 miles) in length. Little was now said about international service. Tupolev wanted engines with forty metric tons thrust, reflecting a preference for brute force and ignorance instead of more refined development of extant engines or paring weight from the airframe. This militated against Western trends in civil air design toward elegance and efficiency. The 144 shown had 140 seats—its full tourist complement—as opposed to the 100 shown in 1973.

Other Soviets at the show were noticed photographing and measuring selected Concorde components, indicating that Soviet technical problems were far from resolved. The TU-144 ended its sojourn in Paris with two sedate exhibition flights at Le Bourget.[8]

The Soviet Search for an Improved Engine

The introduction of the production-version 144 in late 1972 was the last time the Soviets increased the power of its NK-144 engines. Although the aircraft's weight continued to creep up, no evidence indicated further development of the engine. Comparison with Western analogues, however, indicates that considerable potential for development remained. Instead, U.S. writers in 1973 were first to be told of work beginning on alternative engines. The NK-144 was not abandoned, however. Soviets apparently were looking for greater efficiency instead of increased power. The SST had a weak heart: the Soviets shopped for a foreign pacemaker even while they readied a transplant. The Soviet engine designer Koliesov investigated a new engine within the USSR while Soviet agents looked in Europe for more sophisticated control electronics.

Soviet failure to penetrate the secrets of Concorde engine development at Bristol-Siddeley in the late 1960s was followed by commercial approaches to purchase Concorde engine technology in 1972–76. Andrei Tupolev's questioning of Sir George Edwards at the 1969 Paris Air Show regarding air intakes reflected Soviet problems in slowing air to the TU-144's engines over a wide range of high speeds. A more effective and sophisticated control system was needed to keep the shock wave of supersonic air from entering the engine and stalling it. The NK-144 apparently could operate well only at cruise speed. Controlling and evening out the air delivered to the NK-144 from zero to 1,500 mph was proving torturously difficult. This same problem had been one of the most difficult for the Concorde team to crack; half the wind-tunnel hours logged for the Concorde had been spent on internal dynamics, on the air intakes.

The Soviets must have been desperate. Their approach to Lucas in 1972 was the first in a series of approaches to a number of British companies. Remaining NK-144 inefficiencies meant it was abandoned before its potential had been fully explored, even though these engines powered the current Soviet first-line strategic bomber, the TU-116 "Backfire".

A representative of *Air Force Magazine*, during a tour of the Soviet aircraft industry in mid-1973, was the first to be told of the existence of the "hitherto-unreported Koliesov Design Bureau" developing an alternate to the NK-144 engine. This new Koliesov engine was reported to be a variable-geometry, variable bypass ratio type, functioning as a turbojet in supersonic flight and as a turbofan in the subsonic regime. This was the best of all theoretical worlds, but one never achieved in practice because of its terrible complexity; the concept required variable-pitch fan blades in the rotating main section.

Theoretically, this was the optimum engine mode for combined subsonic and supersonic applications. But this Koliesov design—as reported—represented a technical prodigy far in advance of Soviet capability, since no successful variable-ratio jet engine existed in the West, which was ten to fifteen years in advance of Soviet jet-engine technology.[9]

As another possible clue to Soviet failure, Kuznetsov, Chief Designer of the NK-144, led a delegation of Soviet engineers on a fishing expedition to Rolls-Royce—itself in financial trouble in late 1973—to discuss the possibility of collaboration. Apparently not even impending bankruptcy could force Rolls-Royce to consider serious cooperation with Kuznetsov. Soviets traditionally have little hard currency to offer in foreign trade, and Soviet jet-engine technology held no attractions for Rolls-Royce. British memories were long: the sale of Rolls-Royce engines to the USSR twenty-five years before and their eventual copies powering the MIG-15 still rankled. Kuznetsov's mission was fruitless.[10]

In approaching Lucas, the original Soviet shopping list represented a prescription for a broad front of Soviet R & D problems: generators, combustion technology, and fuel-control systems. Lucas experts quickly became convinced that the Soviets were really after the digital fuel-control system, which promised to integrate engine, air intakes, and afterburner as an overall fuel-efficient monitor. Lucas had a digital engine control flying on the Concorde, which was never put into production. It was experimental, employing a U.S.-made ECM processor, in 01, the British prototype.[11]

When it became evident that the Soviet shopping list was only a cover to obtain the digital control system, Lucas consulted the British government. Whitehall advised: go ahead and talk, but come to us for clearance. Lucas spent 1 to 1.5 million pounds sterling pursuing the contract. The Soviets held out the promise of a package deal on the order of 10 million pounds sterling, but Lucas was not convinced the Soviets were serious regarding this.

The original technical specifications and operating parameters for the NK-144 engine provided by the Soviets in autumn 1973 were deliberately distorted. How this counterproductive maneuver served Soviet interests is not clear. It was a gratuitous confusion, imposed unnecessary burdens on Lucas, and cast a pall over the good faith of the negotiations. The Soviets surely should have recognized they were dealing with experts, who would discern such deception. On the other hand, Soviet experts themselves may not have been privy to such secret data. Lucas experts made their own estimates of NK-144 specifications and adjusted the errant Soviet data. These tables were then fine-tuned by Lucas and Soviet technicians working together.

Possibly because of such perverse pragmatism, in late 1974–

early 1975, Soviet Ministry of Aviation Production and factory personnel working with Lucas were all replaced. Their replacements explained that their predecessors had not "met targets on the 144." Specifically, they had been dragging their feet on the Lucas contract. A new Soviet official, met at the Paris Air Show, May–June 1975, noted—half in jest—that the old bunch had been rusticated "to Siberia," together with their entire families. They would, however, eventually return.

Bernard Scott, Lucas's group chairman, took personal charge of the negotiations with the Soviets in late 1974 and traveled to Moscow on several occasions.[12] Other Lucas executives flying to Moscow at the invitation of the Ministry of Foreign Trade were heartened by being whisked through Soviet customs and receiving the general VIP treatment. In the context of a general Soviet scarcity of hard currency reserves, a representative from a second Soviet ministry now accompanied the Soviet negotiators and handled financing issues.

It was obvious to Lucas specialists that the Soviets "didn't have the technology to tie the electronics together and marry various sub-systems." Lucas's digital fuel-control system was the most advanced in the world "as supplied to" the Concorde, a strong Lucas selling point. This applied, however, only to the Concorde prototype: production versions were fitted with an entirely different analogue system. Lucas wished to fit digital control systems to all seventeen Concordes. Pin for pin, it provided the same performance—analogue instead of digital was simply different. What complicated the sale of Lucas's digital system to the Soviets was that its heart was a U.S. microprocessor, controlled as strategic technology. So Lucas was brokering a marriage between a French Crocus microprocessor, already supplied to the Soviets from Thomson CFM, and Soviet hydromechanical actuators. To this end, Lucas was given the specifications of the Soviet mechanical parts.

The Lucas-Soviet accord was a fine Christmas present, signed December 22, 1976, in the Holiday Inn, Birmingham. Lucas then applied for an export license from COCOM, the NATO committee controlling strategic technology. Lucas was then set upon by the British Ministry of Defence, backstopped by the Foreign Office and the Pentagon. Winston Churchill, M.P., condemned the sale, ensuring extensive publicity. Critics pointed out that the most modern and effective Soviet bomber, the "Backfire", was also powered by NK-144 engines. Any improvement made to turn the TU-144 into a viable long-range, transatlantic civil airliner would also enhance the "Backfire" 's capability to penetrate NATO airspace.

Lucas insiders believed the deal should not have been stopped; that the West would learn more about Soviet engine technology if the deal went through. Others privy to the plot cynically added: if the cocktail of hydraulics and electronics the Soviets had asked for were sold to them, it would only widen the technological gap between East and West.

What the Soviets were asking Lucas to do was to cobble together Soviet components obsolete by Western standards, not access to Lucas's state of the art. The system had to be designed using extant Soviet components. When first apprised of this, Lucas experts "were a bit horrified." The Soviets provided catalogues of Soviet equipment. Lucas personnel estimated that this would have doubled the weight of the TU-144's electronics. Soviet avionics at this point were "in the immediate stage beyond thermionic valves", with no integrated circuits. By U.S. standards this was 1950s technology.

The *Times of London* saw a Pentagon conspiracy behind the nonratification of the Soviet-Lucas compact, citing Lucas skepticism about Pentagon speculation that "the Lucas fuel system will be fitted to the 'Backfire'." U.S. machinations masked commercial interests: Lucas was the largest aircraft component maker in Europe, the only one outside the United States to offer complete aircraft electrical systems. With Lucas eliminated, the U.S. aerospace industry "would have the field free to deal with the Russians." U.S. aid would help Soviets become effective competitors in international civil-aviation markets.

Blocked in their approach to Lucas, the Soviets succeeded in purchasing a sophisticated fuel-gauging and flow-metering system from the French firm Intertechnique. This reportedly helped the Soviets develop a high-speed pump to shift fuel during the 144's transition to supersonic flight. This was less sensitive technology than the engine-control equipment, but it did not represent a magic wand for the central issue of engine efficiency.[13]

In the fall of 1977, the press reported renewed Soviet approaches: "Soviet aviation designers have informally asked the British and French manufacturers of the Concorde . . . aid in making [efficient] the inlet doors to the four engines" of the 144. The Anglo-French rejected Soviet advances on grounds that the technology they sought was incorporated in the Toronado, an advanced NATO fighter-bomber. "As jet engines will not accept air approaching them at supersonic speeds," the Concorde and 144 "have to be fitted with doors which open or close depending on the speed at which the aircraft is traveling."[14] Paradoxically, getting the airflow supersonic over an SST's fuselage was easy; more difficult was slowing down the air to the engines. The faster the cruising speed, the more difficult the job; and different techniques had to be devised to dump or divert the air at different speeds.

Ironically, at the time the Soviets were mounting this second series of approaches to the British, the TU-144D, with its much-touted but never-seen Koliesov engines, was within a year of its maiden flight. The standard TU-144, with its flawed and thirsty NK-144 engines, was months away from a highly publicized and strenuously contested entry into "commercial service." Soviet authorities were still serious about improving the 144 as late as mid-1977, if for no other reason than its engines powered their premier bomber.

There is impressive testimony that the Soviets never succeeded in dramatically extending the NK-144's range, either for the SST or for the "Backfire" bomber. "Backfire" range figured prominently in SALT negotiations, U.S. officials asserting that it was intercontinental and strategic in nature, the Soviets responding that it was only tactical. Marshal Ogarkov, the brilliant and articulate Soviet Chief of Staff, brazenly challenged U.S. Lt.-Gen. Edward Rowney in 1979: "I'll make you a deal. I'll give you a chance to fly it. You'll fill up the tank and I will give you a parachute to bail out when the plane does not reach the United States. I'll sign the deal right here."[15] Rowney's response to this offer is not recorded, but ultimately the U.S. side conceded that the "Backfire" could not reach the United States, hardly a point of pride for Ogarkov.

10

THE STRUGGLE
TO ENTER SERVICE,
1975–1977

A blaze of publicity followed the successful first flight of the TU-144 in 1969. But Soviet media treatment of the SST before the launch of passenger service in November 1977 was stumbling, contradictory, and confused, signaling that consensus had broken down in the Soviet leadership and that earlier monolithic SST enthusiasm had shattered. Divided counsels regarding the wisdom of proceeding with the SST were subtly reflected in Soviet media.

Aeroflot Jilts the TU-144

By mid-decade, the TU-144 was slipping off the radar screen of Aeroflot's illustrious future. The SST, showcased as Aeroflot's "future flagship" in early 1970s projections, was reduced to successively smaller billings as the standard-bearer of the airline's future in annual surveys of aircraft soon to enter service. The IL-86 Airbus had usurped the title of future flagship some time before. A final one-sentence entry in January 1976 was a remarkable dismissal of the TU-144. This dethronement was followed by indications that Aeroflot no longer desired the former apple of its eye.

Aeroflot chiefs had been prominent sponsors of the SST from the beginning. In mid-1961, Loginov was the first to tell Westerners that the USSR was designing a civil SST that was not a modified bomber.[1] The progressive disillusionment of Aeroflot Chief Boris Bugayev may be charted in some detail. Bugayev, who had piloted the first TU-104 flight to the United States in 1957,[2] was an ardent early booster of the project, and his vision extended beyond its capabilities. He told a Stockholm audience in 1967 that the Soviet SST would fly before the end of the year, and that it would initiate transatlantic service in 1968. Bugayev's article in *Aviatsiya i Kosmonautika* in August 1968 was so glowing that some Western experts concluded the TU-144 had already flown, four months before the fact. He included it among "the most outstanding aircraft of the near future" and touted its promised capabilities.

Aeroflot had sponsored the 144's futuristic publicity. A 1972 pamphlet prophesied breezily, "In three hours it will whisk you from Moscow to Khabarovsk—that's right across the Soviet Union. London or Paris takes 1.5 hours and you can do Delhi–Moscow in just 2.5 hours." There would be "hardly any noise or vibration to bother you so that you feel really comfortable during your flight." Similar rhetoric marked Aeroflot's fiftieth birthday in 1973. Other detailed route plans were announced later that year. Reflecting high-priority support of western Siberian oil and gas fields, the prime service to Khabarovsk on the Pacific would be broken by stops at Novosibirsk and Irkutsk, a segmentation that may have been a concession to the SST's limited range. It was hoped that Singapore and Tokyo could later be added to this route. Later also, flights to the three Soviet cities would originate from Leningrad. Other routes would go South to Alma-Ata and Tashkent. In 1973, the schedule was for these routes to open in 1975, with service to Europe to follow in 1978–79 and to the United States, Singapore, and Tokyo in the 1980s. Chief Designer Tupolev in 1975 shifted the focus back to servicing internal routes, fourteen of which were 3,000 to 6,000 kilometers in length.

But by mid-decade, Aeroflot was backing away from its flagship, apparently because flight tests revealed its thirst for fuel, its unreliability, and its lack of refinement for passengers. The

144 required special passenger ramps because of its tall landing gear, and baggage had to be carried through the long, cramped passenger compartment to the tail. Aeroflot-London appeared uninformed of the beginning of supersonic air-freight service in December 1975, and this "scheduled service" was not integrated into Aeroflot scheduling or Intourist booking. Aeroflot-London could not quote rates for the freight service.

In the first week of November 1976, Bugayev provided a report to the weekly *Nedelya* that distanced Aeroflot from the SST. The outlook was not promising, indicating that Aeroflot had put its acceptance of the aircraft on indefinite hold. Bugayev made discouraging noises regarding the TU-144: "It's undergoing reinforcing work . . . no prospects of regular service getting underway. . . . It will continue to be tested throughout 1977."[3] Tupolev had affirmed at Paris the previous spring that the TU-144 was ready for commercial service, but he noted that the final decision was up to Aeroflot. Omission of the TU-144 from Aeroflot plans for the next Five-Year Plan, 1976–80, was widely commented upon in the West.[4] An official from the Ministry of Aviation told a Western reporter that deletion of the TU-144 from Aeroflot future plans meant "then maybe there would be no flights." The Western writer concluded that the SST's "ten-year-old technology" made it "a prime candidate for the scrap heap." Goulakov, Bugayev's Deputy, also ignored the SST in a survey of Aeroflot plans through 1980 published in *Trud* on December 31, 1976.[5]

Aeroflot was acting on pragmatic evidence: the TU-144 failed even in the light-duty supersonic air-freight service to Alma-Ata. The twice-weekly service was cut back to weekly in June 1976, and three of the four TU-144s at Domodedevo Airport disappeared. In December 1976, the service was cancelled altogether, without official explanation. *Aviation Week* provided one: sustained use of afterburners cut so deeply into fuel supplies that the TU-144 could only carry a skeleton payload. In reality, the regular airmail runs were still only test flights.[6]

Tupolev KB was still anxious to see its expensive project in service, if only as an air freighter. A likely Tupolev ally in the struggle to obtain Aeroflot acceptance of the TU-144 was Pyotr Dementiev, Minister of Aviation Production. Dementiev, an old Tupolev associate from the 1930s, was alert to Aeroflot assertiveness. He "made it clear he didn't want airline officials interfering with aircraft design or production," properly his province.[7] Many officials in his ministry had a vested interest in the project, having helped to resolve its technical problems or production snags. His death in harness at the age of seventy in May 1977 added an additional element of uncertainty to the TU-144's future.

Tupolev's travails to obtain Aeroflot acceptance of the TU-144 was part of a larger struggle between the Ministry of Aviation Production—which included all design bureaus—and the Ministry of Civil Aviation. Traditionally, the KBs had certified their own aircraft as airworthy after a period of tests. In 1977, the Soviet Union replaced this traditional procedure for one based on Western models: the Ministry of Civil Aviation was given authority for certifying Soviet civil aircraft. This was a major bureaucratic convulsion at a time of immobility in Soviet ruling circles.

This power struggle may backlight Alexei Tupolev's occasional mutterings about Aeroflot and his overemphatic assertions that the TU-144 was ready for service. Accelerating technical complexity of Soviet airliners meant that development times were three times those of the 1950s. Dementiev's passing from the scene after twenty-four years in office may have sped the day of Aeroflot's bureaucratic victory. But certification of the TU-144 quickly followed in October 1977, coinciding eerily with an announcement that passenger flights would begin the next month, to celebrate the sixtieth anniversary of the Great October Revolution.

An irritant contributing to the infighting was the considerable achievements of the archrival Concorde. Transatlantic flights began in May 1976, with service extended to Dallas in February 1977. In October 1977, the first Concorde proving flight landed in New York City in preparation for scheduled service beginning that November. On October 26, 1977, Singapore Airlines announced thrice-weekly Concorde service from London via Bahrain. These substantial commercial achievements must have pricked Soviet pride. Hence the 144 was promoted from an inter-Ministerial irritant occasionally hauling mail sacks to Central Asia to its former role as a standard-bearer of Soviet prestige.

Certification cleared the way to "in service" passenger flights overland in the USSR and its tributaries. But restricting the TU-144 to one Aeroflot route when Tupolev had indicated there were fourteen of 3,000 to 6,000 kilometers in length, with eight TU-144s in flying order, reflects the extent of official Soviet skepticism in 1977 regarding TU-144 viability. International certification was an even greater hurdle. Even in these years of détente, delivering detailed documentation to French, British, or U.S. official bodies and admitting certification inspectors to the assembly hall would have touched upon Soviet pride or security preoccupations.

Though the TU-144 was shortly to commence much-anticipated passenger service, its limited extent indicates that this was a face-saving measure undertaken with many misgivings—a disguised continuation of the testing program.

Ilyushin Displaces Tupolev as Prime Aeroflot Supplier

One result of the failure of the TU-144 was the dethronement of Tupolev KB as premier airliner designer. From the advent of the TU-104 in 1955 until the launch of the TU-154 in the early 1970s, Aeroflot forecasts of new types shortly to enter airline service invariably started with Tupolev equipment. Yet in the decade following the entry into service of the TU-154 in 1972, Tupolev unveiled only one new airliner, the TU-164, which represented a transplant of IL-62 engines to the TU-154. Only in 1983 was a new Tupolev airliner announced—the TU-204. But the new IL-96 had first billing. Ilyushin had succeeded to

Tupolev's former role as provider of long-distance airliners. The new TU-204 had second billing, as the medium-range airliner.

The slowing momentum of the 144 program coincided with a massive shift of Tupolev resources into defense projects: a radical redesign of the TU-116 "Backfire" bomber and development of the TU-160 "Blackjack". The late 1970s were spent updating the "Backfire", with focus probably on the limited-range problem it shared with the 144. The early 1980s saw the "Blackjack" begin flight-testing. The small-scale production of the TU-144 yielded to a massive production program for the two bombers. Although Tupolev benefited from Brezhnev's concentration of resources on the most modern weapons, it experienced again the dynamics of the 1930s: civil airliner production again had been subordinated to combat aircraft.

The Tupolev-Ilyushin Rivalry

Behind the bewildering announcements and confusing counterannouncements, a number of political struggles swirled around the centerpiece of the SST project. The complex interplay of forces will not be better known until some insider reveals all the details, but the outlines may be pieced together from fragments of conversation, the timing of certain announcements in the Soviet press, and what is known of the dynamics of the Soviet aircraft industry.

The first political factor was the comradely rivalry between Tupolev and Ilyushin. Sergei Ilyushin had, like most of his generation, served as an apprentice designer under Tupolev in the early 1930s and worked at TsAGI. Stalin appointed him chief of the entire Soviet aircraft industry in 1937 to succeed Tupolev. Ilyushin renounced the power and peril this position represented and succeeded in returning to head his own design bureau early in 1938, as the elder Tupolev was just beginning his long years in the *Sharashka*.

During the war, Ilyushin distinguished himself as a successful designer of a number of twin-engine combat aircraft. The IL-2 Stormovik armored tank-destroyer proved an indigenous Soviet design without precedent or equivalent in the world. In the late 1940s, like Tupolev, Ilyushin was active in developing twin-engine jets, chiefly for military uses. They were based first on captured German technology and then on the Rolls-Royce Nene engines purchased from Britain in 1947. The IL-28 twin jet, the first mass-produced Soviet jet-bomber, was chosen by Soviet aircrews over the competing TU-70 in a 1948 fly-off and is still in service.

From mid-century on, Ilyushin KB moved "up market" from its earlier focus on twin-engine combat aircraft into the large civil transports and airliners then regarded as a Tupolev preserve. Aeroflot requirements for a group of modern airliners in 1953 found Tupolev and Ilyushin competing against each other repeatedly. The IL-18, a four-engine turboprop airliner, was a smaller contemporary of the TU-114; it could carry only seventy-five passengers and first flew in 1957.

Tupolev's dramatic successes with the TU-104 and its successors in 1955–56 brought a response from Ilyushin—the IL-62 state-of-the-art long-distance jetliner, designed in 1960 and first flown in 1963. It became the flagship of Aeroflot after its entry into service in March 1967, the last design from Sergei Ilyushin's hand before his 1968 semiretirement. As the first viable long-range Soviet jetliner, it displaced the TU-114 on the Moscow–Montreal and Moscow–New York routes in mid-1967. A longer-range version, the IL-62M, began Moscow–Havana service in 1974.

While Tupolev had been engaged on the TU-144 and the more orthodox TU-154, Ilyushin had been developing the IL-76 civil air freighter, powered by four NK-8-4 engines with reverse thrusters. First flown in March 1971, the IL-76 was quickly deployed on proving flight to the Tyumen oil- and gas-producing areas in western Siberia.

The Usurping Flagship

But the Ilyushin product that most dramatically challenged the TU-144 was the IL-86 widebody Airbus. Chosen over rival

Tupolev and Antonov design proposals, the IL-86 had by the mid-1970s usurped the position of future Aeroflot flagship. Its design philosophy and development climate contrasted radically with that of the TU-144. The elitist SST embodied Soviet dreams of shooting "apparatchiks" at speeds faster than a speeding bullet to distant cities and high-priority development projects. The pragmatic, proletarian IL-86 was designed to move Soviet masses between major gateways and population centers. Ilyushin publicity stressed its careful marketing research and its effort to match the IL-86 with Soviet realities, in contrast to the technocratic futurism enveloping the TU-144.

IL-86 design had been "determined in part by a poll of 7,000 Aeroflot travelers and by prolonged study of the traveling habits of Soviet citizens. . . . A 'significant segment' of the traveling public has an average journey of 900 miles. . . . The average weight of baggage is under 33 lbs." This kind of sophisticated, pragmatic market research was light-years away from the unexamined technotopian adventurism that inspired the 144. IL-86 design goals coalesced in 1967–70,[8] so this poll of future IL-86 passengers coincided with the rush to completion of the TU-144 prototype.

Whereas the TU-144 was inspired by greater speed, IL-86 development witnessed steady expansion of passenger capacity, reflecting the dawning age of Soviet mass air travel. The IL-70, 72, and 74 design studies of 1967–70, anticipating the IL–86, saw carrying capacity increased from 150 to 250 to 350 seats.[9] IL-86 publicity contained implicit criticism of TU-144 design values. Its designer, General Novozhilov, noted in a February 1973 interview—several months before the energy crisis in the West—that the IL-86 "will be 25 percent cheaper to operate than existing transports and will be able to compete economically with supersonic transports that fly at speeds up to Mach 1.7."[10] This was not a direct attack on the TU-144; the speed cited was far below the cruising speeds of the 144 and Concorde. But it provided a clue that the SST's questionable economics were under review within Soviet ruling circles.

Now it was a question as to when economic discipline in the form of performance parameters such as "seat-miles per gallon" would come into vogue in the USSR and challenge the older obsession with speed. But this was to require another decade, for so much in the way of prestige and resources had been devoted to the SST that there was no way to gracefully disinherit the flawed creation. The Politburo was a prisoner of the publicity it had set in motion.

It would take yet another decade before efficiency-performance indicators such as "grams per fuel per kilometer" would displace "passenger-kilometers" as an index for Soviet airliners and Aeroflot performance. The ascendancy of efficiency indicators coincided with the final decision to axe the TU-144. But a change at the top would be required first.

As reports of the TU-144's operational failings revealed in route testing began to circulate during 1975–76, the advances of the IL-86 program reflected a vision of a rival, more pragmatic and realistic tomorrow. An experimental IL-86 was described in *Pravda* in March 1976, and its first flight took place on December 23 of that year. The first production IL-86 took shape at Voronezh during 1977.

Different as the IL-86 was from the TU-144 in concept, it suffered from similar drawbacks and failings endemic to the Soviet aircraft industry. The required great leaps in technological sophistication prolonged its development, based on the "longest and most detailed parametric evaluation of any Soviet aircraft" yet undertaken.[11] Gestation of state-of-the-art aircraft in the mid-1970s was taking three times as long as the first-generation jet airliners of the 1950s.

As with the TU-144, the IL-86 suffered from an overweight airframe and engines with insufficient thrust and range. Its entry into service was also unavoidably postponed. Widespread publicity was devoted to the promise that the IL-86 would service the 1980 Moscow Olympics. The IL-86 did not in fact enter service until December 1980, an end-of-the-year date redolent of a political deadline.

The Frozen Heights

In 1976–77, the Soviet SST was slipping into obscurity, as reports circulated among the Soviet elite of its growing weight, fuel dipsomania, and unexorcized vibrations and noise. Aeroflot excluded the 144 from future plans after January 1976. Chief Designer Tupolev seemed happy to restrict it to air-freight duties when accompanying it on its last visit to Paris in 1977. The aircraft could not be improved quickly or radically enough to catch up with a rapidly changing future.

The Soviet civil-aircraft industry was also changing. As with most of the Soviet economy, the wrong things were being rewarded. Aeroflot still touted its burgeoning growth in primitive performance indicators of passenger-kilometers or numbers of passengers boarded. But efficiency-centered operating parameters, long the indices of commercial air operation elsewhere, were given new prominence by the 1972–73 "energy crisis." The Soviet state still distributed awards, promotions, and bonuses in terms of achievement without reference to efficiency. But there were inklings of more sophisticated thinking in pronouncements from Ilyushin KB and a growing emphasis in rhetoric, if not actual performance, on fuel efficiency. The Soviet equivalent of seat-kilometers per gallon had not yet come into currency. But "*effektinost*"—efficiency—was gaining in currency as a bureaucratic incantation, even if indices to track it and incentives to award it were still a matter of the future.

These changing goals for Soviet airliner design and use were paralleled by a generational succession in leadership. One by one, the giants who had founded the Soviet aircraft industry in the 1930s, survived Stalin's cannibalistic purges, designed and built the aircraft which defeated the Nazis in 1941–45, and led the transition to jets after the war, died. During the mid-1970s, a whole generation had passed from the scene.

Old Tupolev, the patriarch, was the first to go, in late 1972. Pavel Sukhoi, who had worked for Tupolev early in his career and whose KB had developed a smaller bomber resembling the TU-

144 in the early 1970s, died in 1975. The death in March 1977 of Pyotr Dementiev, a long-time Tupolev associate and Minister of Aviation Production since 1953, altered the bureaucratic balance of forces in the battle to get the TU-144 into commercial service. Sergei Ilyushin, Tupolev's former Brigade Leader and chief rival in bomber and transport designs, died in February 1978. In October 1978, Myasishchev, a former Tupolev disciple who produced deceptively awesome strategic jet-bombers in the 1950s before carrying out groundwork SST studies joined him.

No corresponding sweep occurred at the top. The Brezhnev generation did not pass from the scene, even after Brezhnev himself died in November 1982. They simply remained in power until the mid-1980s when, in former Moscow correspondent Dusko Doder's metaphor, the dinosaurs were driven from their caves.

This was the political landscape of the Soviet aircraft industry when—in the face of mounting evidence of technical short-comings—Soviet media announced in October 1977 that the TU-144 would begin scheduled once-weekly passenger flights the following month to celebrate the "Diamond Jubilee of Great October." As always with hurried end-of-the-year entries of new aircraft or their appearance on Bolshevik birthdays, the clumsy hand of Brezhnev's Central Committee was obvious.

This was clearly the wrong decision. By 1977, the SST's moment had come and gone. Its prestige potential was a debased currency. Given the successful entry of the Concorde on a number of international routes the year before, launching a once-a-week domestic service for the TU-144 hardly burnished Soviet laurels. Instead, it raised questions. This seems to have been recognized. Restricting flights when eight aircraft were fit for flying indicates that the Central Committee was mindful of further potential for disaster. Brezhnev and his moribund cohorts had some inkling of the 144's failings. Had they been convinced of the aircraft's soundness, they would have ordained its use on a number of domestic routes, as originally planned, rather than on just one. Instead, they decided on a course of action miscalculated to reap maximum propaganda value with minimum risk exposure. The Fates were waiting.

The TU-144's entry into service was a media event providing non-Soviets their first and only opportunity to ride in the TU-144, confirming that it was not ready for premium passenger service. Inaugural passengers reported a cacophony suitable only for combat crews. Comfort would have been possible only for passengers outfitted with helicopter soundproofing helmets.

It is remarkable that this incarnation of early 1960s technology and values got this far. The Central Committee's launch of TU-144 "scheduled service" represented the triumph of hope over experience. Launching this propaganda vehicle for dubious and limited dividends, given Soviet technical inadequacies, reveals the quality of Soviet decision making in general. A similarly shallow assessment of alternatives and consequences would lead to inauguration of the Afghan adventure two years later.

From 1977 on, the TU-144's fate paralleled Brezhnev's. The project survived the Party Secretary by only three months. Brezhnev and the men who overthrew Khrushchev promising "stability of cadres" eventually calcified the system, frustrating badly needed structural reforms. These years saw the climax of the "cronyism" and "toadyism" cited in the post-Brezhnev Soviet press. In his final years, Brezhnev adopted the folkways of an ancient oriental despot, surrounded by sycophants who showered upon him military metals and promotions, and finally the Lenin Prize for his turgid memoirs. The salient achievement of the Brezhnev regime was to reach a rough military parity with the United States. In his closing years, Brezhnev drew instinctively closer to the military, which had benefited most from his largesse. This was not an environment conducive to the examination and cancellation of superannuated prestige projects. Nor is it surprising that the state-of-the-art civil airliner ended its days as a test bed for military purposes.

Inauguration of Soviet Commercial SST Service

Signs were accumulating during 1977 that the TU-144 was in trouble. Yet in early October, Aeroflot announced that the SST would commence "regular passenger service" from Moscow to Alma-Ata on November 1, 1977. Flights to Tashkent and Khabarovsk would come later.[12] Though this was billed as a celebration of the Diamond Jubilee of the October Revolution, careful study indicates that the Brezhnev regime was hedging its bets. The distance between the two cities was just under 2,500 miles, indicating that the TU-144's range problems were unsolved. Only one intercity service was announced, while the Concorde was opening up a number of international routes. At least four TU-144s could be seen at Moscow's Domodedovo Airport and eight were known to be flying, enough to support a variety of routes. The TU-144 would serve as a flawed instrument of Soviet prestige, commissioned by a leadership cognizant of its shortcomings. The flight program meant to showcase advanced Soviet science and technology instead disclosed additional shortcomings.[13]

The official date for inauguration of Soviet SST service had advanced and receded several times, an accurate barometer of the TU-144's manic fortunes. Bugayev in 1968 confidently predicted commercial flights would begin in 1969. The euphoria following the first flight in 1969 inspired reports that airline service would commence in 1971. Bugayev, attending the prototype at the 1971 Paris air show, set this back to 1975. Victor Louis, the Soviet journalist, brought the advent of commercial flight forward again to 1973, just before the crash of the production 144 in Paris.[14] Visitors to Voronezh following the crash were told that service would begin in 1975 from Moscow to Novosibirsk, Irkutsk, and Khabarovsk, indicating that hopes were still held of extending the 144's range.[15] SST supporters had evidently pledged that the 144 would enter service before the end of the Ninth Five-Year Plan: the mail and freight service inaugurated in the last days of 1975 was a face-saving dodge to meet this commitment. After these proving flights were discontinued in

193

December 1976, Bugayev's comments that the 144 would not enter service in 1977[16] reflected Aeroflot's misgivings. The subsequent November 1977 "entry into service" can only represent an ill-advised intervention by Brezhnev and the Politburo.

Behind-the-scenes battles between the Ministry of Civil Aviation and the Ministry of Aircraft Production made it all the more important that the inauguration, a victory for the latter, should be carried out smoothly. A press campaign was prepared. The Moscow weekly *Nedelya*, on October 20, carried a 2,000-word advance report on the 144 in flight. The captain was quoted as saying that other airliners were "difficult, heavy, and complex for the pilot" in comparison with the 144. The correspondent ended with a panegyric: "We need the TU-144 not only because it cuts distances and makes the most of time. No, when an aircraft of this kind soars into the sky it raises our technology, our science, our production and us to a higher level."[17]

TASS followed with a press release on November 2: both passengers and specialists aboard the first passenger flight agreed that the 144 was "ready for regular flights along 'Aeroflot' routes." According to TASS, the first flight had been flawless: "None of the passengers sitting in convenient soft airchairs felt any fatigue." Even when passing through the sound barrier, flight participants "felt no G-loads and did not hear buildup of turbine noise." Stewardesses served breakfast to passengers traveling at 2,300 kph (over 1,400 mph). Chief Designer Tupolev, who took part in the inaugural flight, insisted that "the characteristics of the TU-144 are quite within the standards of the International Civil Air Organization." Takeoff and landing were no more noisy than that of the TU-104 or DC-8.[18]

Westerners on board the 144 had a different story. This was the first occasion that non-Soviets had actually flown the TU-144, and their dispatches revealed how uncomfortable it was. The Soviets had taken pains to make the first "commercial" flight of their flagship as auspicious as possible. Before takeoff, official speeches linked this first Soviet supersonic service to the sixtieth anniversary of the Revolution, as "a great achievement, a huge contribution to the celebrations." But ground services were strictly earthbound. Bugayev, who had assigned the speech making to his deputy, Gulakov, was infuriated by the breakdown of a new motorized embarkation ramp, which delayed departure half an hour. Similar problems occurred on arrival in Alma-Ata, when the plane was towed back-and-forth for twenty-five minutes in an attempt to align it with an exit ramp.[19]

Eighty privileged passengers, selected by the Soviet Foreign Ministry, were served caviar and cognac for breakfast "from serving carts which could barely negotiate the narrow aisle."[20] Reports of vibration problems seemed unfounded. The cabin had shortcomings: several ceiling panels were ajar, service trays stuck, and window shades dropped without being pulled.[21] The five-abreast seating was criticized as cramped. Not all the toilets worked. These shortcomings were normal in a new airliner. A more serious problem remained.

On-board speakers played the theme from *Love Story*, "Gloomy Sunday," and "Raindrops Keep Falling on my Head," but few aboard could hear it. Their dominant impression was not speed but noise. Fed by the onrushing air, the huge air-conditioners and the huge engines created "an ear-shattering roar that could almost have been heard in Queens," according to the *New York Times*. Shouting, Tupolev, explained that most on-board noise originated from the huge air-conditioners designed to keep the high skin temperatures at bay, and that Soviet technicians were at work to cut down the decibels. Passengers complained that the loud onrushing sound of wind made conversation impossible and communicated with each other by passing notes. The cacophony was almost unbearable in the rear of the cabin. Tupolev admitted that the TU-144 was half again as noisy as the conventional TU-154.[22]

The passengers' other prime impression was the tremendous acceleration of which the 144 was capable as it took off. *Air et Cosmos* calculated that it had a power-to-weight ratio almost 20 percent higher than the Concorde.[23] Since the 144 was carrying only eighty passengers—57 percent of capacity—its rate of ascent was truly dramatic. Although the Soviets had devoted top priority to this project for fifteen years, they had been unable to achieve levels of comfort suitable for a civilian airliner. The noise, lack of range, and naked power of the TU-144 reflected the personality of a military aircraft, as did its practice of landing with three popout parachutes instead of thrust reversers. Issuing sound-deadening helmets to passengers, as is done on board helicopters, would have been a cheap, pragmatic solution to the noise problem, but Tupolev was not about to accept defeat.

The Soviet media seem to have received mixed signals on coverage of this inaugural flight, patently designed for foreign consumption. Soviet press coverage of the first passenger flight was less than that of the first freight flight at the end of 1975. This ambivalence seems well founded. Following the media event of the first flight, Aeroflot canceled the next three, although tickets were sold and passengers were waiting. No explanation was given for these cancellations.[24] For the West, this Soviet propaganda splash was anticlimactic: the Concorde had been serving international routes to the Middle East and North and South America for twenty-two months.

11
TWILIGHT AND
LEGACY, 1977–1984

The operational career of the TU-144 was short, not sweet. Starting with the inauguration of service on November 1, 1977, 102 flights were completed between Moscow and Alma-Ata before Flights 499 and 500 was canceled on June 1, 1978. Almost all these flights were flown at half-capacity, limited to seventy passengers and mail sacks, though there was a waiting list for the flights.[1] The 2,400 odd miles of the flight taxed the 144's capabilities enough to require additional administrative safeguards.

Several of the early flights were canceled outright in November–December 1977. The 102 flights involved 181 hours of air time, of which 104 hours were supersonic. The Soviets later reported that 226 malfunctions were discovered in regular service, 80 of these in flight. Although half of the 144's development costs had been devoted to electronics, this area proved the least reliable. Instruments and navigation gear were the most troublesome components, followed by radio and autopilot. Mechanical elements such as the landing gear, engine, and canards gave less trouble. Eighty of the faults were serious enough to affect the schedule, 146 were not. For example, on December 27, 1977, reduced cabin pressure forced a subsonic flight at the lower altitude of 36,000 feet. On January 29, 1978, a faulty switch indicated that the landing gear was down when in fact it was retracted. On March 14, 1978, excessive temperature in an engine exhaust duct forced the 144 to return to base. The 144's seven months of service required 1,170 man-hours of maintenance. A main problem was metal fatigue on the tip of the vertical stabilizer, which was corrected with a titanium doubler plate.[2]

Second Crash

The TU-144's last scheduled flight occurred on June 6, 1978. No immediate explanation for its cancellation was given. Though four TU-144s remained at Domodedovo Airport until late September 1978, the flight schedule had been semisymbolic: irregular, delayed a day or more, often canceled outright.[3] Evidence that surfaced three months later provided the reason for cancellation of 144 flights. The Western press carried reports that a U.S. satellite had recorded the wreckage of an SST several miles east of Moscow.[4] Gradually the story of what happened could be pieced together: one of the new 114Ds—D for Dalnaya, or long-range—with the Koliesov engines had crashed during a test flight on the afternoon of May 23, 1978. Rumors circulating among Tupolev personnel indicated that a fire broke out in the left engines and spread to the fuselage. The pilot, believed to be Edward Elyan, succeeded in shutting down one or more engines, but power was insufficient to reach the main test airfield at Ramenskoye. The plane came down in a field, was gutted by burning fuel, and then blew apart. The Soviets later reported that two crew members were killed and three more were seriously injured.[5] Elyan survived and took part in later TU-144 ceremonies.

Cancellation of TU-144 service as a result of the 144D crash underscores the narrow margin of consensus for scheduled flights. If incomplete reports are correct, the second crash—of a test 144D—originated with experimental Koliesov engines. The Aeroflot hierarchy seized upon this second disaster—though rooted in technology not shared by the flying airliners—as a pretext to unloose the supersonic albatross from their necks. It's clear that they had their supporters in the political leadership because it took only two weeks to scrub the TU-144 from the Aeroflot schedule.

Backstairs skirmishing seems to have continued. At the end of September, the four white TU-144s at Domodedovo Airport—77105,6,7,8—disappeared.[6] By October 1978, supersonic service had also disappeared from Aeroflot's timetable and the 144, according to Aeroflot, was restricted to "special flights."[7] Callers to Aeroflot were told that it was not known when the SST would return to service, though in November an Aeroflot spokesman projected that this would happen within a few months.[8]

Rumors circulating among Tupolev workers responsible for assembling the SST hinted at further crashes and flights aborted owing to last-minute malfunctions. A third crash, unreported by Soviet authorities, was believed to have occurred at the end of a Moscow–Alma-Ata run. The Bolshoi Ballet had reputedly escaped extinction only when the company transferred to another craft at the last minute. This contained a half-truth: services of the 144 were frequently cancelled, but it is highly unlikely that a third crash could have been concealed, owing to the high profile for the SST that Soviet propaganda had created.

Later, Soviet revelations of a few details of the second 144 crash were accompanied by the aircraft's service record during its fourteen-month career as a freight carrier, from late December 1976 to April 1977, and its seven-month service as an airliner. During a visit of Aerospatiale technicians to Moscow in late October 1978, after the Western press had already established the fact of the second crash, Soviet specialists proved "unusually frank." Remaining Soviet advocates of an SST were now approaching desperation. In 1977 they had approached Lucas for help with the electronic management of the 144's engines, and asked both the British and French for assistance in improving their variable-geometry air intakes. Now, in late 1978, they provided the 144's service record together with a request for a broad range of Concorde technology.

The Soviet shopping list reflected a wide spectrum of unresolved technical problems. Some may provide clues to the second crash: de-icing equipment for the leading edge of the air intakes, fuel-system pipes and devices to improve durability of these pipes, drain valves for fuel tanks, firefighting equipment, including warning devices and lightning protection, and emergency power supply. Other requests reflected more generic problems: mud flaps, fireproof paints, navigation and piloting equipment, acoustical loading of airframe and controls, and ways to reinforce fuselage strength to withstand damage.[9]

Informed French observers believed the Soviets were "burning" to use the TU-144 for the 1980 Olympic Games in Moscow, and would try anything to straighten out the aircraft for this prestige occasion.[10] This forecast may have been well founded as a reflection of Soviet wish-fulfillment; in truth, however, the TU-144 did not venture out from behind its imposed iron curtain of obscurity. The Soviet publicity apparatus focused its spotlights elsewhere. Belated Soviet openness to the French does not seem to have garnered much technical assistance. The French were bound to refer such requests to the British, who had already decided that SST technology had important strategic and defense implications.

Testing the 144D

By the end of 1978, it could be concluded that the Soviet SST had failed. The second 144 crash in May, the cancellation of the 144's sole service two weeks later, the appeal by the Soviets for technical help in October, and the apparent lack of Western response, signaled the end to the decade-long struggle to make a commercial proposition out of the Soviet SST. The Concorde had been servicing the Near East and Latin America for over two years; the 144 had been withdrawn from its single, truncated domestic route.

However, Soviet SST proponents were strong enough to mount one final attempt, in 1979–82, to put the troublesome "technological showcase" back on Aeroflot routes. As early as February 11, 1979, Soviet media announced that 144s would be making regular flights to Khabarovsk as soon as the local airport was re-equipped and a new runway was re-lengthened. This seemed to contradict the earlier line that the 144 could use conventional airports without conversions or improvements. Designation of Khabarovsk as destination served notice that the 144's range problems had been resolved, and that the original plan to span the USSR on the Trans-Siberian axis was again a realistic prospect.

The inaugural flight of the new service took place on June 23, 1979, a year and a month after the second crash, and was prominently featured in Soviet media. The 3,480 miles from Moscow to Khabarovsk were covered in three hours, twenty-one minutes, with Chief Designer Alexei Tupolev on board. The date was chosen because it was the fortieth anniversary of the first flight from Moscow to the Pacific, which had taken a Tupolev aircraft twenty-four hours to accomplish in 1939. Soviet TV indicated that this was the inauguration of a new route and showed pictures of its crew being draped in flowers by locals on their arrival. The Chief Designer noted that the weather had been "extremely complicated" with strong winds.[11]

Marshal Bugayev and Deputy Minister of Civil Air Sergei Pavlov, once involved in gleaning Concorde secrets out of Paris, confirmed to the U.S. ambassador and economic counselor that operations of the 144 had resumed. Yet when Aeroflot was contacted for the schedule, it noted that only freight operations were presently being carried out; there was as yet no SST schedule to Khabarovsk published, and no tickets were for sale. In reality, the new flights were a route-proving exercise— but one that stretched 3,480 miles, indicating the Soviets had solved their engine problems and nearly doubled the effective range of their SST. The consensus among foreign observers in Moscow was that the Soviets were dropping their SST program.[12] Bugayev told another group of visitors that the 144s had been modified to correct "nagging design faults" and high fuel consumption. It was "now ready" to resume scheduled flights. But an Aeroflot official stated that "only cargo" was being carried: "I don't know when passengers will be carried again." Moscow experts viewed a Radio Moscow report that the "new version is ready to go into mass production" with skepticism.[13] Soviet domestic broadcasts emphasized that the 144 carried 140 passengers—40 more than the Concorde—and that the proving flights had helped specify the program for improving the aircraft.

The secret of the 144's new range capability slipped out almost accidentally, months after the event. On Radio Moscow's English-language African service on August 4, 1979, the Deputy Minister of Civil Aviation noted that the 144's new engine was 50 percent more economical. Novosti then noted that the "inaugural regular technical flight" was carried out by a new variant, the 144D, powered by Koliesov turbojets, which cut fuel consumption 50 percent. The real purpose of the flights was to provide "a profitable experience" for the aircrews, ground team, and research agency. Cancellation of the previous flights represented "only a page in the TU-144's biography . . . everything is following its pattern." A Soviet "technical flight regulation and commissioning" agency was overseeing the "linkage" of crews, ground personnel, and designers—an obvious reference to the new Soviet certification system set up in 1977.

The reference to the Koliesov turbojet was initially confusing. Previous information regarding Koliesov had centered on a variable-geometry jet engine. This kind of engine involved very tricky technology to function as either a turbojet or with turbofans to attain maximum efficiency in subsonic and supersonic modes. Western experts dismissed such Soviet claims as beyond Soviet capability. Western engine manufacturers on both sides of the Atlantic had long tried to produce a "variable geometry" engine, with rotating vanes and had failed, yet they were known to be far in advance of Soviet design capability. *Air et Cosmos* believed that such claims were simple Soviet propaganda: a Soviet technician at the Paris air show had pointed out that the 144's claimed weight of 150 tons was 30 tons under the true weight.[14]

The USSR had achieved some kind of breakthrough, however, addressing the 144's critical weakness of insufficient range. *Etudes sovietiques* noted that the 144's fuel consumption had decreased while its range had increased. After a recent flight, a pilot had reassured the writer that enough fuel remained to fly another 1,000 kilometers.

By the beginning of 1981, there were signs that the testing was coming to a close. A spokesman for the Ministry of Aviation Industry indicated that the "new round of tests" was "virtually complete" and that the 144 should soon be back in service. Extensive modifications were believed to have been carried out, the "only remaining problems are economic ones." No date was given for restart of service.[15] Other sources indicated that "important modifications were still to be carried out, but that further flight tests had been carried out in the last few weeks."[16] The new engines were said, unofficially, to have 39,690 lbs. thrust—48,500 with afterburner. *Air et Cosmos* established that the new 144Ds were still carrying only cargo and that twenty-two tons of thrust instead of eighteen might make possible the original range goal of 6,500 kilometers. *Interavia* quoted Aeroflot as stating that up to four 144 flights were made daily.[17]

In spite of these hopeful backstairs whispers the 144D never did enter service. In August 1981, the 144 was dropped from future technology listed in the *Economic Gazette*. Although 144s remained visible on the runway at Domodedovo, where they had been prominently displayed for the last six years, the SST was slighted in a 1981 book published by Bugayev.[18]

What had happened? It is difficult to penetrate the armor of Soviet secrecy, but obviously even the new engines had failed to measure up in some ways. The best clue was the official admission that the only remaining problem was economic. The Koliesov engines did endow the 144 with restored range, but we do not know the cost. Fragmentary references indicate that reliability problems had been solved, but that the new engines, while more powerful than the NK-144s, did not have the requisite efficiency for Aeroflot. By the early 1980s, efficiency and fuel economy were receiving attention even in the Soviet Union.

No pictures were released of the 144D; apparently the Soviets regarded it as semisecret. If its engines truly marked a leap in efficiency over those in the earlier 144, this could have some bearing on the range of the "Backfire" bomber. Engines that could be fitted to the 144 could also interchange with the Soviet's front-line medium-range bomber. Because NATO experts agreed that the "Backfire" was not an intercontinental bomber, we can infer that the 144D engines, if fitted to the "Backfire", did not endow it with dramatically increased range. The fate of the Koliesov engines remains a mystery.

The Soviets may have staged the impressive 3,480-mile flights to Khabarovsk with stripped aircraft, for propaganda and publicity only. Without a viable payload, there was no possibility of viable airline service. At this time, Tupolev was becoming more and more involved in production of the new "Backfire" variant and the new intercontinental bomber "Blackjack". Apparently, new-airliner development was relegated to the back burner in the early 1980s, as Brezhnev's military buildup mandated a dramatic expansion for Tupolev.

By the late 1970s and early 1980s, a new emphasis on efficiency and fuel economy had become paramount in Soviet civil aviation. By 1978, Aeroflot was carrying out a nationwide fuel-conservation program. Presentation of new Soviet airliners emphasized their profitability, fuel economy, and efficient use of space. The Soviet industry was reflecting emphases that had overtaken the West in the previous decade. It was not a hospitable environment for supersonic airliners. The production version of the 144 carried over 104 tons of fuel for each flight, and all indications are that there was little of this remaining at the end of the 2,000-mile flight from Moscow to Alma-Ata. If the modified 144D did indeed cut this fuel consumption by 50 percent, as claimed, why wasn't this improved version brought into service? Probably about four 144Ds were produced, either manufactured outright or converted from 144s.

When the 144's conventional sibling, the TU-154, had an economical long-distance version introduced in February 1983, its improved engines were said to cut fuel consumption 15 to 20 percent. Alexei Tupolev, in an aside, indicated that the SST's days were numbered: the operation of supersonic passenger airliners was "economically inexpedient at present." Work was proceeding to make them more economical. But "the question of supersonic aircraft has not been taken off the agenda." Alexei Tupolev looked forward to a second-generation SST that would convey 200 passengers with "enhanced fuel efficiency and greater comfort."[19]

Obituary

Early in 1983, the TU-144D was dropped from Aeroflot's flight plan. This presumably marked the end of the freight-only proving flights to Khabarovsk. Boris Panjukov, head of Aeroflot's International Division, described deployment of the 144D as both costly and difficult. He did not elaborate. The flagship and pride of Soviet civil aviation disappeared quietly after more than 10,000 air-hours. All the modifications and improvements had apparently not brought the hoped-for success. Its great thirst for fuel foreshortened its range, and the cabin din made passenger comfort impossible. Flying a Soviet SST the 6,500 miles from Moscow to Havana remained a dream. Even the thriftier 144D, flying the 3,200 miles from Moscow to Alma-Ata, carrying its full passenger complement of 140, would have required drop tanks if the wind was unfavorable. The end of the 144's career was unhonored and unsung.[20]

An article in *Znamya (Banner)* reflected the changed priorities among Soviet aircraft designers and builders, and the changed emphasis on economics and national economic freight. Aeroflot had been influenced by the importance the West placed on operating economics: Aeroflot was presented as "a commercial organization, whose aircraft must operate profitably." The trend in Soviet airliner development was to add additional seats, as had been done with the 104. The TU-134 had begun with forty-four passengers. Through twelve subsequent versions, this had been expanded incrementally to ninety-six passengers. This more intensive space-utilization raised fuel consumption only slightly. The engines, too, had undergone improvement: every airliner now flying reportedly used little over half the fuel it had previously. The extremely efficient turbofans of the TU-154M were a case in point. The IL-86 was to be the Soviet airliner of the 1980s, if it could achieve good load factors.

Soviet contemplation of the malodorous fate of the Concorde put the TU-144's misfortunes into perspective. Soviet writers occasionally comment upon Western parallels to Soviet problems; Soviet readers realize the intent of the critique is to elliptically address forbidden domestic topics. *Le Point* was quoted, with a touch of malicious pleasure: "Concorde is dying. . . . After years of glory and polemics, its end is drawing nigh . . . a kind of death under anesthesia." British Concorde service to Bahrain and Singapore was discontinued. From April 1982, Concorde flights to Rio de Janeiro and Caracas had been curtailed. Air France Concorde service to Washington and Mexico was discontinued the following November, with load factors of 51 and 44 percent, respectively—close to the 50 percent enforced on the Alma-Ata run as a safety measure to save fuel.

This "sad ending" was a result of "bad luck." Repeated oil-price increases had made the Concorde operation extremely costly—a ton of fuel was burned per passenger on every transatlantic run. It expended as much fuel to transport one hundred passengers as the 747 used to move five hundred. The Concorde's "very high noise level" outraged environmentalists. Reportedly, U.S. firms were putting all kinds of obstacles in its path, allegedly because there was no U.S. counterpart, but no specifics were given. Last, the Concorde was regarded as "obsolescent": its engines could not be developed further, and Concorde operations were heavily subsidized by taxpayers. Concorde had neither a future nor a present. Not all the facts in this Soviet treatment were necessarily true, but it did explain SST shortcomings to a Soviet audience.

The eruption of the energy crisis did not, however, force Soviet aviation designers to abandon hope for superfast airliners. Selyakov, who had been with Tupolev for twenty years and had helped develop both the TU-104 and the TU-134, believed SST technology had a future. Designers do not retreat once a speed has been attained. David Gai, an aviation writer, wrote lyrically of a ride taken during a 144 test flight, which cruised at a 20-kilometer altitude, at the edge of space. The black of the sky, which made the stars seem quite close, turned the 144 into a planetarium. Engineers toiled to produce improved engines. General Ponomarev projected a vision for the year 2000 and a "new generation of winged machines carrying a thousand passengers at 10,000 kph at an altitude of 25 to 100 kilometers." These speeds—six to ten times the speed of sound—might be obtained from liquified hydrogen fuels.[21]

But the stage had been set. All indications were that the TU-144 was moribund: little had been heard from it since the last notes of the Khabarovsk freight flights in 1981. It was indicative that official notification of the end of the program came almost as an afterthought, in response to questions from Western reporters, without the Soviet public receiving much in the way of an explanation. The occasion was the twenty-fifth anniversary of the opening of Sheremetyevo Airport, on August 9, 1984. Nikolai Polyachik, Director-General of Aeroflot's international operations, stated that the TU-144 had become too expensive to run, just like the Concorde. SSTs had proved inefficient in operation in Britain and France; the Soviet cousin had also. The USSR could not afford to operate inefficient aircraft.[22]

Informed Westerners suspected that this was at best a half-truth. Soviet sensitivity to high running costs was a relatively recent development. Operating one or two TU-144s, however prodigiously wasteful and costly, made little difference to Aeroflot's total operations. Operating the 144 expended an infinitesimal fraction of the billions spent developing the SST and making seventeen examples. One Western expert in Moscow judged the 144 as "one of the most expensive failures in history." Another stated, "In terms of investment and return the TU-144 may well rank as the biggest single failure in the whole history of aviation."[23] If so, the Soviet SST may have set yet another record in a heavily contested field.

Western analysts suggested additional reasons for Soviet abandonment of the SST program. Some Soviet officials indicated that the second crash, rather than high operating costs, was the real reason for scrapping the project.[24] The second crash may have indicated serious and intractable problems with the Koliesov engines, for which so much had been hoped. If so, why did test flights continue for three more years? *Aviation Week* believed that the SST program had never recovered from the setback of the first crash. This had grievous effects, but the onset of route proving, entry into service, and the second series of route-proving years after 1973 reflected Soviet perseverance with the project.

The end of the TU-144D testing and the abandonment of the SST program occurred within a year. The 144D must have been written off as marginal indeed, given the tremendous cost and publicity devoted to it. Positioning the 144 in the shadow of the Concorde's known operating expense was in part a face-saving maneuver. If the Soviets had developed a reliable, comfortable airliner capable of the distances they claimed for it, they would certainly have used it. The best estimate available from fragmentary evidence is that the 144D did improve on the dismal fuel consumption of the original NK-144 engines but not enough to make it a viable airliner. Coupled with the loss of Brezhnev's patronage, the continuing cabin noise, and new obsessions at Aeroflot with efficiency and fuel conservation, the project had lost its appeal. Tupolev was increasingly caught up in bomber production, and airliners had become almost a secondary concern. The once-monolithic constituency of Soviet SST advocates had melted away to leave only a residue of enthusiasts: the end had come. Like the huge czar's bell and czar's cannon in the Kremlin, the 144 had hardly ever been used for its intended purpose.

Last Role—Bomber Test Bed, Record Setter

Concorde chief test pilot André Turcat pointed out correctly that the TU-144 was one of the first Soviet aircraft designed purely for civil applications. Its Chief Designer was at pains to point out the distinction between airliners and bombers, noting in

1969 that the "high reliability, comfort, and economy required" usually could not be fulfilled by starting from a bomber.[25] A state-of-the-art supersonic airliner represented a quantum leap forward from Tupolev's previous experience with bombers and subsonic airliners: "The new aircraft had no prototype either civilian or military." Eventually it became clear that the Soviet SST, with its cramped and noisy passenger compartment, had evolved only marginally beyond a bomber's comfort levels, while its engines retained the high maintenance profile and great fuel thirst of combat aircraft.

Airliners had become so sophisticated and specialized in function that they could no longer be evolved from facile conversions of bombers. But was the reverse also untrue? Could a high-speed civil airliner serve as a basis for a bomber? Could not some elements of its pioneering technology be exploited for military purposes?

Khrushchev's blighting of strategic-bomber development at the beginning of the 1960s did not last long. His successors did not share his overreliance on strategic-rocket forces and followed

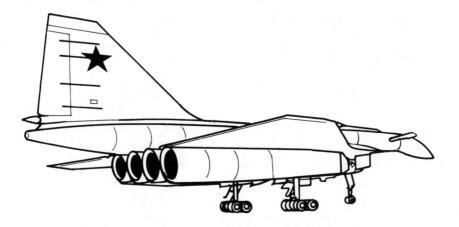

The T-101, the Sukhoi entry in the strategic bomber design competition in the early 1970s, resembled a half-scale T-144. This drawing, believed to provide the first evidence of its wing and engine arrangements, is based on a photo taken at Monino in 1987. (*via Ruffles Archive*)

closely the arguments of manned bomber protagonists in the West. As the Soviets became aware of U.S. low-altitude, terrain-hugging bomber projects during the mid-1960s, they began to study prospects for analogous Soviet aircraft. The first of these was a four-engined delta begun at Sukhoi KB in the late 1960s. This, Sukhoi's first bomber design, was begun at a time when Sukhoi had suspended development of its latest fighter design. In outline it resembled a smaller TU-144 and was designed for a target speed of Mach 2.8, enough to require heavy use of titanium on its leading edges. The prototype, designated T-101, flew in 1972, anticipating later efforts by Tupolev and, reportedly, Lavochin.[26]

This remarkable prototype resembles both the B-70 and the TU-144 in its full delta wing with four engines mounted close to the centerline, with the engines split in pairs to make room for a small weapons bay. It was roughly half the size of the TU-144 and two-thirds the size of the B-70, except that it had a single fin and rudder. Its length has been estimated at 130 feet and its span at 70 feet. Its maximum speed may well have matched the Mach 3 of the B-70, though its range is problematic. An example is on display at the Soviet Air Force Museum at Monino.[27]

"Backfire" and "Blackjack"

The "Backfire", reportedly assigned Tupolev designation TU-116, was—with the TU-154—a contemporary of and sibling to the TU-144. The TU-116 was the first large long-range bomber to be conceived after the fall of Khrushchev, with development commencing in 1964–65 as the first fruits of a policy reversal of Khrushchev's hostility toward strategic bombers. Its variable-sweep wing and turbofan engines point to an intent to achieve long subsonic range. The original design goals are believed to be top speed: Mach 2–2.5 and range 5,500–6,000 miles—both close to the TU-144.

It was a much more transitional, evolutionary design than its SST stablemate, for which it provided the mismatched engines.

Many of its features were drawn from the Tupolev cupboard: its general outline, with long inlet ducts for the engines, and low-set swept wing came from the TU-102/28. The original version echoed the waisted fuselage and landing-gear pods of the TU-28. The variable-geometry portion of its wing was much less ambitious than the fully swept wing of the slightly later B-1.

The prototype that flew in 1969, months after the TU-144, shared the SST's deficient range, ascribed to excessive drag, and like the 144, it was subjected to radical redesign. The second version, designated "Backfire B", had new outer wings of increased span with a double taper on the trailing edge and landing gear that retracted inward into the fuselage. It was operational by 1975, with two squadrons outfitted that year. Although production was estimated at thirty-five a year, the Pentagon believed that only a hundred were in service in early 1980.[28]

A long debate over the TU-116's range was resolved in 1985, when the DIA agreed with the long-term CIA position that the "Backfire" did not have an unrefueled combat range exceeding 3,000 miles. This meant that it was not really a strategic bomber. This would verify the fuel-consumption problems of the NK-144 engine, shared with the SST.[29]

By 1974, flight tests were observed in the USSR of a strategic bomber larger than the TU-22M "Backfire", featuring a slender delta wing like the TU-144's. By 1976, a different bomber was under test, with double-delta wings like the Swedish SAAB Viggen. This combined a heavy weapons-carrying capability with short takeoff and landing performance. Suggestions that this was "a military version of the TU-144" were dismissed as a "gross oversimplification."[30]

The Soviet SST project thus ended as it began: with rumors and reports of supersonic bombers paralleling supersonic airliner development. Military interest would go far to explain the dogged development of the TU-144 up to 1984. It almost certainly served as a test bed for the supersonic cycle of new bombers, much as the Concorde played the role of a penetrating bomber in RAF exercises.[31] Brezhnev's last speech—to Soviet military hierarchs in October 1982—emphasized that "lagging was inadmissible" in military technology, hence the flawed civil SST was suborned to bomber development.

As mentioned earlier, Khrushchev reportedly closed down strategic-bomber development in 1961. This made the TU-144 less strategic and militarily sensitive at a time when the USSR was opening itself up to the outside world. We know as much as we do about the 144 because its technology was temporarily regarded as militarily irrelevant. Coinciding with the need for Soviet prestige, fueled by the hope that the Soviets might export SSTs for scarce and coveted hard currency, the TU-144, like its older sisters—the TU-104 and TU-114—were opened up for outside inspection. Foreigners were allowed to inspect the aircraft close up, inside and out. This license to scrutinize was sometimes capricious, always selective: photos of the vexatious NK-144 engines, the Gordian knot of the Soviet SST, never appeared in *Jane's All the World's Aircraft* alongside other Kuznetsov engines during the nineteen years of the 144's public career. In fact, no photos were ever released.

Simultaneously, the development of the B-1 bomber reflected the changed conditions affecting large bombers after the U2 incident. They were designed for ground-hugging missions to evade radar and the effective high-altitude missiles that had killed off the promising designs of the 1950s. In the United States, the B-1 was conceived as a low-level bomber, and the high-altitude B-70 came to be regarded as a deadend museum piece. Requests for proposals for the B-1 were issued in November 1969, the design was frozen in 1971, and the first flight occurred in 1974. By the end of the 1960s, graduating Soviet pilots were being told by alarmed technical experts that the Soviet Union had no conceivable defense against the low-flying B-1.[32]

Soviet concern over U.S. manned bomber penetration inspired requirements for similar aircraft. There apparently was a standard Soviet design competition for a long-range supersonic bomber capable of a 1,800 mph cruise, which contributed to abiding Soviet interest throughout the early 1970s and early 1980s to plans for a Mach 3 SST. There were three design entries. One of the Tupolev proposals was developed from the TU-144.

Indications that these early projects had been revived began to appear in the Western press in mid-1978, when the second TU-144 crash seemed to dash remaining hopes for its commercial prospects. The Soviets themselves confirmed these indications while signing the Salt II agreement in mid-1979, by announcing what reconnaissance photography had already revealed: three new strategic bombers were under development.

Bombers again became Tupolev's first priority in the 1970s. The first of these was a development of the TU-26 "Backfire"; the other two were direct spinoffs from the TU-144. One, designated initially RAM-P, closely resembled the exterior of the 144. It retained the characteristic full delta wing, but was reconfigured for supersonic operations to carry a twenty-ton payload for the ultra-long-range of 10,000 nautical miles. Little more was heard of RAM-P after the initial reports of 1979. No photos were released of this type, and it is likely that it was passed up in favor of the third, and most promising design.[33]

This third design was RAM-H, designated "Blackjack" by NATO and probably known as the TU-160 to the Soviets. "Blackjack" does not resemble the 144 as closely as does the RAM-P, for it has a variable-geometry wing and a separate tail. A poor-quality photograph of the aircraft, taken at Ramenskoye, the Soviet air test center near Moscow, in November 1981, was published in *Aviation Week* on December 14, 1981.[34] Because it was parked next to two TU-144s, analysts were able to quickly establish its length at 166 feet. Extrapolation led specialists to estimate its probable maximum range initially at 4,535 miles. This range estimate could fall in the future, unless its engines represent a significant leap in efficiency over the NK-144s—a target that eluded Soviet technology for decades. Though its overall length was only 77 percent that of the production TU-144, its assigned maximum takeoff weight at 295 tons—49 percent more than the 144—reflected heavy ordnance and a high fuel fraction.[35]

Although the TU-160 operates primarily subsonically, some of its technology borrows from the 144. The wing-root aerodynamics seem indebted to the 144. The 160 may also employ the internal ducting and intakes of the 144. Landing gear may also be similar. Many believe its engines to be modified NK-144s. *Jane's* opines that the 160 is powered by four Koliesov turbjets, as fitted to the 144D.[36]

Recent editions of the Pentagon's *Soviet Military Power* assign impressive capabilities to the new strategic bomber. Its estimated range of 7,300 kilometers—if an accurate mirror of its capabilities—would allow it to attack the United States in two modes. It could reach any target in the United States from an Arctic base and return in a high-altitude mission. Since heavy losses would make this an expensive means of approach, the TU-160 is said to also have the capability of carrying out a low-level penetration of U.S. airspace at a speed just below the speed of sound, dash at supersonic speed and higher altitude to its target, and escape to refuel at a base in Cuba. These scenarios are based on an estimate of engine performance that should be met with some reservations, given what is known of TU-144D performance. In 1986, five "Blackjack" prototypes were undergoing flight testing; the type was projected to become operational in 1987. Over 100 "Blackjack"s were projected to be built at the new huge airframe plant at Kazan.[37]

The TU-160 was the first new Soviet strategic bomber since Myasishchev's M-50 was seen at Tushino in 1961. Its appearance in 1981 means it was designed in the mid-1970s. It is an entirely new design—unlike the TU-22 or TU-26-116—evolved from earlier designs. Like the "Backfire", it is designed for subsonic cruise and a supersonic dash to the target, but has double the "Backfire"'s weight and four engines instead of two. Its 144 sibling contributed engines, operating experience, landing gear, aerodynamic work, and possibly some electronics.

The 144 inspired another derivative. In March 1984, the International Aeronautical Federation announced that, eight months previously, Type 101, a four-engine delta design, had broken fourteen international air records on July 13 and 20, 1983.

The Soviets did not forward the customary photograph of Type 101, but its description and certification date of January 25, 1982, together with its registration number 77114, made it either the Sukhoi T-101 or one of the last 144Ds fitted with Type 57 engines, a hitherto-unknown designation for the Koliesov jets.

The TU-144, which had begun its career as a futuristic airliner emblematic of Soviet ability to excel in the civil air realm, ended in a 1930s era role, lending its technology to bombers, serving as a bomber test bed, and breaking international records, some set by its conceptual ancestor, the B-58 Hustler, twenty years before.

12
MAGNIFICENT
FAILURE:
HOW DID IT HAPPEN?

Development of tricky, unknown technology under pressure is risky enough in itself. When mandated by the authority of the highest Soviet leadership and aimed at visibly enhancing national prestige within the confines of a rigid time scale, failure is almost axiomatic.

Politicization of the Development Process

The ability of the Soviet state to summon and focus nationwide resources on a national-prestige project is at best a mixed blessing. If the project focus is off target or is not periodically corrected in the course of its long gestation, it is exceptionally difficult, if not impossible, for the authorities to admit the mistake, cut losses, and redeploy funds and resources to more realistic, effective, and pertinent ends. "Mass development" distorts resource-allocation priorities, preempts professional judgment, and sucks resources from the rest of the sector.

In the case of the TU-144, the upper Party leadership proved neither prescient, realistic, nor flexible. Its mobilization of the resources of an entire industry for a risky, glamorous project at a time of political and economic exuberance is understandable: the Kremlin was not alone among national leaderships in lavishing great treasure on an SST. But certain of its mistakes were uniquely Soviet. The inability to radically cut back the TU-144 program when it was clear that it overstretched the country's technical resources reflects the almost-irreversible momentum of mass development and the allure of the myth of technical progress. Failure to cancel the project in the mid-1970s, when the flaws were apparent to Soviet aviation experts, reflects the stagnation and myopia of Brezhnev's later years and a congenital weakness of a planned economy. It is relatively easy to launch a project that inspires the enthusiasm of the Soviet elite for "scientific and technical progress"; it is almost impossible to halt it, even when its spinoff effects are minimal.

National prestige, telescoped development timetables, and tricky, beyond state-of-the-art technology do not mix well. Earlier Soviet success with the space program was a misleading precedent, since it was completely secret and based on many years of research, experimentation, and application of better-known technology. In the Soviet SST program, the early obsession to upstage the Concorde and achieve a commercial Sputnik saw a high-pressure political timetable superimposed on a tricky, unknown technology. This undermined and distorted the development cycle. Hasty, simultaneous development of all subsystems meant their interconnections had to be continually reworked. A relatively primitive and undeveloped prototype TU-144 design was frozen in 1967 for the political purpose of beating the Concorde into the air, while research and development of more advanced variants were carried forward secretly at high speed.

This goal of being the first to launch an SST flight was achieved. But political preoccupations undercut Soviet opportunities to unscramble the mysteries of making the SST comfortable and fuel efficient. Industry-wide energies marshaled to produce a flying prototype in record speed might have been better focused on other goals: long-term research on more sophisticated aerodynamics in the wings and engine inlets; attacks on more radically intractable power, air, and fuel-flow problems in the engines; and development of a quieter and more elegant solution for cooling the kinetically heated fuselage. Taking the long view might have deprived the USSR of the short-term prestige in making the first SST flight, but a possible permanent gain might have been a more satisfactory design contributing to greater ultimate Soviet prestige.

The exertions of Soviet theoreticians, technocrats, and engineers were not equal to the conjoined challenges of national-prestige requirements and pioneering technology. The prototype represented one level of technology, the production version stood for quite another, while study of a Mach 3 Soviet SST absorbed the research institutes. The TU-144's career was characterized by fits and starts: repeated cycles of rapid development and/or production leading to bottlenecks and months of apparent stagnation. The complete redesign, the transformed production version TU-144 of 1972, was recorrected with a radically new wing in 1977 and a new engine in 1979. At least four different wing designs can be identified. Technically, too much of the TU-144 remained unresolved, in flux.

Solving technical puzzles was not helped by requirements that the Soviet SST outpoint the Concorde in specification. The Soviet production version, as its Chief Designer pointed out, was 5 percent higher, 6 percent longer, had a wingspan 13 percent wider, and a wing area 22 percent greater than its Concorde counterpart. By squeezing economy passengers into narrow, five-abreast seats, the 144 could carry 140 passengers to the Concorde's normal 128. This war of statistics could be inverted: Soviet publicity represented the prototype 144's gross weight at 142 tons at the 1972 Hannover air show versus the 173 tons of the prototype Concorde, a figure corrected by its Chief Test Pilot, Edward Elyan, to 180 tons.

Publicity imperatives defined the TU-144's life: its surprise launch at the 1965 Salon Aeronautique; its first flight made in the closing hours of 1968 to honor pledges made in Paris in mid-1965; its entry into (freight) service in the last days of 1975 to fulfill the Five-Year Plan and again preempt the Concorde's inauguration of service; the misguided attempt to inaugurate passenger service to commemorate the sixtieth anniversary of "Great October" in November 1977. Only its disasters were unscheduled.

Nontraditional Development Strategy

Much in the concept and project approach of the 144 offended the dominant folkways of the Soviet aviation establishment. Soviet research, design, and development practice is based predominantly on "design inheritance," a conservative and evolutionary approach founded on incremental improvements and marginal advances. Simplicity, communality, and inheritance of concepts and components are its hallmarks. The SST project emerged at a time when the Soviets were moving beyond this approach into more innovative, indigenous designs and bolder paralleling of Western state-of-the-art technical projects in air, space, and weapons systems.[2]

But the 144, based heavily on Western design concepts such as the delta wing, required of the Ministry of Aviation Industry too much that was new or unknown too quickly. Handbooks still guided Soviet designers both in design approaches and availability of standardized parts and subassemblies. The TU-144 literally and figuratively obliged its designers, manufacturers, and assemblers to throw the book away. Almost all its technology had to be custom built; its state-of-the-art production machinery represented either advanced semi-experimental apparatus assembled by advanced Soviet research institutes or the very latest imported from the West or Japan. Western experts visiting Voronezh were startled by the ultra-high tech mixed with the primitive and incongruous. Impressions of unique Soviet prowess in wrapping huge titanium wingskins around spars jostled with those of a forest of lathes and machine tools recalling conditions of the 1930s. The assembly line producing a passenger aircraft that could fly faster than a speeding bullet paralleled another producing an automated chicken coop. The 144 was unique.

Tupolev's guidelines, set down in the early 1930s, made provisions for "departures from departmental norms," for "crash programs" forced on the industry to combat technological stagnation. TU-144 development fits into this variant programmatic context. Although the 144 was overwhelmingly a civil aircraft, predominant military patterns within the aviation industry strongly influenced its development. Military aviation R & D emphasized the ability to rapidly modify and update designs in response to shifting tactical or strategic developments; this rapidity of response and capacity to tinker and modify characterized the 144's development. The 144's failings—excessive fuel thirst, noise, and discomfort—also reflected a design heritage dominated by combat aircraft, where these problems are perceived as unimportant. The 144's most crucial failing—a combination of insufficient range and high speed—is different. The Soviet quest for range was solved with turboprops; Mach 2 speed could be achieved by jets only in short bursts up to ninety minutes or so, before the tanks ran dry. No doubt, the Soviets have made progress on this problem since the demise of the 144. Their refusal to develop the 144D further suggests that the Soviets did not achieve the breakthrough with the Koliesov engine they had hoped for and had needed; however, reported use of this engine in their latest strategic bomber, the TU-160 "Blackjack," hints that improvement was more than marginal.

Withdrawal of the American SST from the field in 1971–73, and later growth of Anglo-French skepticism regarding the Concorde's prospects, dampened the ardor of Soviet SST advocates. There is nothing so damaging to a system informed by military analogies as voluntary or threatened strategic withdrawal of the competition. This strengthened the hand of those who argued against, or delayed by indecision, such a radical design. Increased Soviet vaunting, after the 1973 crash, of an "SST within one country" serving inland Aeroflot routes may have sincerely reflected the problem of vast distances in the USSR, for which the SST was uniquely suited. It may also have marked a tactical withdrawal and a lowering of profile of the Soviet SST project.

Two factors tempted the Soviets to bite off more than they could chew: overconfidence, bred by the rapid development and technical (if not economic) success of the TU-104 and TU-114 airliners, and the relatively inexpensive successes of the Soviet space program and first-generation supersonic fighters. But conveying over a hundred passengers in comfort, at twice the speed of sound for over two hours, involved solving a galaxy of technical problems. After sixteen years of research and eight years of test flights, the Soviets ended up with a fuel-thirsty, powerful, noisy, cramped, relatively short-range aircraft whose passenger environment was suited more to combat crews than commercial customers. Requirements for economy, quietness, and passenger comfort were never resolved and may have had a low priority. Its designers attacked the problem of claustrophobia in the passenger cabin with colors and decor, but the TU-144 still reflected decades of military predominance in aviation.

Indigestible Western Technology

The very high priority accorded SST data and technology by the KGB, GRU, and other Science and Technology collection organs during the 1960s and early 1970s resulted in reams of material and samples of equipment being delivered to the USSR, including the complete blueprints of the prototype Concorde. But émigré engineers who had worked at Tupolev KB have testified that much of the data was "unintelligible" to Soviet scientists and technicians. Information that could be deciphered often set performance standards that could not be attained with Soviet equipment and materiel. It is possible that Soviet efforts in this field were inhibited and confused by the reported success of the DST, the French security service, in coopting a Soviet science and technology collection network and feeding it doctored technical data.

Most tellingly, the Soviets proved incapable of producing in sufficient numbers the high bypass-ratio turbofan engine they desperately needed for two priority projects: their SST and their new generation of strategic bombers. This failure occurred even when Western engines, which accomplished this, were installed for analysis in their laboratories. Specifically, they could not mass produce a reliable, precision cooling system for the turbine blades. Nor could they produce turbine blades that could reliably withstand the high operating temperatures on which the higher fuel efficiency—hence, range—of jet engines depends. There is some evidence that such engines could have been produced in small quantities by the Soviets in laboratories in the 1970s, but quality control failed when an attempt was made to mass produce them. Reliability and durability of components remained a problem.

Technical secrets abstracted from the West, even when combined with the best that the resourceful Soviet science and technology establishment could serve up, did not solve the SST's trickiest technical conundrums. In 1968, electronics was said to have absorbed half the unprecedented development costs of the TU-144. It remains unclear just where the rubles went. Inadequate range could have been improved through electronic-mechanical couplings regulating the intake geometry and the engine internals, as was done with the Concorde. Rooted in Stalin's longtime proscription of cybernetics as "anti-Marxist," Soviet work in this crucial area of electronic management was left behind by Western technical advances, forcing them to approach Western suppliers several years too late, to ask for the wrong equipment, and then to have the deals blocked because of strategic considerations. The huge air-conditioners that deafened the 144's few paying passengers were necessary because the Soviets did not reproduce the Concorde's effectiveness in using its huge fuel tanks as a radiator/heat sink to cool the kinetically heated fuselage.

Design drawbacks were compounded by inept development. Soviet skill in manufacturing titanium was not followed by its successful application to the airframe. The design target was that titanium would constitute 30 percent of the 144's gross weight; in practice, it was 18 percent. The airframe crept up 50 percent in weight in the course of development. This weight creep—not unusual in aircraft development—was not matched by a commensurate increase in power from the NK-144 engines, which is abnormal. A thirty percent increase in engine power was announced by Soviet engineers in 1972, at which time they apparently threw up their hands and withdrew. Lucas engineers believe the NK-144 engine was capable of much greater power and development. Additional power was potentially on tap, but it would have eroded already-marginal NK-144 reliability and economy.

Because the weight creep was greater than the power coaxed from the engines, the actual speed and range of the TU-144 deteriorated as time went on—a case of retrograde development. The problem was not solely that the engines lagged behind Western standards of performance, but that the Soviets refused to extract maximum results from their own equipment. The Soviets, however, did move quickly to obtain aid from the West: initial Soviet approaches to Lucas for electronic engine-control equipment were made in 1972. This stillborn attempt at a legal technological transfer took three years of negotiation before it was halted. By 1977, the range and speed of the 144 had reportedly dropped to under 2,000 miles and Mach 1.8, respectively.

Lack of three-dimensional modeling computers to generate aerodynamic shapes of maximum efficiency forced the Soviets to depend on time-tested wind-tunnel and flight-testing techniques. There is often a great gulf fixed between Soviet theory and application. Their theoretical knowledge is second to none; shop-floor practice is frequently crude blacksmith work.

The most fateful stratagem of the Soviets was to attempt to join or surpass the West at the technological frontier in a project of such broad sweep that previous localized Soviet gains and successes could not be reproduced. The political program to be first in the air meant that they could not leap-frog from assimilated Western experience, as they had in the past, but were forced to attack technical puzzles simultaneously with the West. This resulted in a succession of prototypes. Fifteen years of improvisation and patchwork produced immensely improved designs, but they never closed the gap with the West or brightened the prospects of the SST concept. Ultimately, enough Soviets came to recognize the project concept as obsolete, if not intrinsically flawed.

Bureaucratic Sniping

Technical frustrations were fueled by bureaucratic frictions among Soviet institutions. Civil air development is shared by the Ministry of Aviation Production (MAP) and the Ministry of Civil Aviation (MCA), with the respective spheres of responsibility remaining unclear, possibly even to the Soviets themselves.

Responsibility for certification of aircraft types shifted in 1977—following the Western model—from the Design Bureaus to the Ministry of Civil Aviation, shortly after the death in office of long-serving MAP Chief Dementiev. This was a strategic defeat for the MAP, a significant turning point in these subterranean struggles in the era of Brezhnevian immobility and stagnation. This event occurred just before the TU-144's own certification and is doubtless related to its protracted travails.

Professional jealousies played no small role in the 144's gestation. Tupolev KB was resented by other design bureaus. They were forced to revert to 1930s-style, largely unacknowledged support roles for the premier design bureau, which they perceived as receiving the lion's share of credit, support, cash, and personnel. While the SST project was going well, Tupolev KB basked in the credit for work performed by the entire aviation industry. As it soured, the Tupolev Design Bureau escaped criticism, it was felt, because the program suffered through interventions in detail by the Supreme Soviet. Resentments festered within Tupolev, styled the "Fathers and Sons" KB by junior designers, because only relatives and well-connected protégés remained at Tupolev after their internship.

Reckoning the Cost

How much did the Soviet SST project cost? What was spent to bring Aeroflot's fallible flagship into service? It is questionable whether precise Soviet data exists to answer these questions authoritatively. If it does, it's not accessible. Even if we had access to the Soviet figures, they might still be difficult to work from. Soviet accounting tends to emphasize labor input more than cost, and TU-144 costs were spread across at least two ministries, various design bureaus, and scores of institutes. As the Chief Designer once stated, "Money is not the problem." There were no budgetary constraints we know of, only technical barriers. Soviet literature made few references to TU-144 finances, except that half of the prototype's development costs had been absorbed by electronics, and that the earliest cost projections were set at three times the rate for the IL-86, then the most expensive of Soviet airliners. In the early 1970s, $30 to $45 million was mentioned as a possible export price range for one TU-144.

Concorde cost overruns became a major political football in Britain and France, after they were revealed by the incoming Labour government late in 1964. French critics termed the Concorde the Fifth Republic's "most expensive hobby." In contrast, the thousands of words dedicated to the 144 in the USSR contained almost no references to financing or expenditure, a reminder that Soviet political leaders were not dependent upon any constituency or economic considerations for resource allocation decisions. Nevertheless, there is a Soviet literary-political convention whereby such issues can be addressed indirectly. By discussing the Concorde project, issues of cost-effectiveness, high fuel consumption, environmental impact, and resource allocation could be raised by Soviet analysts. No Soviet secrets would be revealed by studying Western parallels and no bureaucratic ox would be gored. Soviet specialists, scanning the Soviet writing regarding Western SSTs, would have been alert to oblique references to TU-144 troubles.

Some approximation of TU-144 costs can be reconstructed through parallels to Western projects. The American SST project absorbed about $1 billion by the time it was canceled in 1971, leaving behind a mockup and two partially assembled airframes. Boeing developed three subtypes, including an overambitious swing-wing design that eventually had to be abandoned. Concorde R & D costs approached $2.5 billion, and *Interavia* projected Anglo-French total expenditure on the project through 1982 at $4.32 billion.

An estimate of TU-144 production costs can be made. The second production version of the 144 which crashed at Paris in 1973, was insured for 15 million pounds sterling, or $37.5 million at then-prevailing rates of exchange. This can serve as a benchmark per-unit cost. The production version of the 144 was said to cost 70 percent as much as the prototypes,[3] so the cost of the two prototypes comes to $107 million in 1973 dollars. If we assume that TU-144 production costs echo the 5 percent annual inflation ascribed to leading-edge Soviet military hardware, the cost of the eleven production versions of the 144, when spread out at the rate of three in 1973 and two per year through 1977, works out to $452 million. Production costs for four 144Ds, given a 25 percent surcharge for a new wing and new engines and the same inflation surcharge, totals $258 million. Following this model, production costs for seventeen TU-144s come to $711 million.

The Concorde R & D figure of $2.5 billion is probably useful as an analogue for 144 expenditure. Production costs added on bring the total spending to $3.2 billion. This is a conservative figure considering that the 144 underwent more radical redesign than the Concorde and had a second complete engine redesign. It is likely that total cost may have soared to $4 billion. The total-cost problem is compounded by the issue of the 144's second engine: should it be charged off to the 144, for which it was originally designed in the early 1970s, or to the TU-160 "Blackjack", which ultimately became its definitive application?

If we accept $4 billion as an approximation of the TU-144 cost, how big an impact did this have in the Soviet context? This figure represents only a very small percentage of the annual Soviet defense budget. In the context of hard-currency foreign trade, it is slightly more than annual Soviet natural-gas export earnings from 1981 to 1985, and below the $4.5 billion and $4.85 billion spent by the USSR on grain imports in 1980 and 1983.[4]

If TU-144 cost is relatively insignificant in the context of the total Soviet economy, it looms larger within the aviation sector. The Soviet SST was certainly the most elaborate and ambitious civil aircraft ever developed by the Soviets. The major technical advances it embodied and its protracted development were both greater than any known military aircraft, whose technical advances based on borrowings from previous experience are generally more incremental. So it is by far the most expensive Soviet aircraft ever produced.

The Anglo-French Concorde consortium obtained, for the same amount of money, a more commercially successful aircraft that ultimately flew about eight different international routes. But the revised operating economics that followed a second lurch upward in fuel prices in 1979–80 turned most of these routes into a financial drain. By the end of 1980, Concordes had incurred a cumulative $200 million operating loss, which in some years canceled out the profits earned by the less exotic aircraft of the French and British national air carriers.[5]

Concorde production ended in 1979, just as fuel prices rose for the second time. Soviet writers replayed Western analyses that the Concorde was three times more fuel intensive in seat-miles per gallon than the benchmark Boeing 747. They could not refer to the fact that excessive fuel thirst limited the TU-144 to an effective range of only about 2,200 miles, but they could hope their readers realized that the 144 was almost twice as thirsty as the Concorde. Comparing range with maximum fuel carried, the 144 required 100.16 pounds of fuel per mile flown versus 54.13 pounds for the Concorde.[6] The less the 144 flew, the more the Soviet economy benefited. Figures for the promising 144D are not available, but since it was never launched into service as promised, its vaunted 50 percent improvement in fuel efficiency apparently was not enough to overcome the doubts of Aeroflot.

Possibly the TU-160 "Blackjack" was given first call on the Koliesov engines.

The impenetrable thicket of Soviet statistics, sometimes suspect and then designed to defeat a strategic review of any program, would halt any cost-benefit analyst in his tracks. But a general balance of 144 benefits and debits can be attempted. The Soviets gained a useful instrument of national prestige, set a number of records, and serendipitously picked up useful support for a new generation of supersonic aircraft, particularly in the area of aerodynamics and powerplants.

Indirect costs are more difficult to measure. Energies and resources were siphoned from projects that more realistically answered Soviet needs, particularly the Soviet Airbus, the IL-86, which was never provided with adequate power. Given the generally backward state of Soviet jet engines, development of a afterburner turbofan was an expensive diversion. The 1975–85 decade is notable for stagnation in Soviet civil-air design; the 144 surely accounted for much of this and Brezhnev's redirection of resources into a new generation of weapons took up what slack remained. Tupolev's loss of leadership in civil-airliner design might not have occurred had the 144 project been curtailed in the mid-1970s. Western analysts believe that the Concorde will remain a "sterile" mutant without direct descendants; the same fate seems likely for its Soviet cousin.

In the End a New Beginning?

In 1983–84, as medium-level Soviet officials offhandedly indicated that the Soviet SST project had been ended, stirrings in Western high-tech circles indicated planning activity for a second-generation SST—one that would achieve speeds of Mach 4 to 25 in orbit.

President Reagan kicked off this boom in his State of the Union message in late January 1986, by referring to an "Orient Express" airliner that would reach Tokyo from Washington in two hours. This reference, and the commitment of $450 million of

Federal research to explore its technical possibilities, inspired a wave of speculation by advocates in the press. The HST, or hypersonic transport, is conceptually an extension of the SST. But instead of attaining Mach 2 or 3, its speed range is projected at Mach 5 to 25, from about 4,000 to 17,000 mph, requiring quite different technology.

As with the SST concept a generation before, enthusiasts were not slow to outline the possibilities inherent in these performance levels. Washington to Los Angeles, for instance, could be spanned in thirty-three minutes and Tokyo reached in two hours. This idea was driven by new advances in technology and the faith that faster, more flexible craft were needed for a variety of civil and military applications. Aerospace planners were captivated by the recent fact that trade flows from the United States across the Pacific now surpassed those across the Atlantic, hence the HST airliner was dubbed the "Orient Express." A former X-15 test pilot observed that all current aircraft had in fact been conceived and designed in the 1950s. A presidential blue ribbon panel in the spring of 1985 had recommended that HST research be made a top priority. The Reagan administration was seeking $600 million for HST research for fiscal years 1986–89 and was projecting an expenditure of untold billions that would be "required" through 1995. The research would first benefit a successor to the space shuttle; the commercial HST would become available sometime after the year 2000.[7]

An informed skepticism leads one to wonder whether a commercial market exists for HST airliners. Certainly, the history of Concorde operations has provided a chilling precedent. Six Concorde routes were axed in 1979–84: British Airways to Bahrain and Singapore; Air France to Rio de Janeiro, Caracas, Mexico City, Washington, and Dallas. By 1984, Air France had pruned back Concorde flights to the single, operationally profitable route to New York. But British Airways gave the Concorde a new lease on life by ingeniously repackaging it as a high-tech recreational vehicle. Millionaires could charter the Concorde to provide their friends with a supersonic experience. Special flights were also profitable: by 1984, British Airways had carried out 130 one-way Concorde flights, in which the return was a cruise on the *Queen Elizabeth II*. Special-event charters were also profitable for British airways. By late 1986, the airline was offering a one-time-only chance to fly the Concorde from London to Moscow to attend the Bolshoi Ballet—through Soviet airspace once rigorously closed to foreign SSTs—an event reflecting how little official Soviet interest remained in SSTs.[8] The Concorde is ending its days as a curiosity.

Economic analysis undermined HST passenger prospects. In 1980, the U.S. Office of Technology Assessment (OTA), reviving SST issues after a decade of quiescence, asked Congress to increase fivefold NASA's funding for second-generation SST research. The purpose was to "maintain the SST option," arguing that otherwise America would miss out on a projected $50 billion in sales in the super-SST market of the 1990–2010 period. OTA's own arguments, however, suggested this market might be but a mythical kingdom. Their figures painted a bleak future for the SST, which used 50 to 100 percent more fuel on a seat-mile basis than any other commercial aircraft. A second-generation SST would cost an estimated $1.25 million each in 1979 dollars versus $80 million for the existing Concorde. No private corporation could raise the $6 to $10 billion required to fund its R & D, so government guarantees, if not participation, were mandatory.[9] This was the quandary that helped kill the original American SST in 1971–73: not enough citizens actively wanted it, a vociferous minority despised it, and it had insufficient perceived defense implications to attract the military-industrial constituency.

Despite the unpromising experience of the Concorde and the American SST, President Reagan's call for an HST was echoed by technocrats in ways recalling the SST boomlet of 1955–63. Ironically, in view of Air France's dismal experience with the Concorde, Aerospatiale became an early and prominent publicist for a second-generation SST and the HST. Within days, Aerospatiale dusted off old research studies for a "Son of Concorde" that closely resembled the Mach 3 SST concept developed by Boeing in 1967–71 and researched by the Soviets well into the early

1980s. "Son of Concorde" would attain 1,700 mph versus the 1,350 mph of the Concorde and carry 200 to 300 passengers up to 5,000 miles. Aerospatiale noted it had extensive experience designing a second-generation SST and was looking for partners.[10]

Slightly over a year later, Aerospatiale considerably updated and revised its act. Under the headline "Paris–New York: One Hour," the French press carried renderings of an Aerospatiale HST nestling down to a landing, the twin towers of the World Trade Center and the impressive architecture of lower Manhattan as a backdrop. This completely new French HST, it was stressed, had nothing in common with the Concorde or with "Son of Concorde."

It was revealed that thirty Aerospatiale engineers had toiled for the last two years on this HST concept, shortly to be announced at the 1987 Salon Aeronautique. Its speed was 3,800 mph, Mach 5, at the low end of the HST range. It would appear in the twenty-first century as the equivalent of the U.S. "Orient Express," on which research had already started. Its design goals included: weighing twice as much as the Concorde (300 tons) and carrying 20 percent more passengers (150) at 80 to 98,000 feet up to 7,200 miles. This performance implied the solution of a number of technical problems—cooling down the kinetically heated fuselage skin from 600° C, for example.

But the engines, as with the SST, represented the greatest challenge. Such a craft, it was calculated, would require 120 tons of thrust. The best commercially available 1987 engines delivered 15 tons each. Aerospatiale believed that power might be doubled so that four engines of 30 tons thrust each could be employed; if not, six of 20 tons would do.[11]

Engine power, as with the SST, remains the greatest barrier to HST realization. A research engineer speaking to an audience of specialists at the Smithsonian's National Air and Space Museum in early 1987 revealed that the ramjet required for the HST had not yet delivered a positive power flow—that is, generated more power than that fed into it under laboratory conditions to keep it running.

But the new factor in the equation is that there is a first-rank military-strategic application for HST technology. Unlike the SST agitation of 1955–63, which it superficially resembles, HST agitation in fact covers two different aircraft for two different constituencies. The more remote of these in terms of economic viability and eventual certification is the HST airliner. An expert has noted that a two-hour trip from the eastern United States to Tokyo sounds wonderful until one realizes this requires either embarking or arriving at a most uncivilized hour.[12]

What endows the HST movement with more than a moderate chance of success is its potential as a cheap and reliable alternative to the Shuttle and SR-71. There are many friends out there for a Mach 5 to 25 orbital craft that can land on runways, ferry repair materials up to satellites, make SDI seem more plausible, carry out photographic reconnaissance, act as a rescue vehicle, and, on occasion, serve as an ultra-high-speed airliner. The *Challenger* tragedy, and the recently demonstrated unreliability of other orbital vehicles, appears to underscore the need for a more reliable, safe, shallow space vehicle.

Aerospatiale pinpoints the need for a second-generation space vehicle as the prime mission for an HST. Added to this list, however, are reasons that apply exclusively to an HST commercial airliner: the recent impressive growth in long-range airline routes between Europe and the United States to the Far East, and calculations indicating that, at Mach 5, distance versus fuel consumption is twice that of the Concorde and approaches that of the Boeing 747. The HST airliner that would follow the orbiter would be characterized by technology quite different from the Concorde. Its aerodynamics are different, for example. As speeds rise, the optimum aerodynamic shape more resembles a wedge. Titanium-based sandwiches and composite materials would predominate, while high-temperature motors would feature ceramic components in their combustion sections. These ramjet engines would operate aerodynamically interactively with the fuselage.[13]

What are the Soviets to make of the HST phenomenon? Will history repeat itself? Soviet observers are certainly following the

HST closely. There is concrete evidence that the Soviet research establishment is devoting much effort to HSTs. At the 1981 Paris air show, the Soviet pavilion included a scale model of an HST that emphasized its civilian aspect as a followup to the TU-144. Its wings, in fact, appeared to be identical to the last (1977) 144 wing design—the most aerodynamically sophisticated portion of the 144 but one suited for speeds only up to Mach 2.3, not the Mach 5 to 25 to be attained by the HST. This 1981 model was most likely a conversation piece, a rehash of the Mach 3 studies carried on in the 1960s rather than a new HST design proposal. Soviets at the stand described it as a hydrogen-powered craft that would appear in the twenty-first century. Its four engines stood away from the fuselage and wing surfaces, not like the ramjets of American HST proposals, which feature interactive inlets and fuselage surfaces à la Concorde and TU-144.[14]

Soviet specialized periodicals attest to continuing interest in ultra-high-speed flight and trans-orbital craft. The Soviet reproduction of the U.S. Space Shuttle, which appears nearly identical with the exception of the larger boosters required, is well known. Early in 1987, the *Financial Times* of London reported that there was a second Soviet shuttle design, which may be an HST. Past patterns decree that the Soviets will develop an HST orbital vehicle in parallel with the West, and that it will appear in the 1990s.

The Soviets have abandoned their long studies of a Mach 3 SST, though their research will feed other defense projects. Soviet moves in the direction of a Mach 3 SST are even less likely than a revival of the TU-144. Aerospatiale publicity was probably developed to smoke out a consortium partner to fund the project and develop the engines. But the Concorde debacle overshadows any Western discussion of ultra-fast commercial air transport. With the Soviets having so recently and belatedly buried the TU-144, it is hard to see SST enthusiasm reviving outside a small, rabid coterie of engineer enthusiasts.

The topmost echelons of a new Soviet regime committed to rationality, reconstruction, effectiveness, efficiency, and Leninist populism are likely to regard ambitious civil science and technological projects with well-founded skepticism. More than two years after Aeroflot offhandedly announced the demise of the TU-144 to a group of Western reporters, the Soviet press was still receiving letters from Soviet citizens asking why the TU-144 was no longer flying. In December 1986, *Argumenty i Fakty*, a weekly provided to Party activists to spread the Party line, referred to three of these letters. The answers were an interesting test case for *Glasnost* and represent the Party line.

Argumenty i Fakty's reponse ignored the TU-144's brief period of commercial service. Instead, it noted that a "number of causes"—unidentified and unexpanded—to abandon the TU-144 had surfaced in the course of large amounts of research, flight-testing, and experimental operations. The two main reasons given for TU-144 cancellation figured only peripherally in the nineteen years of its public career. The first was "environmental protection, in particular sonic shock waves." This argument against SSTs in general, and the 144 in particular, had been ridiculed regularly or ignored in the Soviet press. "Sonic boom" was introduced to be dismissed by the observation that the 144 flew, and would fly supersonically only over sparsely settled regions. Soviet scientists argued moreover, correctly, that the SST sonic boom phenomenon had been exaggerated. The second explanation, much closer to the mark, was that the TU-144's "proportionate fuel consumption is several times that of modern subsonic aircraft."[15] This more significant, truthful reason surfaced only at the very end of the 144's career. These two "answers" are likely to be enshrined as the official Soviet explanation for the 144's failure.

In late spring of 1988, five years after the demise of the TU-144, the SST theme resurfaced in the Soviet media. Even in an era of cost-efficiency and rhetorical new departures, the idea had not lost its allure. The Soviet tradition of following Western research and speculation was revived in "two hours to Tokyo" rhetoric and forecasts of speeds at five to thirty times the speed of sound. But in the West, the latest research from Boeing and

McDonnell Douglas indicated that 1,200 to 1,900 mph was a much more realistic goal. They concluded that productivity would come by doubling the range to 5,000 to 6,000 miles and trebling the passenger load of the Concorde and TU-144. Western analysis concluded that there was no commercial payoff in going any faster than Mach 2.4.[16]

The Soviets had reached some of the same conclusions. Academician Georgiy Svichev, director of TsAGI, told TASS that a model was being evaluated that was capable of flying 300 passengers from Moscow to Tokyo in less than two hours. It would feature variable-sweep wings, like the Boeing SST of the late 1960s. Power would be provided by "a compound engine using cryogenic fuel." Power required for hypersonic speeds would come from a multinozzle ramjet underneath the fuselage, as in the earliest TU-144 designs. A "semi-rocket shape" was required for speeds five to six times the speed of sound. Its fuselage, just over thirteen feet in diameter, would be elongated to dampen sonic boom, to over 100 meters, or 329 feet—long enough to put pressure on existing airport facilities.[17]

Tupolev KB was projected to be the future builder of a 300-passenger Mach 5 to 6 airliner, expected to begin flight-tests in 1999—another arbitrary deadline with political overtones. This aircraft would depend on new fuels. Alexei Tupolev had, in April, flown the world's first hydrogen-powered airliner, a modified TU-154. Interviewed by the Soviet press, he emphasized that Kuznetsov had been developing hydrogen engines for the last nine years. The fuel was cryogenic: liquid hydrogen frozen in a vacuum bottlelike tank at minus 253°. Hydrogen is the cleanest fuel available from an environmental viewpoint, but its extreme flammability had been dramatized in the *Hindenburg* disaster. Tupolev was also evaluating liquefied natural gas, more readily available and easier to work with. Tupolev predicted that regular flights with cryogenic fuels might take place within a few years, possibly with the TU-204 and TU-154M airliners. Eventually, Tupolev would design a new airliner exclusively around cryogenic fuels.[18]

It took Soviet ruling circles several years to develop enthusiasm for the SST, many years more to recognize its shortcomings, and several years more—only after Andropov had succeeded Brezhnev—to cancel it. The resurfacing of another SST project in the Gorbachev era, which could again suck up scarce funds for limited gains, shows how seductive are power and speed for the Soviet imagination. An ultra-fast passenger airliner still has its Soviet patrons, but its applicability as a cheap space shuttle will garner the support of the Soviet military and improve its prospects.

The Soviet apparatus is slow to cut losses and acknowledges mistaken strategic decisions rarely, sometimes only twenty to thirty years after the fact. If there is again to be a Soviet SST project, it will mean that Marxist historicism has not improved the Soviet decision-makers' ability to learn from mistakes. SST themes, recast in the mold of the HST, will doubtless continue to reappear in the Soviet media. But Soviet funds will tend to concentrate on the strategically oriented HST space shuttle. Unless the experience of the past is overcome and Soviet technical resources can be marshaled to defeat a further series of unprecedented problems with fuel, ultra high speeds, and materials, an HST airliner will represent a triumph of ambitious vision over bitter experience.

In Book Ten of *The Republic*, Plato observes, "if I were to capture the heart of a people, I would ask to write, not its laws, but its fables." If there is a moral to the TU-144 story, it is distilled in the Russian fairy tale of the Firebird. The young Czarevich becomes intoxicated, with a bewitching, lissome birdlike creature he sees dancing alone in the wilderness. He launches various stratagems to learns her secrets, but the Firebird always dances away out of reach. The Czarevich retains only a tantalizing tuft of her golden plumage. The Firebird escapes with her elusive mysteries intact, after stealing the golden apples that provide the sustenance of the Russian realm.

This Soviet high-level HST discussion precipitated revelations regarding the Soviet SST technopolitical debate. On October 1,

1988, *Red Star,* the Soviet military's weekly, published a retrospective critique of the TU-144 by Yuri Mamsurov, retired Colonel General of Aviation. He confirmed Myasishchev's hitherto unacknowledged pioneer SST work, praising his "thorough analysis as far back as the 1950," before his OKB was obliterated by Krushchev. Myasishchev's engineering teams had attacked problems related to aerodynamics, technologies, and the manufacture of engines and navigation instruments. Myasishchev had focused early on the Soviet SST's Achilles' heel: fuel efficiency. His theoretical studies established that a long-range Mach 1.8–2 SST was "inconceivable" without engines of a certain size and thrust, with "fuel consumption under cruise conditions of no more than 1.16 kilograms of thrust per hour." Myasishchev established the theoretical feasibility of a 100-seat SST with 7000-km. (4340 mi.) range.

The General revealed that unspecified "departmental barriers" impeded the solution of Soviet SST problems during its abortive 1977–1978 service career. "Aeroflot's management evaluated the aircraft's operation soberly . . . design refinements related to increased flight safety were required." Then as now, as the USSR debated an HST, economics should be primary. Complex, expensive aircraft should pay for themselves. The critical question for SST and HST alike: Does Aeroflot need it?

The sensitive issue as to why the Soviet SST failed was gingerly introduced; the Soviet establishment had not achieved unanimity on this point. Some cited "design errors," others the 1973 crash, others "unprofitability." "Our SST did not blend with demands previously considered unimportant regarding cost and reserves of fuel as well as environmental protection." How torturous was the path to scientific truth! The SST experience embodied valuable lessons useful for a new Soviet "approach to the solution of scientific and technical problems," which "should quickly be exploited to the maximum extent" in the context of *Perestroika,* the general restructuring of Soviet industry and production underway, because SST "materials and engineering solutions," if not economics, proved themselves operationally.

The "sad fate" of the "approximately dozen and a half" TU-144s produced was affecting: some were in aviation museums, one was being used "as a laboratory," and the rest were stored at an airport outside Moscow. Mamsurov concluded, "It looks as though they will never again get into the sky. . . . These aircraft resembling huge eagles turned out to be beyond the pale of our aviation life."[19]

APPENDIX:
TU-144 Production

Prototypes

68001. Original prototype, first flown December 31, 1968; shown at Shermetyevo May 1969, Paris 1971, Hannover May 1972. A well-worn prototype; two engines stopped on the way home from Paris, June 1971.

68002. No pictures found, but Gunston says two aircraft originally commissioned in 1963 and probably first flown 1971(?). Recurring rumors of one prototype heavily damaged with landing gear going up through wing from early 1969 on. Curious that Soviets would fly only one prototype from late 1968 to mid-1972, while usual Tupolev practice involved three to four and Concorde had two to three. Was it repainted with number 68001 for crash insurance?

68003. Static testing?

Production

77101. First (pre) production, used in late 1972 for publicity and as scene of April 1973 press conference.

77102. Flown to, and destroyed at, Paris air show, May–June 1973.

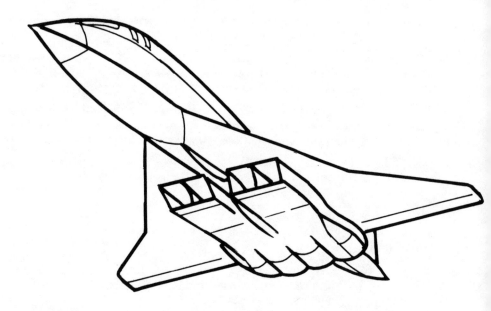

June 1965: The TU-144 scale model as first seen at Paris air show. Flat-bottomed fuselage and engine nacelles on center line were soon abandoned. Fuselage is double oval in cross section, and shallow S (ogival) leading edge to main wing.

June 1967: Second scale model. Engines moved back into two semiseparate nacelles, with four square inlets. Wing now double delta; fuselage retains semiflat floor.

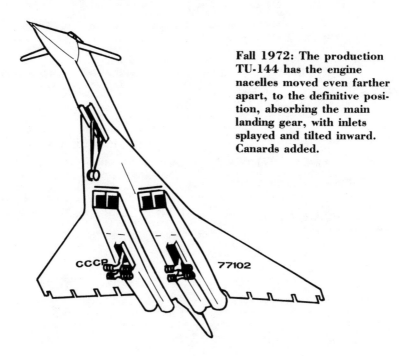

December 1968: Two steps backward, one step forward. Engine nacelles now fully separated, with rectangular inlets now angled and more pronounced splitter plate on center line. The landing gear is now slightly outboard of the engines, retracting into the wing and eating up fuel-storage space. This full-size aircraft of 1968 employs the 1965 wing, not the improved double delta shown in scale in 1967.

Fall 1972: The production TU-144 has the engine nacelles moved even farther apart, to the definitive position, absorbing the main landing gear, with inlets splayed and tilted inward. Canards added.

77103. Used in Soviet publicity. Visit of U.S. journalists to factory show; five in assembly June 1973, presumably 77103,4,5,6,7.

77104.

77105. At Domodedevo, 1978.

77106. Believed used in early route-testing; flown into Soviet A.F. Museum at Monino, 1980. First SST to land on dirt runway.

77107. At Domodedevo, 1978.

77108. At Domodedevo, 1978.

77109. Used to inaugurate passenger service from Moscow to Alma-Ata, November 1977.

77110. Shown at Paris, 1977.

77144. This believed to be generic registration number to disguise extent of total production, shown at Paris, 1975; in *Parade* magazine, 1976.

77114. Used as registration number for "Aircraft 101," to establish international speed and distance records, July 1983. Possibly Sukhoi T-101.

Three to four possible 144Ds, registrations unknown. Registrations known are 77101 and 77114, plus two prototypes, signifying seventeen completed aircraft.

Krasnaya Zvesda, October 1, 1988, states, "about a dozen and a half"

NOTES

CHAPTER I

1. Michael Gladych, "Andrei Tupolev." *Air Force Magazine,* July 1958, 40.
2. *FBIS Daily Report,* Supplement 15 January 1960. Also Supreme Soviet, 11 January 1960.
3. Bill Gunston, *Aircraft of the Soviet Union* (London: Osprey, 1983), 305. Also John Erickson, *The Soviet High Command: A Military-Political History 1918–1941* (Boulder: Westview, 1984), 408–409.
4. Gladych, 40, 42.
5. K. E. Bailes, "Technology and Legitimacy: Soviet Aviation and Stalinism in the 1930s," *Technology and Culture,* January 1976, 55–81.
6. Charaguine [Gregoriy Ozerov], *En prison avec Tupolev* (Paris: Albin Michel, 1973), 76–77.
7. Ibid., 78.
8. Ibid., 79–81.
9. Ibid., 83.
10. A. S. Yakolev, *Fifty Years of Soviet Aircraft Design* (Jerusalem: Israel Program for Scientific Translations, 1970), 8.
11. Alexander Boyd, *The Soviet Air Force Since 1918* (New York: Stein and Day, 1977) 61–62.

NOTES

12. Nikita Khrushchev, *Khrushchev Remembers: The Last Testament* (Boston: Little, Brown, 1974) 38. Also Gunston, 300; Fruma Genevsky, an eyewitness. Interview with author, July 1986.
13. Gunston, 305.
14. Ibid.
15. Enzo Angelucci, *World Encyclopedia of Civil Aircraft* (New York: Crown, 1982), 141, 143, 155, 167.
16. Gunston, 303.
17. Bailes, 67, citing *Industria* 21 June 1937.
18. Gunston, 168.
19. Leon Volkov, "Tupolev, Red Bomber Designer, a Traitor . . . and a Hero." *Newsweek*, 23 August 1954, 32.
20. Gladych, 42; David Gai. "Performance of Duty." *Moscow News*, 48-1987, 13.
21. Gunston, 313.
22. Ozerov, 65.
23. Gunston, 315; Robert Conquest, *The Great Purge.* (New York: Macmillan, 1968), 331.
24. Gladych, 42.
25. Yakolev, 52.
26. Gladych, 42.
27. Khrushchev, *Testament*, 158. Also Ozerov, 86–88; David Gai, "Performance of Duty." *Moscow News* 48 (1987), 13.
28. Gunston, 322–23. Also W. T. Lee and R. F. Starr, *Soviet Military Policy Since World War Two.* (Stanford: Hoover Institution, 1986), 12, 14, 220.
29. Ibid., Lt. Col. Howard R. Jarrell, "The Man Who Gave Ivan the Bird." *Air Force Magazine*, February 1957, 102–109. Also William Green, "The Brick Bomber." *Air Pictorial*, July–September 1971.
30. Gunston, 323.
31. Ibid., 324.
32. Boyd, 215–16. Alternately, Vasily Stalin is said to have ordered this.
33. Ibid.
34. Werner Keller, *Are The Russians Ten Feet Tall?* (London: Thames and Hudson, 1961), 348–50.
35. *New York Times*, 28, 29 June 1959, 1.

36. John W. R. Taylor, ed., *Jane's All The World's Aircraft, 1960–61*. (London: Jane's, 1960), 221. Also Gunston, 339; *Aviation Week*, 6 July 1959, 38.
37. Nikita Khrushchev, *Khrushchev Remembers* (Boston: Little, Brown, 1970), 120.
38. Vaclav Nemeček, *The History of the Soviet Aircraft Industry From 1918*. (London: Willow, 1986), 2xx.
39. Boyd, 226.
40. *FBIS Daily Report*, supplement, 15 January 1960.
41. Gunston, 336.
42. Nemeček, 107.
43. *Aviation Week*, 3 August 1959, 40.
44. Gunston, 337. Also *Aviation Week*, 20, 27 July 1959.
45. *Khrushchev Remembers*, 406.
46. *Aviation Week*, 3 August 1959, 40.
47. Gunston, p. 336.
48. *Aviation Week*, 9, 16 July 1956.
49. Ibid., 6 July 1959, 19.
50. Ibid., 27 July 1959.
51. Washington *Evening Star*, 23 March 1956.
52. *New York Times*, 23 March 1956, 1.
53. *Evening Star*, 23 March 1956.
54. *New York Times*, 23 March 1956.
55. *Aviation Week*, 2 April 1956, 38–39.
56. *New York Herald Tribune*, 26 March 1956.
57. *London Times*, 17 April 1956, 16.
58. Ibid., 24 April 1956.
59. Gladych, 40.
60. *Aviation Week*, 2 September 1957, 40.
61. Ibid., 2, 9, 30 September 1957.
62. *New York Times*, 28, 29 June 1959, 1.
63. *Aviation Week*, 6, 9, 13, 20 July 1959.

CHAPTER 2

1. Gunston, 346.
2. Boyd, 223.
3. *Jane's 1985–86*, 248.

4. John Ranelagh, *The Agency: The Rise and Decline of the CIA* (New York: Simon & Schuster, 1986), 173.
5. Khrushchev, *Testament*, 39.
6. *Jane's, 1976–77*, 431; Boyd, 223–34.
7. *Air Pictorial*, October 1971, 265.
8. Vladimir Bogdanov, *The US War Machine and Politics* (Moscow: Progress, 1986), 259.
9. *Air Pictorial*, October 1971, 210; *Jane's 1960–61*, 219.
10. Gunston, 210; *Supersonic Air Transports. Hearings before the Special Investigating Subcommittee of the Committee on Science and Astronautics. U.S. House of Representatives.* May 17 1960, 126–132.
11. *Jane's 1961–62*, 229.
12. Colin Munro, *Soviet Air Forces.* (New York: Crown, 1972), 96.
13. *Aviation Week*, 31 July 1965, 36.
14. *Jane's 1964–65*, 324.
15. Boyd, 223.
16. R. B. Maloy, *History of the Supersonic Transport Program—International* Federal Aviation Administration, 11 August 1966.
17. J. S. Butz, "Those Jolly Red Giants." *Air Force Magazine*, November 1968, 65.
18. Karl-Heinz Eyermann, *Lufttransport: Spiegelbild der Luftmacht* (East Berlin: Deutscher Militarverlag, 1967), 382, 378.
19. *Aviation Week*, 1 June 1959, 52.
20. *FBIS Daily Report Supplement:* Material from Supreme Soviet Session, January 1960, 2–3.
21. Arcady Genevsky. Interview with author, August 1986.
22. *Aviation Week*, 17 July 1961, 3.
23. Najeeb Halaby, "Will Russia win the SST Race?" *Look*, 7 February 1967, 72–77. Also, Bill Gunston. Interview with author, 11 December 1986.
24. *Aviation Week*, 31 July 1961.
25. *New York Times*, 5 April 1962, 66.
26. *Aviation Week*, 31 July 1961.
27. *New York Times*, 5 April 1962, 66.
28. *New York Times*, 17 May 1963, 66.
29. Najeeb Halaby, *Crosswinds* (New York: Doubleday, 1978), 183, 193.

30. Ibid., 199.
31. Ibid., 200.
32. Ibid., 206. Also, Najeeb Halaby. Interview with author, 22 January 1987.
33. Arcady Genevsky. Interview, August 1986. Also, *London Times*, 7 June 1963, 12.
34. *New York Times*, 7 November 1963, 7.
35. Halaby, *Crosswinds*, 168.
36. Geoffrey Knight, *Concorde: The Inside Story* (New York: Stein & Day, 1976), 88.
37. *New York Times*, 8 July 1964, 70.
38. London *Times*, 10 December 1964, 10.; 8 July 1964, 70.; 10 November 1964, 12.
39. *New York Times*, 23 February 1965, 65.
40. *Jane's, 1967–68*, 168–69; *1968–69*, 182.
41. Bill Yenne, *History of the U.S. Air Force* (London: Exeter, 1984), 161. TU-22: Paolo Matricardi, *The Concise History of Aviation* (New York: Crescent, 1985), 229.
42. *Aviation Week*, 12 June 1961, 28–30.
43. Robert Wall, *Airliners* (London: Quarto, 1980) 240.
44. Gunston, 16–18.
45. Ibid., 27, 122.
46. *Krasnaya Zvesda*, 3 January 1969, 1.
47. David Gai, *Nebesnoe Pritcheniye* (Moscow: Moskovski Rabochi, 1984), 180.
48. Ibid.
49. A. S. Yakovlev, "Aircraft Building." In *Razvitie Aviatsionnoy Nauki i Tekniki v SSSR* (Moscow: Nauka, 1980), 91, 96.
50. Gai, *Nebesnoe*, 180.
51. *Jane's 1964–65*, 324.
52. Ozerov, *En prison avec Tupolev*, 31–32.
53. Khrushchev, *Testament*, 39.
54. Ibid., 42.
55. *Khrushchev Remembers*, 395.
56. Khrushchev, *Testament*, 376.
57. Ibid.
58. Ibid., 41–42.
59. Ibid.

60. Leonid Brezhnev, *Vospominaniya* (Moscow: Politizdat, 1981), 16.
61. *Great Soviet Encyclopedia*, translation of Third Edition (New York: Macmillan, 1981), 31, 594.
62. Leonid Brezhnev, *Pages from his Life* (New York: Simon & Schuster, 1978), 149.
63. J. Dornberg, *Brezhnev: The Masks of Power* (New York: Basic Books, 1974), 286–7, 291.

CHAPTER 3

1. *Flight International*, 24 June 1965, 1000–1003.
2. London *Times*, 15 June 1965, 10.
3. John Costello and Terry Hughes, *Concorde: The International Race for a Supersonic Passenger Transport* (London: Angus and Robertson, 1976), 108–111.
4. Proceedings, U.S. Senate, 9 August 1964, 17865–73.
5. *New York Times*, 16 October 1966, 16.
6. Ibid., 4 December 1966, 10.
7. Mel Horwitch, *Clipped Wings: The American SST Conflict* (Cambridge: MIT, 1982), 209–10.
8. *New York Times*, 30 January 1967, 5; 7 March 1967, 81; 19 April 1967.
9. Halaby, *Look*, 7 February 1967, 72–77.
10. Ibid.
11. *Flight International*, June 1967.
12. Costello & Hughes, *Concorde*, 153.
13. Kenneth Owen, *Concorde: New Shape in the Sky* (London: Jane's, 1982), 156.
14. *Jane's, 1968–69*, 434; *Interavia Air Letter*, 15 May 1968.
15. *Aviation Week*, 29 July 1968, 24–25.
16. *Aviatsiya i Kosmonavtika*, August 1968.
17. London *Times*, 4 August 1968, 1.
18. A. N. Tupolev, "Into the Supersonic Era." *Science Journal*, 1968, p. 3.
19. Bill Gunston. Interview with author, 11 December 1986. Also, John W. R. Taylor. Interview with author, 12 December 1986.
20. Tupolev, *Science Journal*, 1968, 3.

21. "Our Aviation Showcase." *Teknika Molodezhi,* December 1977, 40–41.
22. Ibid.
23. Gunston. Interview with author, 11 December 1986. Also, Taylor, interview 12 December 1986.
24. A. A. Tupolev, "Going Ahead of Time." *Teknika Molodezhi,* April 1969.
25. Ibid.
26. Ibid; George Michaelson. "Airplane Designer Aleksei Tupolev: Russia's Supersonic Man." *Parade,* 21 March 1976.

CHAPTER 4

1. Edgar Ulshamer, *Air Force and Space Digest,* October 1968.
2. Horwitch, *Clipped Wings,* 210.
3. Ronald Payne, *Private Spies* (London: Barker, 1967), 179–80.
4. André Turcat, *Concorde: Essais et Batailles* (Paris: Plon, 1977), 48, 349. Also, Seattle *Intelligencer,* n.d.; Jay Tuck. *High-Tech Espionage.* (London: Sidgwick & Jackson, 1986), 114.
5. Jean-Marie Pontaut, "Espionage: les trucs du KGB." *Le Point,* 25 April 1983, 120.
6. Payne, 179–86.
7. Raymond Palmer, "Operation Brunnhilde." *The Observer* (London), 7 December 1969, 9–10.
8. Payne, 179.
9. Palmer, 9; Payne, 180–81. Also, "TU-144: Operation Brunnhilde." *Der Spiegel,* 22 December 1969, 92–93.
10. Palmer, 9. Also, *London Times,* 6 December 1966; 15 May 1969, 4. Also, Payne, 180.
11. "Concord Spy Alert." *Daily Express* (London), 14 November 1966, 1.
12. Pontaut, 120. Also *Infra Red,* February 1983.
13. Payne, 181–82; Palmer, 10.
14. Turcat, 350.
15. Tuck, 168.
16. Turcat, 349.
17. Halaby. Interview with author, 22 January 1987.

18. *Le Monde,* 18 February 1965; 9 July 1965, 6; 18 November 1965, 15; 24 March 1966, 27; 27 April 1967. *Figaro,* 18 February 1965.
19. *New York Times,* 15 May 1976, 36.
20. Turcat, 348.
21. Turcat, 343–44.
22. Keller, *Ten Feet,* 347.
23. Payne, 180; Turcat, 348.
24. Turcat, 354.
25. *Le Nouvelle Economiste,* 9 December 1984, 83.
26. Payne, 177, 182.
27. Pontaut, 120.
28. "Ce Tupolev qui vole grâce aux espions." *Paris-Match,* 1969, 1028.

CHAPTER 5

1. *Take-off.* Central Film Studio, Moscow, 1969. At National Air and Space Museum, Washington, D.C.
2. TASS, 1937 GMT, 31 December 1968; TASS, 10 January 1969.
3. Ibid., 12 January 1969.
4. *Izvestia,* 1 January 1969, 6.
5. *Take-off;* Henri Ziegler. *La Grande Aventure de Concorde.* (Paris: Grasset, 1976), 55.
6. *Business Week,* 24 May 1969, 35; *Newsweek,* 24 May 1969, 35.
7. *Air et Cosmos,* 14 June 1969, 21.
8. Ibid.
9. *Flight International,* 29 May 1969.
10. *Air et Cosmos,* 31 May 1969, 112–13.
11. *Wall Street Journal,* 17 April 1969, 8; *London Times,* 5 September 1969, 18; *New York Times,* 4 June 1969, 2. Also, *Summary Status Report: U.S. Supersonic Transport Program and Foreign Supersonic Transport Programs,* FAA, April 1969, 35.
12. *Air et Cosmos,* 14 June 1969, 21.
13. *World Airline Fleets Directory 1986–87* (London: Aviation Data Center, 1986), 62.

14. Gunston, 347.
15. *New York Times*, 29 July 1969, 74.
16. Ibid., 31 July 1969, 70.
17. Ibid.
18. Ibid., 17 August 1969, 82.
19. *Aviation Week*, 25 August 1969, 26.
20. London *Times*. 5 September 1969, 18.
21. *Aviation Week*, 25 August 1969, 26–28.
22. Ibid., 27.
23. *Wall Street Journal*, 25 February 1969, 20.
24. London *Times*, 5 September 1969, 18.
25. *Wall Street Journal*, 17 April 1969, 8.
26. Ibid., 11 June 1969, 12.
27. *New York Times*, 20 October 1969, 4.
28. *Wall Street Journal*, 6 November 1969, 1.

CHAPTER 6

1. Gunston, 16, 121–22, 125–26, 402–404.
2. *Jane's, 1964–65*, 221.
3. TASS, 31 December 1968.
4. *Jane's, 1976–77*, 732, 803.
5. *Aircraft Engineering*, January 1969, 20.
6. Charles Alley. Interview with author. February 1986.
7. Ibid.
8. Ibid.
9. London *Times*, January 7, 1977. 1; April 23, 1976, 26.
10. Brian Calvert, *Flying Concorde* (London: Fontana, 1981) 50–51.
11. *Teknika Molodezhi*, April 1969; *Jane's, 1976–77*, 443; Gunston, 347.
12. London *Times*, 14 September 1977.
13. Calvert, 74–75; *Flying*, April 1985, 64.
14. "Wings of Great Hopes," *Krasnaya Zvesda*, 1 January 1969, 6.
15. Calvert, 147.
16. *Krasnaya Zvesda*, 1 January 1969, 6.
17. *Parade*, 21 March 1976, 26.
18. *Krasnaya Zvesda*, 1 January 1969, 6.
19. Ibid.

20. *Newsweek*, 24 May 1969, 35.
21. *Izvestia*, 1 January 1969, 1; *Krasnaya Zvesda*, 1 January 1969, 6; *New York Times*, 1 January 1969.

CHAPTER 7

1. *New York Times*, 18 March 1970, 33.
2. *Washington Post*, 21 March 1971, 25.
3. *Air et Cosmos*, 2 May 1971.
4. *Leninskoye Znamya*, 27 May 1971.
5. *New York Times*, 25 May 1971, 3; Gunston interview, August 1986.
6. *New York Times*, 29 May 1971, 46; *Aviation Week*, 21 June 1971, 43.
7. *Flight International*, 21 June 1971, 9.
8. *New York Times*, 28 May 1971, 1–2.
9. *Air et Cosmos*, 29 May 1971.
10. *Flight International*, 27 May 1971, 741.
11. Ibid., 3 June 1971, 813.
12. Ibid., 817; 10 June 1971, 844.
13. *Aviation Week*, 21 June 1971, 36.
14. *New York Times*, 28 May 1971, 2.
15. *Aviation Week*, 21 June 1971, 36.
16. Ibid., 40–41.
17. Ibid., 41, 47.
18. *Air et Cosmos*, 29 May 1971.
19. *Aviation Week*, 21 June 1971, 46.
20. *Air et Cosmos*, 15 May 1971, 38ff.; *Interavia*, July 1971, 787–95.
21. *Soldat und Technik*, 8 November 1971, 442–43; *Air et Cosmos*, 15 May 1971, 38.
22. *Interavia Air Letter*, 17 November 1971; *Air et Cosmos*, 15 May 1971, 38.
23. *Interavia Air Letter*. 17 November 1970; *Interavia*. July 1971, 442–43.
24. *Aircraft*, July 1971, 1015.
25. *New York Times*, 18 June 1971, 7.
26. Air et Cosmos, 26 June 1971, 29; London *Times*, June 1971,

4; *Aviation Week*, 4 October 1971, 28; *Flight International*, 24 June 1971, 911; *Skrzdlata Polska*, 23 July 1971.

27. *Air et Cosmos*, 2 October 1971, 24; *Aviation Week*, 20 September 1971, 28.
28. *Aviation Week*, 4 October 1971, 28.
29. *New York Times*, 3 May 1971, 32.
30. *Air et Cosmos*, 2 October 1971, 24–25, 47.
31. *Interavia*, May 1972, 532.
32. Ibid., June 1972, 597; *Aviation Week*, 10 January 1972, 14.
33. London *Times*, 12 January 1972; 20 January 1972.

CHAPTER 8

1. Novosti dispatch, 27 May 1971.
2. Col. W. F. Scott, "A. N. Tupolev," *Air Force Magazine*, March 1973, 66.
3. *Great Soviet Encyclopedia* (1977) Vol. 26, 318; *Izvestia*, 19–20 August 1968.
4. *Pravda*, 7 March 1984.
5. *Izvestia*, 17 June 1969, 5.
6. *l'Humanité*, 26 May 1971, 10L; private information.
7. *Izvestia*, 23 September 1971; George Michaelson. "Airplane Designer Aleksei Tupolev," *Parade*, 21 March 1976.
8. Ibid., 2 October 1977, 4.
9. TASS, Trud February 1983.
10. *Aviation Week*, 21 June 1971, 41.
11. *Jane's, 1976–77*, 90, 443–44.
12. *Soviet Aerospace*, 16 October 1972, 17; *Interavia Air Letter*, 11 October 1972, 4; *Flight International*, 12 October 1972, 478; 26 October 1972, 555; 9 November 1972, 634; *Aviation Week*, 30 October 1972, 26. Also, Jean Alexander, *Russian Aircraft Since 1940* (London: Putnam, 1975), 404–405.
13. *Aviation Week*, 26 February 1973, 20.
14. Ibid., 22–23.
15. Ibid.
16. *Air et Cosmos*, 2 October 1972, 24.
17. *Washington Post*, 25 May 1973; *Aviation Week*, 26 May 1973, 31.

18. *New York Times*, 2 June 1973.

19. *Air et Cosmos*, 9 June 1973, 31.

20. *Aviation Week*, 11 June 1973, 18.

21. London *Times* 4 June 1973, 4; 5 June 1973, 1.

22. Ibid., 4 June 1973, 1.

23. *New York Times*, 4 June 1973, 1.

24. *Air et Cosmos*, 16 June 1973; *Lo Specchio* (Rome), 24 June 1973.

25. London *Times*, 4 June 1973, 4.

26. Viktor Suvorov (pseud.), *Soviet Military Intelligence* (London: Hamish Hamilton, 1983), 49–50. Same cemetery as for ANT-20 victims, 1935.

27. Private information.

28. *Flight International*, 14 June 1973, 907.

29. *Aviation Week*, 11 June 1973, 19; *Air et Cosmos*, 9 June 1973, 31.

30. Alexander. *Russian Aircraft*, 408–410; private information; *New York Times*, 28 July 1974, 7.

31. Turcat, *Concorde*, 359–62.

CHAPTER 9

1. *Aviation Week*, 25 June 1973, 12–17; 2 July 1973; *Paris-Match*, 7 July 1973, 68–69.

2. *New York Times*, 28 July 1974, 7.

3. London *Times*, 6 June 1973, 6; 7 June 1973, 7.

4. *Aviation Week*, 26 March 1973.

5. "The Soviet Concorde." 9 April 1973.

6. *New York Times*, 6 May 1974, 48.

7. London *Times*, 18 June 1974, 25.

8. Ibid., 13 May 1975; *Aviation Week*, 15 June 1975; 4 August 1975, 32–33.

9. *Jane's, 1976–77*, 802.

10. Ibid.

11. Most details of the Soviet-Lucas negotiations are based on private information.

12. London *Times*, 7 January 1977.

13. *Air et Cosmos*, 5 November 1977, 1339–40.

14. London *Times*, 14 September 1977.
15. Dusko Doder, *Shadows and Whispers* (New York: Random House, 1986), 230.

CHAPTER 10

1. *Aviation Week*, 31 July 1961, 36.
2. Ibid, 30 September 1957.
3. *Financial Times*, 8 January 1977.
4. *Christian Science Monitor*, 7 December 1976.
5. London *Times*, 31 December 1976, 4b.
6. *Aviation Week*, 6 December 1976, 25.
7. Halaby, *Crosswinds*, 171.
8. Gunston, 125.
9. Ibid.
10. *Aviation Week*, 26 February 1973, 28.
11. Gunston, 125.
12. *Flight International*, 12 November 1977.
13. *Aviation Week*, 10 October 1977, 28; *Washington Post*, 1 October 1977; London *Times*, 1 October 1977, 5.
14. *Le Monde*, 1–2 April 1973, 17.
15. *Aviation Week*, 2 July 1973.
16. *Financial Times*, 8 January 1977.
17. FBIS-SOV-77-207: LD261131.
18. FBIS-SOV-77-212: LD022008; TASS, 2 November 1977.
19. *New York Times*, 7 November 1977; *Time*, 14 November 1977.
20. London *Times*, 2 November 1977; *Washington Post*, 2 November 1977; *New York Times*, 2 November 1977.
21. *Time*, 14 November 1977.
22. Ibid.; *Washington Post*, 2 November 1977; *Christian Science Monitor*, 2 November 1977; *Der Spiegel*, 7 November 1977, 274, 276; *Flight International*, 12 November 1977.
23. *Air et Cosmos*, 12 November 1977.
24. *Interavia Air Letter*, 22 November 1977. 4.

CHAPTER 11

1. *Aviation Week*, 20 August 1984.
2. Ibid., 4 December 1978. 26–27.

3. London *Times*, 15 September 1978, 6.
4. *Washington Post*, 19 September 1978, A17; 15 September 1978, A20.
5. Ibid., 23 October 1978, A23.
6. *Aviation Week*, 4 December 1978. 26–27.
7. *Christian Science Monitor*, 13 October 1978, 1, 10.
8. *Interavia Air Letter*, 1 November 1978, 2.
9. *Aviation Week*, 4 December 1978, 26–27.
10. *Le Point*, 18 December 1978, 80.
11. *BBC World Broadcasts* W1022, A23; W1038, 24; W1040, 17. *Christian Science Monitor*, 25 June 1979, 4.
12. Ibid., 25, 29 June 1979.
13. *Aviation Week*, 2 July 1979, 30.
14. *Air et Cosmos*, 1 September 1979, 14.
15. *Interavia Air Letter*, 7 January 1981; *Flight International*, 31 January 1981.
16. *Aviation Magazine International*, 1 February 1981.
17. *Air et Cosmos*, 28 February 1981, 14; *Interavia*, April 1981.
18. *Journal of Commerce*, 7 August 1981.
19. *BBC WB*, 13 February 1983 SU/W1224/i1225, A19.
20. A. Johansen, "Das Ende eines Supervogels." *Frankfurter Allgemeine Zeitung*, 23 March 1983, 9.
21. David Gai, "Heaven and Earth." *Znamya*, September 1983, 198–212.
22. London *Times*, *Washington Post*, *New York Times*, 10 August 1984.
23. *Washington Post*, 10 August 1984, A20; *New York Times*, 10 August 1984. A3.
24. *Washington Post*, 10 August 1984.
25. *Teknika Molodezhi*, April 1969, 22.
26. *Flight International*, 23 October 1982, 1164; 18 June 1983; *Jane's*, *1982–83*, 226–27.
27. Bill Gunston, *Air Enthusiast*, December 1985.
28. Bill Sweetman, *Soviet Military Aircraft* (London: Hamlyn, 1981), 174–75.
29. *New York Times*, 1 October 1985, A8.
30. Bill Sweetman and Bill Gunston, *Soviet Air Power* (London: Salamander, 1978), 16.
31. Robert Ruffles, Interview with author, August 1986; Doder, *Shadows and Whispers*, 100.

32. John Barron, *MIG Pilot: The Final Escape of Lieutenant Belenko* (New York: McGraw Hill, 1980), 72.
33. *Interconair Aviazione*, January 1979, 28–29; *Aviation Week*, 19 February 1979.
34. Ibid.
35. *Jane's, 1985–86.* 261–62; *Jane's, 1986–87*, 909.
36. *Jane's 1986–87*, 909.
37. *Soviet Military Power 1985* (Washington: Government Printing Office, 1985), 85; *Jane's, 1986–87*, 269.

CHAPTER 12

1. *Flight International*, 4 May 1972, 612.
2. Arthur J. Alexander, *Weapons Acquisition in the Soviet Union, United States, and France* (Santa Monica: Rand Corp., 1973) 7–12.
3. *Paris-Match*, 7 July 1973, 68–69.
4. *Soviet Foreign Trade: Facts and Figures*, August 1986, 12.
5. Horwitch, *Clipped Wings*, 341.
6. Figures extrapolated from *Jane's, 1976–77*, 90, 443.
7. *Christian Science Monitor*, 13 February 1986, 3.
8. London *Times*, 30 March 1984.
9. *Congressional Record*, 11 April 1980, 157.
10. *New York Times*, 22 January 1986.
11. *Le Point*, 10 March 1987, 91–92; 17 March 1987, 28.
12. Ron Davies, Curator of Air Transport, National Air and Space Museum.
13. *Le Point*, 10 March 1987, 91–92; 17 March 1987, 28.
14. *Aviation Week*, 22 June 1981, 42.
15. *Argumenty i Fakty*, 9–15 December 1986, 5.
16. *Aviation Week*, 29 February 1988, 60–61; 28 March 1988, 88–90.
17. TASS, in English dispatch, 28 May 1988.
18. *Izvestia*, 20 April 1988, 3; *Aviation Week*, 16 May 1988, 31; *New York Times*, 24 May 1988, C1.
19. Colonel General Yuri Mamsurov. "Aborted flight: Why did the TU-144 Supersonic airliner leave the airways?" Krasnaya Zvesda. 1 October 1988, 3. JPRS-UEA-80-043. 54.

GLOSSARY: A GUIDE TO SOVIET AND AVIATION TECHNICAL TERMS

Soviet Terms and Acronyms

KB *Konstruktorskoe Bureau,* or Design Bureau. An engineering design establishment, in the aviation context comparable to an aircraft manufacturing company. An OKB, or Detached Design Bureau, is limited to research, testing, and development, as opposed to manufacture.

D After type number, signifies long-range variant of an aircraft, usually achieved by fitting additional fuel tanks and cutting the payload.

GUAP Main Directorate of the Aviation Industry; later Ministry of the Aviation Industry.

KURATOR Caretaker. In KGB and Party parlance, person charged with overall supervision, overt or covert, of particular project or establishment.

RAMENSKOYE The chief Soviet aviation test center, southwest of Moscow.

SAM Surface-to-air missile, used to destroy aircraft.

SHARASHKA Slang for SKB, or Special Design Bureau. A design-bureau-behind-bars, where imprisoned engineers worked together under NKVD supervision with free subordinates, which flourished 1930–50.

STARETS "Old One," a wise, holy man or guru of the Russian Orthodox tradition.

TEKNIKA MOLODEZHI *Technology to Youth.* A sought-after science and technology monthly directed at Soviet teenagers, published by the Komsomol Central Committee.

TSAGI The Central Institute of Aerohydrodynamics, founded in 1918, the earliest center of Soviet aviation scientific and applied research.

VOZHD Charismatic leader, close to sense of *Führer* in German; an affectionate reference to Lenin or Stalin.

Aviation Terms and Acronyms

AREA RULE A design approach mainly for supersonic aircraft, driven by a concern to limit frontal area. It is characterized by a pinching in of the fuselage by the wings, popularly called the "Coke bottle" effect. The theory is that the diminished cross section of the fuselage helps limit the shock effect produced by the wings.

BYPASS RATIO The percentage of air that enters the engine inlets but does not enter the engine proper. Subsonic jet engines have a high bypass ratio and move a large mass of air slowly. Supersonic aircraft have a low bypass ratio and move a relatively small mass of air much faster.

CAMBER The amount of upward arching in the wing, from root to tip.

CG SHIFT As aircraft go above the speed of sound, the center of lift moves backward, in an SST about six feet. This shift in center of lift, or center of gravity (cg), must be compensated for by weight shifting, usually by quickly pumping fuel forward, in auxiliary trim tanks devised for this purpose.

CONTAGIOUS ENGINE FAILURE If jet engines are installed too close together, the shock wave from one stalled engine may disrupt the air flow to its neighbor, stalling it, too.

DROP TANKS Auxiliary fuel tanks fitted externally to an aircraft for extending its range; most commonly used for combat or record-setting aircraft. The tanks are jettisoned when empty or a combat situation develops.

ELEVON A control surface at the rear of the wing combining rudder and moveable airfoil, controlling both left-to-right and up-and-down maneuvering.

FAI Federation Aeronautique Internationale in Paris, repository of records.

FAIRING   A structure added to the fuselage or wing to streamline and optimize air flow.

HST   The still-theoretical hypersonic transport, with projected cruise speeds of Mach 4 to 30, as opposed to the Mach 2 to 3 speed of an SST.

MACH   The speed of sound, 670 to 720 mph at sea level, according to atmospheric conditions, lessening with altitude as air thins.

NACELLE   An enclosed housing on an aircraft for an engine, or rarely, crew.

NUMERICALLY CONTROLLED MACHINE TOOLS   Machine tools that carry out their functions directed by tapes in computers, usually for repetitive metal shaping and machining tasks. Also, CADCAM—computer-aided design, computer-aided machining.

OGIVAL   A lazy-*S* curve of expanding radius, as in the profile of a church bell, Gothic church vault, or TU-144 prototype front wing edge.

REVERSE THRUST   A means of slowing an aircraft on landing by deflecting the jet engine blast sideways or forwards.

STRATEGIC BOMBER   As opposed to a tactical bomber employed as flying artillery in support of ground forces in combat, a strategic bomber carries out independent operations at long range against enemy cities and production potential.

TURBOJET (pure jet)   An engine that derives its power from direct thrust produced in the combustion chamber.

TURBOFAN   A development of the jet, in which an additional set of fans at the front of the engine is driven by the engine and moves a larger mass of air more slowly and quietly.

VARIABLE-GEOMETRY WINGS (swing wings)   As aircraft speeds rise, the wings move back from a position vertical to the fuselage for takeoff and landing to a swept-back position for high-speed; the arrangement promises the best of both worlds.

VARIABLE INLETS AND EXHAUSTS   Internally moving airfoils used to slow and direct incoming air before it reaches engine intake.

VENTRAL SPINE   Reinforcement on mid-lower belly of the fuselage.

SOURCES

There are over fifty entries in the Library of Congress for the Concorde; there are none for its Soviet counterpart. The chief challenge in reconstructing the TU-144's story is the imbalance in sources. In contrast to the accessibility of every aspect of the Concorde story, its Soviet sibling must often be painstakingly reconstructed from a tangle of scattered, obscure sources. Indirect angles of attack sometimes fill in large gaps: photographs of scale models on exhibit reveal early design disagreements and evolution. Research and development strategies and the interactions of Soviet personalities and institutions can be pieced together from known history and observations. The Concorde experience provides insight into SST technical challenges, though the Soviets often resorted to cruder solutions.

Soviet treatment of the TU-144 oscillated widely, from fulsome publicity during the years of optimism (1969–73) to traditional secrecy after 1978. For example, no photograph of the TU-144D or its Koliesov engine have ever been published. There are many aspects of the Soviet SST story that remain mysteries: the fate of the second, and possibly a third, prototype; a definitive explanation for the 1971 emergency landing in Warsaw; the 1973 and 1978 crashes; the abandonment of the 144D after apparently impressive test results, and so on. Imaginative reconstruction and occasional conjecture are necessary to crack this conundrum of contemporary history.

Standard reference works offer factual outlines. A general introduction to world airliners is provided by Enzo Angelucci's *World Encyclopedia of Civil Aviation* (Crown, 1982); *The Illustrated Encyclopedia of Commercial Aircraft*, edited by Bill Gunston (Phoebus, 1980); the

261

similarly titled *Illustrated Encyclopedia of Commercial Aircraft*, by William Green and Gordon Swanborough (Salamander, 1978); and Robert Wall's *Airliners* (Quarto, 1980). These are all lavishly illustrated coffee-table works with accessible texts. The middle two books concentrate on aircraft in current service, while books by Wall and Angelucci are historical surveys. Some information is available in smaller format, as *World Aircraft—Commercial 1935–60* (Rand McNally, 1979). See *Jane's All the World's Aircraft* on the relevant years for reams of detailed technical data, though entries often appear only once.

Two recent works of high quality treat the whole spectrum of Soviet aircraft. Bill Gunston's *Aircraft of the Soviet Union* (Osprey, 1983) is authoritative and indispensible, a benchmark reference containing many obscure facts from Soviet sources, with a highly informative introduction and text organized by design bureau. The only work comparable is Vaclav Nemeček's *The History of Soviet Aircraft from 1918* (Willow, 1986), originally published in Czech but now available in an expanded English-language edition. It is organized by type of aircraft, making for interesting comparisons across design bureaus. An excellent older work with the same kind of exhaustive detail is Jane Alexander's *Soviet Aircraft Since 1940* (Putnam, 1975).

English-language histories on Soviet aviation gravitate to the military side. Robert Kilmarx's *A History of Soviet Air Power* (Faber & Faber, 1962), Colin Munro's *Soviet Air Forces* (Crown, 1972), and Alexander Boyd's *The Soviet Air Force Since 1918* (Stein & Day, 1977) provide good detail through the 1960s; Boyd is especially thorough on the 1930s and World War II. *The Soviet Air Forces* (McFarland, 1984), edited by Paul J. Murphy, is a collection of articles on more recent developments in long-range aviation and on Aeroflot in particular.

Specialists have produced a few finely focused vignettes on Soviet aviation history. K. E. Bailes's seminal essay "Technology and Legitimacy: Soviet Aviation and Stalinism in the 1930s" appeared in *Technology and Culture*, January 1976; it is essential for understanding aviation's central role in the Soviet cult of progress. William Green's series, "Billion Dollar Bomber," in *Air Enthusiast*, July–October 1971, explains the evolution of the TU-4 from the B-29. Green likewise covers Tupolev's first jets in "Jet Pioneers," *Flying Review International*, April 1969.

The two volumes of *Khrushchev Remembers* (Little Brown, 1970 and

1974) contain the usual selective distortions of retired statesmen, but is free of normal Soviet blandness and reticence. The former First Secretary provides a gossipy potpourri of vignettes and indiscretions: the chapter on "Tupolev and Air Power" in the second volume contains many intriguing clues. Khrushchev must be treated with caution, but he does provide a unvarnished portrait of Soviet power at the top. Dredging insights from Brezhnev's various productions—such as *Pages from His Life* (Simon & Schuster, 1978)—is more laborious.

Another Soviet memoir comparable in freedom with Khrushchev's—and also unpublished in the USSR—is Ozerov's volume describing the Tupolev prison design bureau. Originally a samizdat document, it was published by Possev in Frankfurt as *Tupoleva Sharashka*, subsequently as *En prison avec Tupolev* (Albin Michel, 1973). It has the best descriptions of the elder Tupolev's personality and work habits, observed by a faithful paladin, but like many jail documents, it is weak on chronology and causality.

Soviet specialist works tend to focus on the narrowly technical, skirting incendiary subjects such as resource allocation and the implications of less-than-inspired decisions of the senior leadership. As time passes, controversy recedes. The 1930s is known in more detail than the 1960s, but the effects of Stalin's purges on the aviation sector are addressed only obliquely. V. B. Shavrov's *History of Aircraft Design in the USSR to 1938* (Mashinostroenic, 1986) has been recently translated by Wim Shoenmaker into English; the second volume covering 1938–50 (Mashinostroenie, 1988) is still available only in Russian.

A. S. Yakolev was the first head of a Design Bureau to write a history. His *Fifty Years of Soviet Aircraft Construction* (Israel Program for Scientific Translations, 1970) is more accessible than his second volume, *Aim in Life*. Andrei Tupolev's life is still frozen in hagiography, probably because of the uncomfortable issues it raises, but two of his former deputies, Myasishchev and Petlakov, have recently been the subject of full-length biographies by D. Gai. The Petlakov volume—*Profil' Kryla* (Moscow, 1981)—provides new details on the 1930s. Illustrations in Gai's *Heavenly Aspirations* (*Nebesnoye Pritcheniye*, Moskovski Rabochi, 1984) indicates Myasishchev's important role in the early years of Soviet SST development. Karl-Heinz Eyermann provides further details of this period and a picture of the M-52 in airliner guise in *Lufttransport: Spiegelbild der Luftmacht* (Deutscher Militärverlag, 1967). Yakolev provides details of the delta wing wars in *Razvitie*

Aviatsionnoy Nauk i Tekniki v SSSR. (Nauka, 1980). *Sovyetskaya Aviatsionaya Tekhnika (Soviet Aviation Technology)* (Moscow, 1969) is a glossy, well-illustrated overview of Soviet aviation achievement.

Soviet journalistic and periodical treatment of the TU-144 varied dramatically from secrecy to ostentation, an accurate barometer of its technopolitical fortunes. The monthly *Tekhnika Molodezhi,* aimed at young technologists, published interviews with both Tupolevs, providing details on its early development. So did also *Krasnaya Zvesda* (Red Star), the armed services weekly. *Pravda, Trud, Izvestia, Znamya,* etc., over the last twenty-five years, carried articles occasionally providing real insights, though the general pattern is of bland and repetitive public relations releases.

The same could be said for much of Western press treatment, though the sheer volume of references to the TU-144 in the London Times and New York Times was the first indication that a book-length study of this esoteric subject was possible. The *London Financial Times, New Scientist,* the *Economist, Daily Telegraph, Observer, Le Point, Le Monde, Figaro, Los Angeles Times, Washington Post, Christian Science Monitor, Business Week, Wall Street Journal, Time, Newsweek, Der Spiegel,* and *Frankfurter Allgemeine Zeitung* occasionally produced superior and penetrating reporting. The bulk of Western press reporting was straightforward, if inevitably repetitive. The popular U.S. weekly *Parade* produced an interesting on-board interview in March of 1976.

Specialized aviation periodicals provided contemporary commentary and otherwise inaccessible details. Aviation writers tended to be caught up in SST excitement and overrated Soviet capabilities. Reporting by *Aviation Week* was usually copious and on the mark, at its best approached only by the restless curiosity of Jacques Mourisset in *Air et Cosmos. Aviation Week's* coverage of the earliest reports of a Soviet SST, its comparison of the TU-144 and the Concorde prototypes in June 1971, and Robert Hotz's story of visiting the Voronezh factory in July 1973 were distinguished. *Flight International's* coverage of the 144's appearance at four Paris air shows and at Hannover in 1972 captured many fugitive details and nuances of the project. *Air Force Magazine* early published several prescient articles.

Memoirs of Western principals run from the exuberant to the evasive. Najeeb Halaby's *Crossroads* (Doubleday, 1978) is a remarkable chronicle of the SST on the American side from the inmost insider, reflecting his pilgrimage from technocratic enthusiasm to second thoughts about speed as the ultimate goal of civil aviation. Behind the scenes, R. B. Maloy's 1966 *History of the Supersonic Transport Program-International* gives a picture of the early years, while the annual FAA *Summary Status Reports* reflect changes through the 1960s. André Turcat's *Concorde: batailles et essais* (Plon, 1977) contains recollections of Soviet inquiries and espionage and an eyewitness account of the 1973 crash. Henri Ziegler's *La Grande Aventure de Concorde* is discreet to the point of opacity.

Of the many books on the Concorde, John Costello and Terry Hughes's *Concorde: The International Race for a Supersonic Transport* (Angus & Robertson, 1976) is the best study of the technopolitics of the Anglo-French SST. Brian Calvert's *Flying Concorde* (Fontana, 1981) is excellent on the technical problems overcome by the Concorde designers, providing insight into technical challenges confronting their Soviet counterparts, as is Geoffrey Knight's *Concorde: the inside story* (Stein & Day, 1976). Mel Horwitch's *Clipped Wings* (MIT Press, 1982) addresses the political controversies that enveloped the abortive American SST project, supported by ninety-five pages of small-type footnotes.

The written word was supplemented by interviews with specialists and authorities connected with the Soviet SST project. Aviation writers such as Ron Davies, Bill Gunston, Robert Hotz, John W. R. Taylor of *Jane's*, Von Hardesty, and Bill Sweetman all provided illuminating comments and sound advice, some of which was heeded. Certain British and French industrial and government figures shared facts regarding Soviet approaches to the West for technical help and the inner story of the Franco-Soviet inquest following the 1973 crash. Soviet émigrés who had worked at Tupolev KB and in the Soviet aviation industry provided testimony regarding the atmosphere at Tupolev and other design bureaus during the SST project. Najeeb Halaby granted time to describe his visits to the USSR in the 1960s.

An airliner is a terribly tangible artifact. Careful pursuit of photographic detail sometimes reveals secrets not otherwise available. In particular, the evolution of TU-144 scale models reflects unreported design debates and controversies. Robert Ruffles unearthed significant photographic and textual evidence: Myasishchev's designs hint at the design ferment behind the scenes, while photographs of the Sukhoi T-101 suggest parallels between the 144 and the reborn Soviet strategic bomber program in the early 1970s. Wim Schoenmaker's color brochures from air shows encapsulate the Soviet approach to publicity. The 1969 Soviet film *Take-Off* contains unique details that illuminate the gestation of the 144. Film footage of the 1973 Paris crash shows the last fatal moments of 77102 and the devastation of Goussainville. The DOD Stills Center in Anacostia provided renderings of older Soviet combat aircraft, while DOD Public Relations sent pictures of the B-1 and "Backfire". NASM supplied additional stills.

Three-dimensional evidence in the form of a 1:100 scale model of the prototype made by VEB Plasticart (East Germany) was obtained from the Squadron Shop in Carrollton, Texas.

The murky area of technological espionage has surfaced in a number of sources. Werner Keller's *Are the Russians Ten Feet Tall?* (Thames & Hudson, 1961, originally *Ost Minus West=Null*, 1960), details the contribution of German air technology to postwar Soviet aviation, at the cost of underestimating indigenous Soviet innovation. British reports of espionage against the Concorde surfaced early, in Ronald Payne's *Private Spies* (Barker, 1967) and in two books by Peter Hamilton: *Espionage and Subversion in an Industrial Society* (Hutchinson, 1967) and *Espionage Terrorism and Subversion* (Heims, 1979). These revelations were replayed later by Raymond Palmer in "Operational Brunnhilde: How Russia tried to steal the Concorde's secrets" in the *Observer* (London) December 7, 1969. Jay Tuck's *High-Tech Espionage* (Sidgwick & Jackson, 1986) is a sprightly survey of the problem.

The atmospherics of the Brezhnev era have many able analysts. Timothy J. Colson's *The Dilemma of Reform in the Soviet Union* (Council of Foreign Relations, 1986), J. Dornberg's *Brezhnev: The Masks of Power* (Basic Books, 1974), and Selwyn Bialer's *Soviet Paradox* (Knopf, 1986) all describe the years of immobilism and decay. Dusko Doder's *Shadows and Whispers* (Random House, 1986) extends his narrative into the years of transition.

The role of aviation designers and design was addressed by J. S. Butz in "Those Jolly Red Giants" *Air Force Magazine*, November 1968. Arthur Alexander carried the theme further in *Weapons Acquisition in the USSR, United States, and France* (Rand, 1973) and *Patterns of Organizational Influence in Soviet Military Procurement* (Rand, 1982). John Hoagland's *Current Trends in the TU-144 Program* (Wellesley, 1975) pinpoints the Soviet press in the critical mid-1970s. Col. Clyde Dodgen's *Adaptability of the Soviet Supersonic Transport to a Bomber* (Professional Study 3900, Air War College, 1970) is a plea for an American counterpart, for strategic reasons.

ACKNOWLEDGMENTS

Many friends at the Smithsonian's National Air and Space Museum contributed to this project and improved its quality. Ron Davies, Curator of Air Transport, prodded the author into scaling up early tentative studies of the subject into a book-length typescript. Von Hardesty, Director of the Division of Aeronautics, introduced additional Soviet sources and helped locate rare photographs. Mark Taylor provided the film *Take-off* and helped with photographic details.

In Britain, Bill Gunston vigorously debated ideas, facts, and mysteries; Robert Ruffle supplied rare Soviet texts and a cornucopia of photographs. John W. R. Taylor provided reminiscences of both Tupolevs and their work. Wim Schoenmaker of Holland loaned artifacts and pictures from his personal collection.

Perly Draughn, Librarian of the Air Force Association, provided rare photographs. Her colleague Bob Shannis helped with artwork. Arcady Genevsky gave freely of personal recollections, translated Russian texts, and was a critic of interpretations. Roger Leonard checked the text and made useful suggestions. Nick Komons provided access to FAA records.

At Crown Books, Walter Boyne, Contributing Editor, proved a stalwart patron; Jake Goldberg, Steve Topping, and Carl Apollonio helped steer the manuscript through the production process. Jerry Gross edited the text with surgical restraint. This book has its origin in an idea introduced by Ray Blood in 1979: early concepts were honed by Walter R., Jim B., and Jerry P. Julie Gagnon and Peter Brauman provided indispensible support in typescript production. Ermyn King carried out research at Boeing. Ed Ezell provided provocative interpretations of Soviet science and technology mysteries, as well as crucial support in the early months of writing. Charles Alley and the staff of General Electric-Lynn introduced me to the mysteries of jet engines. Several American, British, and French authorities who asked not to be identified made disproportionate contributions. This list is incomplete: what errors survive are my responsibility.

Howard Moon
Falls Church

INDEX

270